SO GREAT A PRINCE

SO GREAT A PRINCE

The Accession of Henry VIII: 1509

LAUREN JOHNSON

PEGASUS BOOKS
NEW YORK LONDON

So Great a Prince

Pegasus Books Ltd
148 West 37th Street, 13th Floor
New York, NY 10018

Copyright © 2017 by Lauren Johnson

First Pegasus Books hardcover edition October 2017

ISBN: 978-1-68177-541-8

10 9 8 7 6 5 4 3 2 1

Printed in the United States of America
Distributed by W. W. Norton & Company, Inc.

CONTENTS

INTRODUCTION

'The rose both white and red, in one rose now doth grow'[1]

IN 1509 KING Henry VII died and his son succeeded to the throne of England as Henry VIII. Behind that simple fact lies a complex story of ruthless political manoeuvring, greed and deception. For 1509 stands at a crossroads between two very different kings, and between equally different worlds. It is a point in time we think we recognize, sitting in the long sixteenth century of the Tudor age, with its Protestants, playwrights and printing presses. It seems comfortably settled between the bloodshed and chaos of the Wars of the Roses, and the bloated tyranny of Henry VIII's later reign. From a modern vantage point we know that the Tudor dynasty would last another hundred years.

But we forget. This is not quite the Tudor world we imagine. To the men and women living in 1509 the future would not have seemed so certain. Civil war was still a visceral memory for many and the old rivals of Henry VII and the Lancastrian line – exiled, deprived or imprisoned Yorkist claimants like Thomas Grey, marquess of Dorset, and Edmund de la Pole – were still very much alive. Tudor rule was associated not with harmony and plenty, but with oppressive interference, thanks to the king's micromanagement and the avarice of his chief councillors, Edmund Dudley and

Sir Richard Empson. Monarchical meddling in guild business, city privileges and noble freedoms meant there was not a corner of English or Welsh life that seemed free from the king's oppressive attention. Disgruntlement was rife and the notion of a country united around the Tudor dynasty looked increasingly hollow.

According to his own frequently repeated rhetoric, Henry VII had swept to power by divine sanction, winning his crown on the battlefield. This Lancastrian had married a princess of the House of York, thus restoring peace to a land shattered by civil war. Henry fervently promoted the image of the 'Tudor rose', coupling the well-known white rose of York with the rather less commonly used symbol of Lancaster, the red rose. In the prince and princesses who survived to adulthood – Margaret, Henry and Mary – this Tudor rose was made flesh. But for fifteen years the next in line to the throne, the eldest rose, had been Prince Arthur, who in 1509 lay entombed in Worcester Cathedral. His magnificent chantry chapel, covered with symbols of his own dynasty and those of his foreign bride, Catherine of Aragon, stood as an embodiment of the country's uncertain future. Now his seventeen-year-old brother Prince Henry stood to inherit, an adolescent who had spent most of his childhood in the company of his sisters, his mother, his grandmother and their women. Since being removed to the company of men, he had still been kept 'like a girl', always under his father's watchful eye, forbidden to join in fully with the dangerous martial pursuits of his peers. But now all of the hopes of the Tudor line fell on his broad shoulders. The precedent of the past century was not good for the young Prince Henry. The last adult prince to inherit the throne peacefully on the death of his father had been Henry V in 1413, and between that time and this lay a century of bloodshed, minority rule and usurpation.

The world seemed no more secure for the king's subjects.

Beyond courts and manors the world of the labouring class was also in flux. The effects of the Black Death of the mid-fourteenth century still lingered, not only in the sporadic outbreaks of sickness that continued to ravage the country in new and horrifying forms, but in the diminished population and the resulting increase in the bargaining power of labourers. Common men and women felt emboldened, turning to the courts to appeal against unjust lordship. Serfdom, the ancient English form of slavery, had virtually disappeared. All the same, the vast majority of the king's subjects who made their living from the land had little cause for celebration. The enclosure of fields to create parkland or to feed sheep was an acknowledged problem, for while it lined the pockets of lords it caused waste, depopulation and unrest among the poor. Famine was an ever-present danger. One bad summer, one poor harvest, and scarcity could lead to starvation.

Under such circumstances, for most of the population, the accession of a new king meant little. The rhythms and rituals of daily life went on unchanged. Only in the immediate vicinity of London, or for those who had had dealings with chief royal ministers, was the change visible. For the largest part of the population the only alteration would have been the addition of a letter 'j' to the end of the name of their king – instead of Henry vii, now it was Henry viij. The face of the monarch was unknown, and since Henry VIII did not change the face on England's silver coinage until sixteen years into his reign, the only royal likeness most of the population knew was the profile of his father. Even when Henry went on progress in the summer of 1509, to display himself to his new subjects, he stuck snugly to the Home Counties.

The early years of Henry VIII's reign have been overlooked by many historians, who prefer to leap from the bloodshed of the Wars of the Roses to the religious and cultural upheaval of the English

Reformation, when there is the added spectacle of Henry's tangled love life to consider. But we ignore this period at our peril. How can we make sense of Henry's almost pathological desperation to sire a legitimate male heir – which famously led to six queens occupying the consort's throne beside him – if we do not understand the precarious circumstances of Henry's own accession? How can we comprehend the impact of the Reformation if we do not first appreciate the vibrancy of the all-encompassing Catholic ritual that it shattered?

Henry VIII's reign is probably the most tumultuous and transformative in English history. When he came to the throne, the country was Catholic, part of the 'universal' church of Rome. By the time Henry's son Edward succeeded him, England had cut itself adrift. Henry VIII had made himself supreme head of the church in England, allowing no pope to serve as intermediary between himself and God. In 1509, translating the Bible into English was heresy, a crime against God. By 1547, when Henry VIII died, there was an English Bible in every church – by royal command. Although not yet a Protestant nation, in 1547 England had cut itself off from much of the ritual and tradition of Catholicism. This was no small change. The entire structure of the year had been founded on a shared concept of religion: days to fast, days to feast, days to celebrate, days to work, days to have sex, days to abstain. Even the hours of the day were based on the liturgy of masses and prayers, and tolled by church bells. In 1509 we see, almost frozen in time, the high point of a world that would be destroyed within half a century. Looking back on it through twenty-first-century eyes, this world appears to be teetering on a precipice, but to those living through it, 1509 was a time of hope, the moment of release from a rule that had become increasingly tyrannical.

Those political players who dominated the scene in 1509 may

not be as famous as Thomas Cromwell, Anne Boleyn and Thomas More, but they are every bit as fascinating and complex as their more celebrated successors – and they deserve equal attention. Among their number were the high-handed Henry VII, who thought that the route to authority lay through his subjects' purses; his pious, indomitable mother Margaret Beaufort, the real champion and defender of the Tudor family; the despised and increasingly desperate Sir Richard Empson and Edmund Dudley, who were the first Tudor ministers to think themselves untouchable and to find to their cost that they were anything but; the gaunt and worldly Richard Fox, warrior bishop of Winchester, the archest of politicians, capable of ruthlessness to his rivals and perhaps trusting a little too much that he could bend a teenage prince to the will of the royal council.

But this was also the time of Thomasine Percyvale (née Bonaventure), a Cornish servant who had risen to become a London gentlewoman and tailor, training apprentices and keeping servants in her own right; of the coroner John Rastell, who fled Coventry to establish himself in the perilous trade of printing, to spread his ideals of education and justice; of William Green, who wanted more than his father's Lincolnshire drudgery of husbandry and labour and whose love of learning was already evident in grammar school; of the immigrants Frederick Freez, Catalina of Motril, Brancino Marini and John Blanke.

Through the eyes of those who lived through it, we can experience the wealth of a world that was vibrant, vivid and exciting, where London streets fluttered with cloth-of-gold to welcome a new king, the shrines of Canterbury Cathedral groaned under the weight of precious stones and vast pageants played out the ideals and fears of communities across the country. A world of peace and of danger. Of prosperity and plague. A world that would be swept away during the course of its young king's reign.

A NOTE ON DATES,
SPELLING AND MONEY

So Great a Prince follows the structure of the ritual year, as it would have been understood by those living five centuries ago. The 'new year' formally began on 25 March, also known as Lady Day or the Annunciation. Although 1 January was called New Year's Day, Lady Day was generally understood as the date that the calendar year changed until 1752. For this reason our story begins on 25 March.

In 1509, the currency was made up of pounds, shillings and pence: twelve silver pennies made up a shilling, and twenty shillings a pound. Henry VII had introduced new silver coins into circulation, bearing his profile: four-pence groats, two-pence half-groats and shillings. He also introduced a gold pound coin that was known as a sovereign. A mark was two-thirds of a pound, or thirteen shillings and four pence.

The sixteenth century enjoyed some truly idiosyncratic spelling, so where quotes have been taken from contemporary sources I have modernized the spelling. Names in the royal court have been standardized, but for those beyond its remit, original spelling has been maintained (e.g. Percyvale not Percival).

I

LADY DAY 1509

Time to pay your debts

25 MARCH 1509. Lady Day dawned over England with a collective kindling of fires. Apprentices and servants rolled up their bedding from where they had slept on the floor, bundled it away and gathered sticks, coal, flint and tinder. In households the breadth of the country, wives, widows and mothers, keepers of the hearth, watched with a keen eye or on bent knee as flames licked into life. In the tapestry-draped homes of the nobility, teenage pages scattered sweet-smelling herbs into the flames and laid out their master's clothes to warm. Waiting women brought linen and water scented with rose to their lady's bedside. Yawning and cricking their spines, old and young headed out to work. On the Northumbrian coast bare-legged figures with their shifts tucked up dug for sea coal in the chill morning sands, making the most of the low tide. In Cheshire, saltworkers banked up their furnaces, pulling piles of firewood from the stacks leaning against their dwellings, drawing briny water from the channels funnelled between their homes and watching it evaporate into profit. High in the Welsh uplands, shepherds watched their flocks grazing across vast expanses of craggy hillside. Church bells chimed the hour while monks chanted and fishermen put out to sea. As the city of London opened its gates,

a babble of languages drifted through the air and and boats of all sizes began their daily task of bearing passengers from bank to bank of the Thames. It was business as usual.

But upriver, deep in the belly of Richmond Palace, in a chamber several rooms removed from the business of servants and courtiers, the king lay dying.

His chamber was dark as a cave. The only light came from flickering flames in the hearth, a few good wax candles and the occasional glint of gold thread in the tapestries surrounding the bed. Shrunk between carved pillars and heavy curtains, beneath a coverlet of silk and Holland linen, lay the wasted body of King Henry VII. His cheeks were sunken almost to the bone, his gimlet eyes dulled by shadows. With painful effort he clasped at the crucifix on his chest and wheezed out a prayer. He had been dying, by degrees, for almost a decade. Every spring his illness had returned, a suffocating quinsy and tuberculosis that laid him low for longer each passing year.* This would be his last such sickness.

It was not an end befitting a warrior king – a man who had won his throne by conquest and kept it by dogged suppression of rebellion. By the time of Henry's birth in 1457, the first great battle had already been fought in the conflict history would come to know as the Wars of the Roses. His birth had been suitably dramatic for such a period of unrest. His mother was thirteen and his father already dead when he was born in the midst of winter in the storm-swept castle of Pembroke. This king, who during his reign would prize privacy above all things, first entered the world in the furthest reaches of the realm.

War had dragged on for thirty bloody years as the houses of

---

* Quinsy is a complication resulting from tonsillitis, where an abscess develops beside the tonsil causing considerable discomfort and fever.

Lancaster and York wrestled for control of the crown. Across the shires of England, from the northeast to the southwest, bitter disputes had flared between rival families in localized imitations of the national conflict. Every lord, lady and abbot worth their salt had a retinue of men to call on should argument turn to violence. Stockpiles of armour and sharpened billhooks seem to have lain concealed in half the households of the realm.

Land was almost always the cause of conflict. An enclosure, a road, a dyke, a bridge, a tenement – they were built up and pulled down, fought over and disputed, in court and in armed clashes. Henry had seen his own lands granted to lords of the House of York when their kings were ascendant. His own royal blood – thin and tainted by bastardy as it was – made him just dangerous enough for flight from the country to be wise. And so he had spent fourteen years at the courts of the duke of Brittany and the king of France. After so many years observing the workings of French and Breton statecraft, by the time he returned to England in 1485 his ideas of sovereignty were more Gallic than English or Welsh. All the same, it had been under the red dragon of his native land that he marched in 1485 and he was hailed by Welsh bards as *mab darogan*, the son of prophecy. The prophecy seemed fulfilled in the clash of royal claimants at Bosworth Field. Henry VII wrestled the crown from the head of Richard III and, five months later, in a display of diplomatic shrewdness that was to characterize his reign, married the eldest princess of the House of York, Elizabeth.

Yet for all the rhetorical insistence by chroniclers, historians and poets that Henry VII had restored peace to a shattered land, the country still bore the scars of war. In Tewkesbury, where whole families tended flocks and fulled and spun to produce the wool that made their wealth, there were still some who could remember the battle that had been fought in the surrounding ditches and meadows, and describe a defeated queen seeking sanctuary nearby.* Only twelve years earlier, armies had gathered on Blackheath, the king's men facing rebels led by the Cornish blacksmith Michael *an Gof*. Numbering in their thousands, the rebels denounced excessive royal taxation. Meanwhile, on the king's northern borders, a Scottish army mustered in support of a rival claimant to the English throne by the name of Perkin Warbeck. The whole country had been in turmoil. By 1509, Michael *an Gof*, Perkin the pretender and many of the rebels were barely even scraps of carrion. Their dismembered bodies had long since been removed from the gates and bridges where they had been displayed. But the disgruntlement that they had represented lived on.

And there were still some claimants alive who could pose a threat to Henry VII's line – descendants of his queen's family, young Yorkists with a grudge. Men like the imprisoned Edmund de la Pole, earl of Suffolk, a grandson of Richard, duke of York, and thereby first cousin to Queen Elizabeth. Dissatisfied with Tudor rule, Edmund had fled the kingdom in 1499 and again in 1501, but after being batted between international powers for the best part of a decade, he was eventually handed over to Henry VII's mercy as part of a deal with that continental powerhouse, the Habsburg family.† Edmund was now lodged comfortably enough, if with an uncertain future, in the Tower of London. His younger brother

---

* The Battle of Tewkesbury was fought in 1471. This was the last conflict of the Readeption, during which the son of the Lancastrian King Henry VI fought and was killed, while his queen, Margaret of Anjou, took sanctuary in a nearby religious house. She handed herself over to the Yorkists for imprisonment after the battle.

† The Habsburg family was led by Holy Roman Emperor Maximilian, and through various diplomatic unions had carved out an empire that stretched from the Low Countries (modern-day Belgium and the Netherlands) to Austria. They also had claims on the kingdom of Castile in Spain.

Richard de la Pole remained in a state of impoverished exile, sheltering with King Ladislaus of Hungary. Another unfortunate victim of Henry's rule was Queen Elizabeth's cousin Lady Margaret Pole – the daughter of the infamous Yorkist turncoat George, duke of Clarence, who had been drowned in a butt of malmsey wine in the Tower in 1478. Her younger brother Edward, earl of Warwick, had been executed and her whole inheritance confiscated ten years earlier, leaving her now just poor Dame Pole. The queen's mother, Elizabeth Woodville, had been one of eleven children, as well as a mother of twelve more, and she had seen it as her duty to marry off as many of her relatives to as much of the English aristocracy as possible. As a result, there seemed barely a courtier in the country who was not a blood relation to Queen Elizabeth. The earl of Essex was her mother's nephew; the marquess of Dorset her half-brother's son; the duke of Buckingham not only her cousin but also a distant relative by descent from Edward III. All three of these men had jousted publicly in the king's honour, but all privately felt themselves hard done by. Perhaps worst off was Dorset, who had become embroiled in a Yorkist plot that briefly saw him keeping company with Edmund de la Pole in the Tower. Five months ago he had been imprisoned in Calais Castle, and many suspected that he was not long for this world.

The symbolic union of the white and red roses of York and Lancaster had been sundered for half a decade. In February 1503 Henry's queen, Elizabeth of York, had died giving birth in the Tower of London. She now lay cold in the crypt of Westminster Abbey. Her husband would soon be joining her there.

It was Lady Day, 25 March. The first day of the new year of 1509. Sometimes called the feast of the Annunciation, Lady Day commemorated the visit of the angel Gabriel to the Virgin Mary, when he announced to her that she would bear a son named Jesus, the son of God. This date, when new life was springing forth across the kingdom, had been considered the beginning of the calendar year since at least the twelfth century. It was apposite that the reign of Henry VII, a fiscally prudent monarch, was drawing to an end as Lady Day dawned. For this day was the traditional time for the payment of wages, rents and taxes – people's minds were on money.

Among the servants who were retained by their masters, wages were paid quarterly: often on Lady Day in spring, on the feast of St John the Baptist at Midsummer (24 June), at Michaelmas (29 September) in autumn and at Christmas in winter. Many household servants like clerks, grooms of the chamber and nurses received clothing, food and lodgings at their master's expense, as well as monetary wages. A trusted servant overseeing the management of a master's estate and his other workers could expect to earn anything from seven shillings to a mark per quarter. An unskilled labourer might receive only a daily wage for casual work: four pence, more or less (generally less in the north). For that he could buy two chickens or four Thames oysters, or if he wished to invest his money in his spiritual wellbeing, he could buy a cheap, unbound, printed prayerbook in Latin. It was little enough compared to the income of the wealthiest landowners, who could hold estates worth hundreds or even thousands of pounds, but it was better than those who were paid for the product of their labour. Donyng the gong farmer* of London was paid two shillings per ton of dung he cleared out of local toilets.[1]

---

* Gong was a colloquial term for a privy and its contents, deriving from gang, 'to go'. Gong farmers dug out the ordure from often overburdened cesspits and carted it away.

In the past decade Henry's subjects, who agreed on few things, seemed all to concur that the king's grasp on their purse strings had tightened. This was more than the usual antipathy towards taxes that had inspired the Blackheath rebels of 1497. Henry VII and his councillors used money as a means to control his people's loyalty, setting sky-high bonds of good behaviour for noble and worker alike. Royal control was starting to look decidedly tyrannical.*

The two chief architects – and abusers – of this system of bonds were the lawyers Edmund Dudley and Sir Richard Empson. They had enjoyed a rapid rise from gentle but unimpressive urban backgrounds, and now numbered among the closest of the king's councillors. Their own loyalty to the king was absolute, but it was combined with a ruthless efficiency bordering on, and sometimes leaping unashamedly into, avarice. In the previous five years they had overseen a reign of bondage and financial extraction that had bolstered royal coffers and lined their own pockets. Long-forgotten bonds of good behaviour and debts to the crown had been called in, the slightest of infractions seized on, to enable Dudley and Empson's men to siphon money from all corners of the country. Abbots, earls, heiresses, London drapers, Italian merchants, the imprisoned and impoverished and orphaned – the list of debtors abused by this system of forfeiture was staggering. Those who spoke out against the pair found themselves bundled into prison cells, like the king's chapel master, William Cornish, who penned vitriolic verses against Empson during his incarceration. Dudley had even grown so confident as to extort money from the king's mother. In the summer of 1507 he made a substantial profit by demanding a payment from Margaret Beaufort for the privilege

* A bond was a contract of good behaviour between an individual and the crown, enforced by a financial debt called an obligation or recognisance. If you broke the agreed terms, your money would be held forfeit.

of acquiring Creake Abbey for Christ's College, her foundation in Cambridge. In rousing the wrath of the implacable Margaret, Dudley was playing with fire, and it is a sign of how sure he felt in the king's confidence that he dared to even attempt it. That he not only succeeded but got away with it is an indication that even before his final illness the king's grip on his chief ministers was slipping.[2]

Beyond these financial exploitations, the king had actively interfered in the business interests of his subjects. As the Mercers of London welcomed new freemen to their company in March 1509 – among them a young lawyer called Thomas More – the members of the city's oldest livery company might well have muttered about royal meddling. The Mercers were the most influential of the sixty guilds and fraternities in the City of London, comprising a number of merchant companies involved in the export of cloth. In recent years the king had seemed determined to curtail their power, promoting rival guilds to undermine the Mercers' dominance of the city. He had interfered in their elections and, the previous winter, threatened a new tax on cloth exports that would seriously damage the Mercers' interests.

Like many of his brother Mercers, the merchant John Middleton divided his time between the city and his home estates in Essex. It had been a stressful few months and, as he paid his servants and workers on Lady Day, he must have contemplated the future with anxiety. In the city people had to watch their words. 'Questmongers' in the pay of Dudley and Empson were on the hunt for any sign of disloyalty. Carpenters, fullers and fishmongers, these questmongers hid in plain sight, waiting to pounce and receive a share of the profits once their victims had been arrested and fined. In the sanctuary of his own home, with his two daughters safely in bed, John could vent his frustrations to his wife. Alice Middleton was not a woman who suffered fools gladly. It is probably just as well no questmongers heard her opinion on the king's treatment of the Mercers.[3]

At the opposite end of the country, in his workshop in York, the alderman Thomas Drawswerd would have contemplated the king's illness with more mixed emotion. Drawswerd was the third generation of his family to work as an image-maker in York, carving alabaster and marble. He would have heard bitter tales of the king's interference in civic business at the start of his reign, trying to force the city to accept his choice of swordbearer despite manifest evidence of his appointee's embezzlement and lechery. The position of swordbearer was one that carried great respect in the local community and to have it laid on the shoulders of John Eglisfield, a man who had slept 'with many wife's servants and other women of the said city' was viewed as an insult.[4] (In fairness to the king, Eglisfield himself had presented a rather different version of events when he petitioned for the role.) Despite his city's sometimes troubled relationship with their monarch, Drawswerd himself had enjoyed Henry's patronage, designing image-work for the king's proposed chapel in Westminster Abbey.

Further up the social scale, noblemen found the king's financial controls especially offensive. In his Gloucestershire manor of Thornbury, Edward Stafford, duke of Buckingham, moaned loudly about the £7,000 he owed the crown. Every feudal exaction possible had been charged against this portly, litigious nobleman: when his widowed mother remarried without royal permission, Buckingham was fined; when the king arranged the duke's marriage to an orphaned heiress, Buckingham was fined; when he entered his estates before the king believed he was of age, Buckingham was fined. The debts had mounted to such a degree that he had been forced to seek the services of a Lombard banker, despite the desperately unfavourable terms for his loan.*

In theory, the nobility had more money to lose than the merchants and citizens of England, but in a worldview that safeguarded many of the privileges of the aristocracy, financial manipulation like that carried out on Buckingham was viewed as morally reprehensible. Even the royally patronized historian Polydore Vergil took umbrage at the king's excessive financial demands on the rich, grumbling that his officers 'proceeded against not the poor but the wealthy, churchmen, rich magnates, even the intimates of the king himself, and any and every individual of fortune'.[5] The duke of Buckingham had more reason to complain than most. To add insult to injury, the king still denied him the hereditary title of constable of England, despite years of petitioning. He was a proud man; it was not in his nature to beg for what he saw as his right.

Whatever his subjects muttered about Henry VII's rule, there was one area in which he had succeeded where his predecessors had not. Despite the ravages of infant mortality and sudden sickness sweeping five of his eight children into early graves, one son had survived. For the first time in almost a century, an adult male would inherit the throne from his father: Henry, Prince of Wales, then seventeen years old. The last time this had happened was in 1413, when English rule stretched all the way to the south of France. By coincidence, that dying king and hotheaded prince had both been called Henry as well. In the intervening decades, the throne had been inherited by a baby, a twelve-year-old, usurpers and more than one murderer. When Henry, prince of Wales, acceded to his kingdom, it would be with a clean conscience and bloodless hands. That was Henry VII's greatest success.

---

* A Lombard was a native of Lombardy in northern Italy. At this time, the most powerful bankers in Europe were almost all from the Italian peninsula.

But it was success by the slimmest of margins. For most of Henry's reign the people of England and Wales had expected their next king to have quite another name. The first-born child of Henry VII and Queen Elizabeth of York was named in honour of the most famous – if mythical – ruler of Britain. Prince Arthur had been brought up from infancy to rule. He had the finest tutors, the most advantageous marriage arranged, and had set off west to preside over the Council of Wales and the Marches at Ludlow, part of his duty as Prince of Wales, when disaster struck. At Shrovetide in 1502 he fell ill, and for two months endured a 'piteous disease' that finally snuffed out his young life at Ludlow Castle in early April. His sixteen-year-old bride, Princess Catherine of Aragon, returned to her in-laws as a widow, through the churned mud and rain-sodden fields of a land drenched in grief.

Some seven years later, Princess Catherine waited as anxiously as all the other courtiers at Richmond for word of the king's condition. Her years of widowhood had seen the slight, auburn-haired girl with rosebud lips grow into a pale and tired woman. Since Arthur's death she had lived close to the English court, first at Durham House on the Strand in London, surrounded by squabbling Spanish courtiers, and then officially as part of the royal household. Yet, despite her proximity to the royal family, her status was still unresolved seven years after Arthur's death. Rumours had at one point reached her parents that King Henry intended to marry her himself, a union that in her mother's opinion would be 'a very evil thing'.[6] Fortunately, in 1503, Catherine had been betrothed instead to Prince Henry. Thanks to a protracted diplomatic wrestling match between the rulers of England and Spain over Catherine's marriage portion, the prince and princess's union had not moved any closer to realization since then. Catherine's father, King Ferdinand II of Aragon, could not – or would not

– pay the marriage portion, and King Henry insisted that without it he and his son were not bound to uphold the betrothal. Caught between these obstinate monarchs, Catherine had grown increasingly desperate. On 9 March 1509 she wrote to her father appealing to be allowed to return to Spain and live a religious life. She had more than most to fear, or perhaps to hope, from the succession of the young prince.

Catherine did not visit the dying king in his apartments. Only the most important lords spiritual and temporal were allowed access to Henry's deathbed. Richard Fox, the bishop of Winchester and Lord Privy Seal, had been a constant at Henry's side since his exile in France, even leading an army overseas in 1492 despite his ecclesiastical rank. His hard work had seen him grow pale and thin with a recurring stomach upset, but as leading member of the Prince of Wales's household and executor of the king's will his loyalty to the Tudor regime was unwavering. Another of the royal executors was Fox's ally Sir Thomas Lovell, who, with his lined face, down-turned mouth and sunken eyes, was even more serious than usual. Lovell had faithfully served as Henry's chief military commander, and as a menacing inquisitor of those suspected of treasonable plots. Until very recently, the most constant presence in the privy chamber of the king – the most private royal apartment – had been Hugh Denys, his groom of the stool. Responsible for the king's purse and attendant on him even during his most intimate moments (the 'stool' of the title was the close stool, a velvet-covered box that served as a portable toilet), Denys had found himself edged aside during the final weeks of Henry's life. Technically he was still head of the privy chamber, but in practice a rival had emerged in the shape of Richard Weston, once a member of the queen's household. This son of a Lincolnshire knight was increasingly prominent in the last weeks of the king's life – the first dim shadow of a conspiracy unfolding at the very heart of the court.

In the midst of the pack of male courtiers at the king's bedside was a small figure in black velvet and gold-rimmed spectacles, the most important of them all: the king's mother, Margaret Beaufort. Margaret was now sixty-five years old; her hands were crippled by cramp and her knees weak from bending in prayer, but that would not keep her from her dying son. She knew with grim certainty that this illness was different from the spring sicknesses Henry had suffered in the past. Settling in for the last weeks of her son's life, she had moved herself and her servants to Richmond, bringing her favourite bed and personal 'kitchen stuff' with her. Like many noble mothers, she had not raised her son in her own home, but the bond between them had proved unbreakable despite years of war, exile and conspiracy. She would not leave him now.

Elsewhere in the palace, Prince Henry contemplated his future. What did he imagine as he awaited the news of his father's death? He had been kept stiflingly close to the king in recent years, allowed little of the freedom that a prince might expect. A Spanish ambassador reported that he was cloistered more like a girl than an heir to the throne. In some ways his fate must have seemed similar to that of his younger sister Mary, who also waited in the depths of the royal palace. Both had been dragged about wherever their father had gone, both raised by the firm but devoted hand of their grandmother – particularly since the death of their mother – and both now seemed to have their futures planned out for them. Mary was betrothed to Charles of Ghent, child heir to the mighty Habsburg empire that stretched across half the Continent (and unfortunate heir, too, to the pronounced Habsburg jaw). If they married, Mary would leave England and forge an alliance with a crucial international ally. Henry's destiny was, of course, to rule

England, and exactly whom he would marry was still very much in question. While the king's men buzzed around his deathbed like flies, his heir had simply to sit and wait.

Noticeably absent from Richmond Palace were Sir Richard Empson and Edmund Dudley. They were some miles downriver in the city, in the comfort of their own homes. Dudley's well-appointed house on Candlewick Street took up 180 feet (55 m) of the busy mercantile street's frontage. Through the small windows could be viewed a network of chambers lined with tapestries, foreign glassware and expensive furniture nestled alongside coffers stuffed with papers – the same papers that had been used so effectively to extract money from Henry's subjects. The house even had its own private water supply, coming off the Cheapside public conduit. The furnishings and rooms of the house on Candlewick Street were little different from any wealthy merchant's home in the city, but what marked out Dudley's house as unique were the throngs of desperate-looking men clustered in the hall. These were the unfortunates who found themselves accused of petty offences and punished with a hefty fine, sometimes twenty years and a full generation after a bond for good behaviour had been signed. Among their number may have been a petitioner on behalf of the Plumpton family of Yorkshire. Sir Robert Plumpton had, since 1502, been engaged in conflict with Empson over the right to an estate that Plumpton had occupied for more than twenty years. Royal protection had been the only restraint keeping Plumpton from debtors' prison. With rumours of the king's imminent death, Sir Robert would have been wise to make a last-ditch appeal to Empson's mercy.

The absence of Empson and Dudley from the king's death-bed did not mean that they were ignorant of his condition. Their 'questmongers' and 'promoters' were as ubiquitous in the royal court as they were in London's streets, chief among them Hugh Denys, the king's groom of the stool. Denys's usurpation by Richard Weston, his colleague in the privy chamber, carried an implicit threat against Empson and Dudley. Weston, unlike Denys, was not considered one of Empson and Dudley's creatures. When seeking allies against Empson in his ongoing legal wrangles, Sir Robert Plumpton had secured the support of Bishop Fox, Sir Thomas Lovell and Richard Weston, who – he was told – was a man who could be trusted. What was good for Plumpton was, implicitly, bad for Empson. Perhaps it was for this reason that, behind the domestic façade of Candlewick Street, away from the coffers of documents and heavy tapestries, was hidden a stockpile of weapons: sharpened billhooks, longbows and crossbows. All that was missing were the men to wield them.

Towards half past six the sun set on Lady Day, the darkness falling over the Northumbrian moors in the furthest reaches of Henry VII's kingdom. Starlight twinkled over the ships in Newcastle harbour, groaning with sea coal bound for London. Creeping darkness followed the herders of the Pennine uplands as they drove their animals from valleys to mountain pasture, and the setting sun lengthened the shadows of West Country clothiers as they silenced their looms and wheels. In Cornwall, where memories of slain rebels and dismembered blacksmiths did not fade, night slunk into tin-miners' dwellings as heather spluttered in the flames of their hearths. Twilight reached across the Channel and touched the tip of France in the Pale of Calais, the last French lands still to fly the English flag. Within Calais's thick walls Alice and John Middleton's wool factor had spent a fraught day over the accounts, chasing payments, dealing with exchange rates and ensuring wages were doled out according to his master and mistress's wishes. As the wool-house was closed up and nightwatchmen began their rounds, he retired to his bed in a local family's home. Laughter and drinking songs in broken French and English drifted out of the nearby tavern, mingling into one dull cacophony as he laid his head on his thin feather-stuffed pillow. He would not have known that the reign of Henry VII was drawing to a close.

II

EASTER

To everything a time and place

EASTER WAS A time of resurrection, but there would be no recovery for Henry VII. On Easter morning, 8 April, he crept on aching knees, his parchment-thin skin cushioned by carpet, to receive the sacrament in his privy closet. As the dying king received the sacrament, elsewhere the youngest of his two million subjects were squealing over baptismal fonts – Easter was always a popular time of year for baptisms – while the more advanced in years stared at the figures of Christ and his saints, their stomachs rumbling as the long ceremony ran its course. Offerings of eggs and apples, or money for those who could afford it, had been collected and the cloths that had covered the images of Christ and his saints for the duration of Lent were removed. After weeks of fasting, it was almost time to enjoy meat and plenty again.

Religion was at the very heart of life for king and commoner alike, shaping not only their morality, but also their behaviour, their sense of hierarchy and of time. The shape of the year followed a church-prescribed procession of holy days, marked by fasts, vigils and feasts. The rhythm of the week was similarly influenced: Wednesday, Friday and Saturday were fast days, and Sunday was an enforced day of rest with mandatory attendance at mass. The hours of the day were tolled by church bells and marked by the chanting of the religious in monasteries, chantry chapels* and churches. The church was the focus of the community, symbolically and physically: whether people lived in town or in the country, hillside or flatland, it was highly likely that the tallest building in their view was the local church tower. It dominated the visual world of Henry VII's countrymen.

An Italian visitor described the religious habits of the English during this period. 'They all attend mass every day,' he wrote:

> And say many paternosters in public (the women carrying long rosaries in their hands, and any who can read taking the office of Our Lady with them, and with some companion reciting it in the church verse by verse, in a low voice, after the manner of churchmen), they always hear mass on Sunday in their parish church, and give liberal alms.[1]

As such, it is unsurprising that local pride was often expressed through parish churches, which were decked in precious items:

> Above all are their riches displayed in the church treasures for there is not a parish church in the kingdom so mean as not to possess crucifixes, candlesticks, censers, patens and cups of silver.

The church gave people their notion of time, as hours were measured according to the canonical 'hours' when service was said, whether in parish churches or in larger households. A bell would

---

* A chantry chapel was an appointed area within a church, endowed for a priest to sing daily mass for the souls of its founders, or for others chosen by them.

be rung to register these hours from prime (around dawn) through to vespers (about nightfall). The time of these services, when the whole household might be expected to gather on holy days, varied between winter and summer, since dawn and nightfall fell earlier or later as the year progressed. Originally cathedrals and monasteries had used water clocks to track the passage of time, by the regular dripping of water through a narrow opening from an upper reservoir into a lower one. As water accumulated in the lower reservoir, a float carrying a pointer rose and marked the hours.

Since the thirteenth century, mechanical clocks had also started to be installed in larger churches and religious houses. Mechanical clocks used arrangements of gears and wheels, turned by weights attached to them. As the weights were pulled downwards by gravity, the wheels turned in a slow, regular motion and a pointer attached to the wheels indicated the hour. These mechanical clocks were less delicate than water clocks and required less maintenance, so they were called upon to toll bells for the hours of the day and to call attendance at church services. Exeter Cathedral had one of the earliest mechanical clocks, appearing in records for the first time in 1284. This marked the beginning of a flourishing of church investment in timekeeping. From the early fifteenth century, smaller churches in towns and villages followed suit with their own mechanical clocks. But contemporary logic meant that hours were not standardized into inflexible chunks of time. Instead, the twenty-four-hour day was divided into two periods of dark and light, then subdivided again so that there were twelve equal hours of daylight between dawn and sunset. This meant that as the year revolved hours lengthened and shortened accordingly: in winter, an hour of darkness was considerably longer than its summer counterpart.

This was one of a few idiosyncrasies exhibited by mechanical clocks, which had to be wound daily and repaired on a regular basis to maintain good running. Even the best mechanical clocks would gain or lose up to half an hour a day. Clock keepers were appointed to watch over the timepieces, often adding clock maintenance to their existing duties. In churches it was frequently the sacristan or sexton who took on the job with a few shillings given as reward – Canterbury Cathedral's timepiece was referred to in its records as 'the sacrist's great clock'.[2] The porter of Lincoln Cathedral close, John Barnes, was paid the princely sum of twenty shillings a year in 1509 for extending his duties to clock maintenance and overseeing the cathedral's festival pageants. When smaller churches and towns first installed clocks they needed to call on the services of experts from further afield. In 1439 Henry the clockmaker and *ducheman de Dertmouth* ('dutchman of Dartmouth') installed the town's clock. He may well have been an artisan who had brought his knowledge of the trade with him from the Low Countries. However, as clocks became more widespread throughout the century, such work fell more and more often to locals, with 'clocksmiths' and 'clock keepers' appearing in records in greater numbers. In St Albans the smith Robert Grave took responsibility for maintaining the striking clock on the local clockhouse as part of his tenancy agreement for living there. All the same, Rye in Sussex still depended on outside assistance to build its clock in 1516: a 'man of Winchelsea' made it for six shillings and eight pence.

From the very beginning, timekeeping was associated not with the visual but the aural. Clocks tolled or chimed the hours rather than showing them. The word 'clock' itself derives from the word for bell, whether taking its origin from French *cloche*, Latin *clocca* or German *glocke*, and was first used in an English document in 1370, which referred to the tower *clok* in Gloucester. In York, the image-maker Thomas Drawswerd could enjoy a cantus for eight bells ringing out from the minster every hour. Where imagery was used in early clocks it was designed to impress onlookers, not necessarily to inform them of the time, as is suggested by John Barnes's responsibilities at Lincoln Cathedral. He was expected not only to tend to the clock, but also to contribute to the pageantry celebrating Christmas, Pentecost, Passion Week during Lent and the festival of St Anne's Day. During Pentecost week Barnes was responsible for the lowering of a dove and incense-fuming censer through the roof of the cathedral and on Christmas Day he prepared a star for the nativity play. It is likely that both dove and star were mechanically operated set pieces, whose movement was designed to awe onlookers. In a similar way, the astronomical clock installed in the fourteenth century in Glastonbury Abbey was intended to impress visitors with its mechanical 'movements and spectacles'. The great clock made for Salisbury Cathedral went even further, with moving figures showing the three kings bringing gifts to Mary and Jesus. The baby Jesus reached out to take the gifts and Mary and Joseph bowed to the kings, who subsequently disappeared. Exceeding all of these was the clock in Norwich Priory, which showed a procession of fifty-nine images with music and bells as well as an astronomical dial. Even outside cathedrals and monasteries church clocks made use of mechanical movement. Sometimes the clock bell was struck by a figure, like 'Jack the Smiter' in Southwold parish church, Suffolk. This four-foot (1.2 m) tall jack was dressed in armour and struck a bell with his battleaxe when a cord was pulled. The first recorded reference to a dial on the outside of an English church is on the newly built tower of Magdalen College, Oxford, in 1505. Rye church in Sussex followed suit – it had a dial in its steeple before 1515. These circular dials were often made of wooden boards painted with chapter numerals, although St Mary's church in Launceston had a stone dial.

Clock-making in towns was leading to more precision in time-keeping. In 1496, a journeyman capper (a maker of woollen hats) at Coventry was enjoined 'to come to his work at six of the clock in the morning, and to leave at six at night'.[3] Whereas once work hours were defined with reference to light and dark, now they were set by the tolling of the local clock. These clocks did not yet have minute hands, although they did sometimes divide hours into fractions. Clocks with minute hands clearly existed in Europe, for the German monk Paulus Almanus made notes on clocks he repaired during a stay in Rome around 1475 and described one showing division of the hour into minutes.

The measurement of time was bound up with the myriad identities Tudor people possessed. As subjects, they dated their year from the king's accession (21 August)*; as Christians, from the conception of Christ on 25 March (Lady Day or the feast of the Annunciation). In local records there was an almost perverse diversity, with the date of the mayor's inauguration usually marking the turning of the calendar. In Bristol, the year was dated for this reason from 15 September. As individuals, people probably knew their date of birth and sometimes recorded it for posterity. Births were noted in small personal items like Books of Hours. These devotional texts were available to the nobility and gentry in beautifully illuminated and bound editions, and to the middle classes – following the advances in printing made by the end of the fifteenth century – in printed versions on cheap paper that could be acquired for a few pence. Sometimes, though, even the year in which a person was born was in doubt. When questions of majority arose, generally in relation to inheritance, they were answered by

* In fact Henry VII won his throne on 22 August (the date of the Battle of Bosworth) but he dated his reign officially from the day before – making all those who had fought against him traitors.

the memories of people's neighbours. William Clopton was born in St Bridget (or St Bride) parish in London on 2 March 1505, but we know this only because witnesses were called when he reached the age of twenty-one to testify that they had stood godparents to him, attended his baptism and indeed one widow proudly claimed to have been in the chamber when he was born. Sometimes all that could be remembered was a person's date of baptism, marked by the carrying of candles to the local church.

Easter was the most important date in the Christian calendar, when the community of a parish was expected to gather, in new clothes and recently confessed, for the miracle of the mass. Even Henry VII's extreme infirmity would not keep him from Easter mass, which he celebrated privately, in a remote corner of Richmond Palace. For most, however, the Easter service was the most public of observances. Religion was the frame on which much Tudor self-identity hung, and anyone who divested themselves of it could expect some hostility from their community. During that Easter service, as during all church masses, rituals of behaviour were enacted which demonstrated the believers' sense of their place in the universe and of their understanding of time. Churches held much to remind parishioners of these facts of life. When they entered, it was through a porch where newborns arrived to be baptized at the nearby font; where couples were legally married before moving within to celebrate a blessing; where brass and stone memorials lay to the memory of the dead. Birth, marriage and death: the three crucial stages of life all celebrated within that small passageway.

Inside the church, walls were painted in red or yellow ochre with scenes from the Bible to provide parishioners with morally uplifting examples and to warn them against sin. In one image the Virgin Mary might stand proudly displaying her pregnant belly as her cousin Elizabeth felt the Christ-child move within it. In another, an adult Christ stood scourged and bleeding as around him floated the tools of people's trades – saws, sickles and scythes – in a grisly visual metaphor of the moral damage done by those who worked on a Sunday. In front of these wall paintings, sometimes in railed-off chapels with their own altars, were the polychrome figures of saints particularly favoured by local families or guilds. Each chapel might have a priest attached to it who would say mass on Easter morning. The most important part of the church, separated from the laity by an intricately carved screen called the rood, was the chancel where the high altar stood. In the most magnificent churches and cathedrals this stone altar rested before a sumptuous reredos in which rows of saints stood, symbols of martyrdom or sanctity in hand. Since Good Friday, the rood screen had been veiled in painted cloths as a symbol of mourning, but on Easter morning these were pulled down to reveal the miracle of the mass once more. During the rest of the service parishioners could move about – reading their prayer books, whispering among themselves, even gossiping and laughing – but during the sacrament of the eucharist the whole church was expected to fall to its knees in silence. The rood screen, panelled to waist height, had glassless windows through which they could watch as the priest said the words that would transform bread and wine into the body and blood of Christ.

The ritual of the mass was known in the bones of those observing it, who had witnessed it since their infancy, even if the Latin words used throughout were unintelligible to them. The genuflection, lowered heads, kneeling, raised hands with palms pressed together, crossing of the body, even the orientation towards this eastern end of the church – all were rituals of behaviour that reiterated the hierarchy of the known world. God came at the top of a pyramid of understanding, which put everyone in their place. Beneath God was the pope in Rome (as head of the Catholic Church); the king in England (head of state); then the lords spiritual (archbishops, bishops); the lords temporal (dukes, earls, marquesses, barons); and so on down the social orders to the lowest labourers, who could still technically be serfs – bonded people who had to work for their lord and were tied to their land. There were female counterparts to most of these roles, positioned one step lower on the pyramid, although in matters spiritual they were to be found only in nunneries and never on the papal throne. In the secular domain, only once had a woman been appointed successor to the English throne: the Empress Matilda, who four centuries earlier had fought a desperate civil war with her cousin Stephen but never actually achieved coronation. Henry VII crawled to the cross that Easter morning because even he – the most powerful man in the country – was inferior to God. He knew his position in this chain just as well as he knew his people's.

Much was written by political thinkers about this understanding of social order, which demanded that everyone play their part to ensure continued harmony. In 1509 Henry's unpopular councillor Edmund Dudley wrote *The Tree of Commonwealth*, an allegory of governance with a tree representing the people, its roots in Christian faith, justice, trust, concord and peace; its fruit prosperity, honour of God, tranquillity and good example. The health of the tree could be maintained only by everyone, from every social group, performing their proper duties and acting under the guidance of the king. For this communal effort, people were to be rewarded 'after their degree', which fell into three categories: the clergy, the chivalry (i.e. the nobility) and the commonalty. However, just because they were an integral part of this structure, the 'commonalty' should not expect to move far beyond their origins:

These folk may not grudge nor murmur to live in labour and pain, and the most part of their time with the sweat of their face. Let not them presume above their own degree, nor any of them pretend or counterfeit the state of his better.[4]

Frequently the 'chain of being' from God through the king to the people was conceived as a body. The chancellor of Henry VII's predecessor Richard III described the king and his council as the 'womb of this great body politic of England'. Earlier in the fifteenth century Sir John Fortescue, experienced in matters of law and order thanks to his time as Chief Justice of the King's Bench, used the phrase 'body politic of this realm' in relation to the mythical foundation of England by the Trojan Brutus. In Henry VIII's reign politics would still be expressed in this way. The courtier Thomas Starkey wrote that the 'under offices of princes' were like the eyes and ears of the body politic:

For as much as they should ever observe and diligently wait for the weal [health] of the rest of this body. To the arms are resembled both craftsmen and warriors which defend the rest of the body... To the feet the ploughmen and tillers of the ground, because they by their labour sustain and support the rest of the body.[5]

This theory of a 'chain of being', in which every person had and knew their place, was borne out in practice. In 1509 there was a very real sliding economy of light and warmth. The wealthiest lords, such as the duke of Buckingham and the earl of Northumberland, could afford to have fine wax candles burning in their many chambers and sea coals blazing in their fireplaces. Meanwhile, poor labourers like Stephen Green of Lincolnshire toiled in the hours of daylight and slept in darkness. The central hearth of Stephen's home was his family's primary – perhaps sole – source of heat, insulated by the residual warmth of beasts sharing their space and the smoking stink of tallow. For those of the middling sort, economy was crucial. The mercer's wife Alice Middleton saved her candle ends to reuse – even artificial light had to be rationed. To guard against the animal odours of the home and the musty smell of floor rushes, which were refreshed every week or so, people put herbs on their windowsills: rosemary, sage and thyme. These herbs had the added benefit of driving away certain insect pests.

This sense of one's place in the order of things was constantly reinforced by people's behaviour when they interacted with one another. Bending the knee and – for boys and men – uncovering the head were the universal indicators of respect. An Italian visitor to England was impressed by the courtesy displayed among its people:

> [They] are extremely polite in their language... In addition to their civil speeches, they have the incredible courtesy of remaining with their heads uncovered with an admirable grace whilst they talk to each other.[6]

This sign of respect was even more important when in the presence of a superior. The humanist scholar Desiderius Erasmus, a friend of the lawyer Thomas More, wrote a book on good manners for the young in which he advised that if they met someone on the road 'who deserves your respect on account of his seniority, or reverence due to his calling, or who is dignified by his rank', they 'should remember to give way, and remove [their] cap respectfully, and even make a slight bow or curtsy'. It was even claimed by some visitors that the English sent their children away from home for education just so they 'might learn better manners', like saying 'Christ help you' when someone sneezed or covering the mouth and making the sign of the cross when they yawned.[7] Corporal punishment was used to enshrine these lessons of deference, as the early fifteenth-century advice poem *How the Good Wife Taught Her Daughter* described:

And if thy children be rebel and will not bow them low...
Take a smart rod and beat them in a row.[8]

For all the formality and reverence expected across social divides, the English were not so restrained in their behaviour among friends. Many foreign visitors were surprised by the traditional English greeting: kissing on the mouth. Erasmus visited England in 1499, and again in 1505–6, and reported on this fashion with amusement: 'Whenever a meeting takes place there is kissing in abundance; in fact whatever way you turn, you are never without it.'[9] A Bohemian visitor explained that 'to take a kiss in England is the equivalent of shaking hands elsewhere'.[10] Embracing was also a universally recognized sign of friendship, used diplomatically between rulers and affectionately among comrades.

To avoid *faux pas* in showing deference to one's inferiors or – far worse – failing to show it to one's superiors, all that was necessary was to look at the person in question. In 1509 it would have been immediately apparent who was less or more important. The first thing to draw the eye would be the number of people surrounding an individual. A lone figure on foot was probably unimportant. A person on horseback attended by swarms of followers wearing the same colours and badges was clearly very important indeed. The king and his family were rarely, if ever, truly alone. Their household, an entourage of courtiers and servants whose purpose was to make the lives of their royal employers easier, could number into the hundreds. The nobility had long emulated this public show of numbers. When the duke of Buckingham rested in his Gloucestershire estates he had over a hundred and fifty people in his household, but the number fell to around sixty when he visited his London home. Buckingham was the only duke in the country in 1509 but earls too were likely to have over a hundred people in their households. Gentle- and noblemen further down the social scale had households numbering around twenty to eighty people – the latter figure was the size of the household of Lord Darcy, a prominent magnate in the West Riding of Yorkshire. The idea that the size of one's household reflected one's authority did not apply only to the secular lords and ladies. Bishops, priors and abbesses would also travel with servants.

Indeed, servants were such an important expression of rank that expenditure on their food and drink alone could take up a third of a nobleman's income. In many monasteries the servants, guests and corrodians (elderly laypeople in residence) outnumbered the monks. When the gentlewoman Elizabeth Stonor found herself 'right bare of servants' at her London home, she wrote to her husband asking that he send over some of his to attend her – without such attendance, her status was undermined. During her widowhood, Catherine of Aragon pawned her own jewels and plate in order to maintain a respectably large household: testament to the importance of presenting an honourable retinue to the wider world.

If by some peculiarity a lord or lady was unattended – perhaps they had entered the most elite realms of the court and could not bring their servants with them – then their dress would give clues to their status. In 1509, people wore their wealth. As the courtier Sir Thomas Elyot later wrote in his *Book Named the Governor* (1531),

'We be men and nay angels, wherefore we know nothing but by outward significations.' The English took pride in their appearance and wore 'very fine clothes', often furred to guard against the notoriously bad weather. One European observer noted that the rain 'falls almost every day during the months of June, July and August; they have never any spring here' and another that 'in England it is always windy, and however warm the weather the natives invariably wear furs'.[11]

In the first years of life, English children were dressed in similar fashion: babies were swaddled, then infants of both sexes moved on to long gowns. At around the age of six a change occurred that would endure for the rest of a person's life: they would dress as adults, according to their sex. Men's clothing emphasized their mobility, both physically and socially. They wore stockings and hose to display their legs, with a knee- or hip-length doublet secured at the waist worn over the top. Gowns – with large shoulders, puffed sleeves and slashes to reveal expensive lining for those rich enough to afford it – hung lower at the back, even reaching to the calves. Older gentlemen might wear floor-length gowns, but shorter ones that showed off the legs were increasingly fashionable. In wool or velvet, heavily furred, men's clothes were bulky but not as restrictive as women's. The wealthier a woman, the tighter her bodice and the longer her train and sleeves, which meant the heavier the gown pulling at the edges of her shoulders and pressing on her lower back. Bending over and reaching up were restricted movements for noblewomen. Working women and housewives wore more practical clothing, their long skirts pinned up at the back or side, or tucked under the arm when they walked. From the waist down never more than an ankle would be on display, petticoats hiding their modesty. In such clothing bare skin was barely seen. The exposed collarbones of female courtiers and slashed doublets of their male counterparts allowed alluring glimpses of a naked body or linen underclothes otherwise concealed. Even hair was tantalizing. Both sexes covered their heads, although men removed their caps or bonnets as a mark of respect. For women, a hood in the French style with a glimpse of parted hair at the front was the most risqué hairstyle generally encountered, except on rare occasions like first weddings or the coronation of a queen. Elizabeth of York had worn her 'yellow hair' down her back for her coronation in 1486.

This is not to say that people did not wear different types of clothing at different stages of their lives. As throughout history, young people disdained the fashions of their elders. When the retainer John Husee sought fur for the gown of his mistress's son he rejected one for 'it had been too ancient for a young gentleman'.[12] Likewise, women's clothing would change as they went through pregnancy, exposed and loosened lacing on their bodice proudly displaying their expanding waistline. When comfort became more important, both sexes adopted gowns like long coats, women wearing them over under-dresses called kirtles, and men eschewing the popinjay padding and slashing worn by their younger selves to accommodate the gown's bulk.

The mercer's wife Alice Middleton was a woman who enjoyed fashion and made efforts to follow it, tightening her bodice and scraping back her hair as style demanded. Perhaps she also inclined to excess, for she was said to be 'penny wise and pound foolish, saving a candle's end and spoiling a velvet gown'.[13] It would not have been difficult to spoil a fine gown in London's streets. When Alice went out to purchase goods or call on neighbours, she might have first donned wooden pattens, clog-like shoes that strapped over a person's normal footwear to physically raise them above the worst of the filth and wet. In the early sixteenth century many urban streets were paved, to the extent that the traveller and anti-quary John Leland specifically mentioned when they were not. He complained about Droitwich, where most of the traffic passed over unpaved streets – presumably consisting mostly of churned mud – leaving it 'rather unpleasant and dirty'. The streets of Kingston upon Hull were cobbled with stones, some of which had jour-neyed all the way to Iceland and back. Trade in Icelandic cod played a crucial part in the local economy, and the cobbles were used as ballast in merchant ships. Henry Chetelle was employed in May 1501 to be 'paviour' to do the common paving within Nottingham, mending and making all the pavements. He was to be paid thirty-three shillings and four pence and provided with a gown for the task as well as being given all the necessary stones and sand. These efforts to maintain the streets were not always successful in a country as damp as England. An Italian visitor in 1497 complained about the slippery paving of England's streets, full of 'evil-smelling mud' that had to be scraped off with rushes when entering some-one's home.[14]

Royal feet were less practically attired. Courtiers' shoes resem-bled slippers: delicate velvet and silk creations swiftly ruined by exercise. The teenage Princess Mary had her shoes provided from the royal purse, and between 1510 and 1514 she was issued with sixty-eight pairs. Such footwear did little to support the arches or provide cushioning from hard tiled floors and after hours of dancing and feasting, the princess and her companions would have had throbbing feet eager to slip into soft, fur-lined slippers.

The passing of the reins of power from Henry VII to Prince Henry saw a change in fashion. Long male gowns drooping to the floor and close-fitting cuffs on female sleeves gave way to men in doublet and hose, their legs and codpieces prominently on display, while for women sleeves widened to reveal flashes of expensive lining. For the royal households wool livery had always been the order of the day, but the last royal provision for noblewomen to wear cloth livery was made in 1509. After 1517 wool livery gowns disappear from royal accounts even for the lower ranks of women, replaced by silk, satin and velvet. It is telling that while Henry VII passed only one statute on clothing, dealing with the price of hats and caps, his son laid out extensive rules of fashion from his first parliament onwards. It may have been simply the difference in their ages – a teenage prince compared with a father in his fifties – but perhaps it speaks of a deeper contrast in temperament, a greater quota of vanity on the part of the young prince. Prince Henry was more concerned with outward display, with the crucial importance of magnificence, than his father had been. He was more than a little vain.

In Tudor England it was easy to have your head turned by fashion. The streets Alice Middleton walked through might be dirty and crowded, but they were also colourful. Although black was the colour of clothing most frequently mentioned in Tudor wills, over forty other possible hues appear in contemporary testaments.[15] Brightly dyed native English wools or expensive imported silks greeted Alice at every turn. Perhaps among the apprentices and servants bustling past her in vivid blue wool was Ralph Walker, apprentice to the tailor's widow Thomasine Percyvale. He might be hurrying to fulfil his mistress's wishes – or sneaking away to waste coin in local taverns. The blue cloth he wore was created with woad, a plant dye so popular that it had to be imported from France to satisfy English demand. Perhaps Alice even passed Thomasine Percyvale herself, resplendent in her crimson velvet and fur gown, riding a horse trapped entirely in blue velvet. Thomasine had once been a servant girl in London, wearing the violet gowns that were a cheap, pale imitation of the bright Tyrian purple worn by the royal family. Members of the royal household, especially those in military roles, marched the streets in Tudor livery colours: green and white. A pocket of black-clad men in clerical coifs muttering together might be lawyers like Thomas More – black was ever more popular as the choice of the professional man, being sober but also reassuringly expensive. Even more costly were the scarlet and crimson coats of their younger colleagues, briefly enjoying an education at the Inns of Court before returning to more gentlemanly pursuits. Creating their rich red outfits demanded significant quantities of a crushed insect-derived dye called *kermes*.

Wool was the prevailing fabric choice for high and low alike. The main industry of England was woollen cloth production, but the most expensive woollens were exported to the Continent to be finished, then returned before sale. Only the cheaper wools, worsteds and kerseys (all types of woollen cloth that appear frequently in household accounts) were extensively produced in England. The cloth might come from abroad, but it was usually dyed in England – English dyers were considered particularly skilled, able to dye in the yarn or in the piece, even colouring delicate silks or over-dyeing to change the colour of clothing. The London dyers worked along the Thames, streaking the river with their work, and the metropolis was a major site for the import of dyestuffs. Bristol and Southampton also saw their fair share of this trade. Port books show brazilwood arriving from Portugal and Spain, orchil lichen, woad, madder and alum from Cologne, Caen and the south of France.

The dyers' hands were stained by their work, and their bodies polluted by the smell of it. They were often exiled to the edges of settlements, where water and firewood were readily available and their stench did not offend. In London, the dyer John Baryns had a house stocked with two dye vats, a boiling vat, a woad vat and a mill for grinding orchil lichen. He needed ready supplies of alum and wood ash to 'fix' the dyes into the fabric. Dyeing woad demanded that woad balls be fermented in wood ash, lime or urine for three days, bubbling noxious gases into the air. When wool was left in this heady concoction overnight, it emerged the next morning transformed into a rich blue. If the dyer did his job properly, the wool would be a single bolt without any fading or patches. Unsurprisingly, John Baryns's own wardrobe was full of greens, violets, murreys* and russets.

If Alice Middleton's mind was on her purse, she might have been wearing clothes that had been patched or cut down from old pieces. Certainly any female servants who attended her on her walk through the city streets were likely to be wearing hand-me-downs. To keep finances balanced, expensive gowns which had grown tired could be dyed – black was a popular choice.[16] For those unable to fund wholly new outfits, second-hand clothing, sometimes left by the dead, could be bought from fripperers, or a bodger could rework old clothes. If only the lining needed attention, one could appeal to the services of an upholder, who dealt in small wares like second-hand furs. However, this trade in second-hand goods was monitored carefully, and in times of plague it was forbidden, since it was believed that sickness could lurk in the fabric. John Husee was on another mission to organize clothing for his mistress Lady Lisle's son when sickness hit London. He waited to buy a coat for the boy because the tailor's man had fallen ill: 'I thought it better he to be without a new coat than to abide the danger of the plague.' When he did make a purchase, it was of 'very good velvet', carefully researched, which he was confident 'shall serve him any day this five years with little reparation'. Lady Lisle had

---

* Murrey was a deep reddish purple or blood red.

requested damask or silk for the coat, but Husee demurred since such fabrics 'were skant to serve him one year'. Even the nobility had to watch their purses when it came to investment in fashion.[17]

For all this, 'outward signification' was sometimes misleading. People aped their social superiors, wearing clothes that were better than their station, even at the highest levels of society. Henry Clifford, a youthful companion of Prince Henry, endured the censure of his father for doing so. In a parental grumble that echoes down the ages, Lord Clifford complained bitterly about his son Henry's inappropriate dress, condemning him for strutting about the country in cloth-of-gold, 'more like a duke than a poor baron's son as he is'.[18]

Monarchs shared Lord Clifford's concern about the potential of fashion to mislead, and for centuries had made efforts to prevent such imitation by imposing 'sumptuary laws'. After succeeding to the throne, Henry VIII passed legislation that prohibited certain cloths, furs and quantities of fabric based on the rank of the wearer. The earliest English sumptuary legislation had been passed in 1337, and the most recent in 1483, during the reign of the Yorkist Edward IV. Foreign imports of silk and fur – even of wool itself – were desirable because they displayed the wealth and cosmopolitanism of their wearer, but they also threatened native industry by driving people away from investing in domestic fabrics. By legislating to control clothing, the king was thus protecting English work while also attempting to limit social mobility.

Women were excluded from the rigours of sumptuary law, perhaps because their identity was subsumed within that of their husband, and it was expected that he would attend to any disciplinary issues on the fashion front. For anyone else contravening the labyrinthine clauses of sumptuary law, the penalty was generally a fine and forfeiture of their illicit, expensive clothing to the crown and royal chamberlain. For servants, shepherds and labourers, a worse punishment awaited: they would be given three days in the stocks for the crime of wearing hose that cost more than ten pence a yard. Under these laws only the royal family could wear purple silk or purple cloth-of-gold, and only a duke – or his horse – would dare to be seen in gauzy tissue of cloth-of-gold. The wearing of non-native woollen cloth ('native' meaning it derived from England, Wales, Ireland or Calais) was forbidden for anyone beneath the rank of lord, just as sable fur was prohibited for any but earls and their superiors. Exemptions were granted: ambassadors were not bound by these rules, nor were heralds or men in the king's livery. There was also exemption for minstrels and 'players in interludes', which is to say actors. Perhaps royal patronage of music and drama made the monarch more soft-hearted towards these professions.

Clothes were an investment, and those fortunate enough to own expensive items guarded them as such in carefully designed presses and coffers. Lady Lisle kept her clothes in a number of locations: a wardrobe, a fur chest, 'a great chest of white boards', and in strongboxes. In smaller houses, clothing was stored in the privacy of the bedchamber, folded away in chests. Caps had special cases of their own, and so sometimes did more expensive doublets or gowns. The clothes were maintained by brushing, to remove dirt and dust from the surface of a garment – the king's Wardrobe of the Robes regularly bought new brushes for this purpose. When John Husee found Lady Lisle a new employee to care for her clothing he sought a 'gentlewoman, which is a maiden and unmarried… a good needlewoman and also she can embroider very well and will be content to wash and brush'.[19]

Silks and woollens could not be properly cleaned – spot-cleaning of stains with sponge or fuller's earth was the best that could be hoped for.* In his book of advice to a chamberlain, the usher John Russell recommended shaking out and brushing woollen clothes once a week, and more regular checks on furs and expensive items, to stop moths taking up residence. Smell was the primary concern for wearers, and sweet-scented herbs and flowers were used to imbue clothing with their perfume, either by fumigation or by wrapping crushed petals into fabric balls. To ensure that clothes did not get too malodorous, people wore a layer of linen between themselves and their clothing – fine bleached Holland linen for the wealthy, and for the poorer a coarser undyed native fabric. Linen could be changed regularly on a hot day, although in practice most did not have the time – and supply – to allow such fastidiousness. When the duke of Buckingham spent the summer in London his two henchmen, Anthony Woodville and Edmund Berners, changed their shirts only once a week at best. The duke himself was a bit more fastidious, with spare shirts, head-kerchiefs and linen sheets provided for him by his laundry on a more regular basis. Linen was much easier to clean than silk and wool. Cakes of black, grey or white soap were bought for this job and in extremis linen could be bleached clean again with stale urine.

Of course, there were always those for whom outward appearance was not a priority. When the humanist scholar Desiderius Erasmus wrote *A Handbook on Good Manners for Children* he felt it necessary to warn them not to have snotty nostrils, and that:

> drying or wiping your nose with your cap or your clothing, or
> on your sleeve or arm is a habit only for fishmongers. Not that
> it's much better to wipe your nose with your bare hand if you're

---

* Fuller's earth is a clay-like substance that can draw out grease from cloth. Its name derived from its use in the fulling industry to absorb the lanolin and oil in wool.

only going to wipe that on your clothes... Disgustingly some
people stain the hems of their shirts and tunics, spattering them
with urine. Others plaster their chests and sleeves with shameful
crusts... of phlegm from their noses and mouths.[20]

Just as life was governed by certain expected codes of behaviour,
so too was death. Those on their deathbeds should make amends
for any wrongs they had done others, ensure that their wills were
written up to acknowledge debts, and have their minds on the next
life. Like most men close to death, Henry VII sought to atone for
his wrongdoing. For a king, that meant receiving absolution from
his subjects. He had already dispensed alms and released prisoners.
Now, on 16 April, as he neared his end a week after that agonizing
Easter mass, a general pardon was proclaimed. In granting this,
Henry was fulfilling a promise he had made his mother's confessor, John Fisher, at the beginning of Lent. Henry had waited until
late in the day to keep his vow. Droves of petitioners filed into the
Chancery offices off Westminster Hall to pay a fee to gain their
pardons, for everything from forfeitures and forgeries to felonies.
The king knew how unpopular some of his policies had been – not
to mention certain of the 'officers and ministers of his laws' – and
now he endeavoured to leave his subjects with a better impression of his reign. Just to be on the safe side, he also ordered ten
thousand masses to be said for his soul. Henry VII had done all he
could to ensure the safe succession of his son, and the peaceful
progression of his soul to the afterlife.

But, unknown to the king, men were gathering in the vast city
downriver. In the dark streets of London a glint of steel could be
glimpsed in the shadows. Silent but for the soft rattle of their brig-
andines, bands of men made their way to Candlewick Street and
the Thameside manor of Le Parsonage. With a blaze of torchlight

they were ushered in, the door firmly bolted behind them. Soldiers were mustering to the homes of Dudley and Empson. Were they simply moving to protect themselves, or to ensure that when the king died they were ready to assume control of government themselves?

III

ST GEORGE'S DAY

An education

ON SATURDAY 21 April, an hour before midnight, King Henry VII died. He held a crucifix on his chest and a taper in his hand, lighting the path of his soul to God. His closest advisers and attendants were at hand, foremost among them his old companion in exile Richard Fox and the groom of the chamber Richard Weston. His mother Margaret Beaufort cannot have been far from her son's bedside. But from that day until the evening of the feast of St George two days later, something very strange took place in the chambers of Richmond Palace. News of the death of Henry VII was not released. Not that night, as the midnight hour tolled in Richmond Palace, nor the following day when logic suggested it would be more convenient to make such an announcement. A full two days later, on the afternoon of the feast of St George, Richard Weston had a 'smiling countenance' as he went in and out of the room where the king had died; a royal offering was made at mass and largesse given to the heralds to celebrate the saint's anniversary, both in the name of Henry VII. His son Prince Henry ate supper and attended evensong while still being addressed as 'prince' rather than, as he now was, 'king'. In short, life went on as if Henry VII had never died at all.

49

There were subtle signs that something was amiss. After dinner on St George's Day, Weston asked the archbishop of Canterbury William Warham and other select lords to join him in the king's privy chamber, where they remained for some time in secret conversation. The prince and Lady Margaret were among the few privy to news of the king's death, a carefully chosen band who were working swiftly now, with a very specific purpose. They needed to ensure Prince Henry's smooth succession, and they needed to exclude from power anyone who could not be trusted to enable it. The gathering of the Knights of the Garter on St George's Day gave them the perfect opportunity to do so.

St George had been England's patron saint since the fourteenth century, supplanting his rivals St Edward the Confessor and St Edmund the Martyr in popularity. Henry VII had associated himself with the warrior patron since his earliest days, arriving into London as a victorious king in 1485 beneath the saint's red-cross banner. His identification with St George was internationally known, and in 1504 the king of France had presented him with a holy relic: the saint's leg, encased in silver gilt. St George's name had been invoked repeatedly during the Hundred Years War with France and it was during the early years of that conflict that another symbol of English chivalry, inextricably linked to St George, had been born: the Knights of the Garter. The knights represented the flower of English chivalry – men whose personal power, honour and loyalty to the crown earned them election by the existing representatives of the order. Positions were highly prized. When the knights marched in their velvet robes and blue garters from chapter house to chapel and back on the feast day of the patron saint of England, they symbolized an ideal of English honour and reciprocal loyalty between ruler and ruled.

The bond of loyalty exemplified by the Knights of the Garter worked to the advantage of both parties: the ruler was provided with loyal support against enemies and honest counsel in his decision-making; the ruled were protected and rewarded by their master. This system was also the basis of a king's council and of the royal court. But the ideal would always be tested in reality, for in personal monarchy, where reward followed service to an individual, some would always seem to be better rewarded and afforded more power than others, leading to inevitable resentment. So it had been under Henry VII in the last years of his reign. Long-term loyalists such as Richard Fox and Sir Thomas Lovell had served Henry VII for decades and their promotions in service had been hard won. Yet in recent years their authority had been usurped by the *parvenus* Empson and Dudley, administrators whose rapid rise to power and receipt of a series of royal grants had isolated them from their fellow councillors. Dudley had become president of the King's Council a mere two years after being made Speaker of the House of Commons, while loyal men like Giles Daubeney, who had served Henry VII when he was just the exiled earl of Richmond and faithfully acted as lord chamberlain to him as king, found themselves financially ruined for minor indiscretions. As illness robbed the king of vision and energy, he had delegated increasingly to Empson and Dudley, and they had grown fat on the profits of their labour. Nor were they the only dangerous faction vying for authority in the wake of Henry VII's death. Noblemen such as the brothers-in-law Edward Stafford, duke of Buckingham, and Henry Percy, earl of Northumberland, saw themselves as the natural advisers of kings but had not always been well treated by Henry VII. The dawn of a new reign afforded them an opportunity to improve their prospects and assert their dominance.

It was the influence of rival factions that Henry VII's close councillors, chief among them Fox, Lovell and Margaret Beaufort, were moving now to oppose, and they could hardly be doing so at a more opportune moment. The celebrations of St George's Day called many great men to the royal court, but Empson and Dudley would not be among their number. Neither had been admitted to the chivalric Order of the Garter, so had no excuse to join its celebrations. Northumberland and Buckingham, little realizing what was unfolding at the heart of the court, had also stayed away from the celebrations. The party controlling access to Henry VII's deathbed, however, were intimately connected to the order: Margaret Beaufort had been given Garter livery in 1488, Fox served as prelate of the order, and alongside Lovell wearing the robes of the Garter that day were men whose strategic importance equalled their loyalty to the old regime: the warhorse earl of Oxford, constable of the Tower of London; the royal chamberlain and 'knight of the body' Charles Somerset, Lord Herbert. The group could not act without including the young prince, of course, but for now his role was simply to maintain the pretence that nothing had changed. These were early days in the renegotiation of Prince Henry's relationship with his councillors and grandmother. For many years they had been his respected elders, and he probably stood somewhat in awe of them.

Isolated from events by their absence from court, Empson and Dudley may have underestimated the prince's willingness to criticize the regime of his father. For Prince Henry was happy to act as the mouthpiece for his respected elders, the prominent counsellors of Henry VII: Bishop Fox, Lovell the chamber treasurer, and especially the matriarch Margaret Beaufort. All three knew they had to walk a finer line than most, for their own wealth and status had been made by allegiance to the Tudor king. They must now emphasize their loyalty to the Tudor dynasty without associating themselves with its unpopular choices. They needed the reign of Henry VIII to begin with a clear gesture, sweeping away both opposition to the regime and rivals for power. Henry VII himself, the *paterfamilias*, could not be overtly criticized, but his excesses must be acknowledged. What was needed was a scapegoat. Conveniently, Henry VII had left two.

The deaths in recent years of high-placed allies like the influential Sir Reginald Bray left Dudley and Empson dangerously exposed at court, and now their enemies were ready to strike. The first act of the new king, acting on the advice of Margaret Beaufort, Fox, Lovell and their allies in the Order of the Garter, would be to issue a pardon that superseded that written by his father less than a fortnight before, being a 'more ample pardon for all things'. 'Any person wronged may seek remedy at law,' it promised, and 'merchants, clothiers and artificers' in particular were encouraged to 'continue their occupations without fear of untrue informations by customers, comptrollers or searchers, or persons calling themselves promoters'. The message was clear: things were going to be different from now on. Under cover of the celebrations for St George's Day the oppressive regime of Henry VII was going to be swept away once and for all.[1]

IN THE HUSHED conversations in holy day closets and private chambers, and in the loud public subterfuge of his first forty-eight hours as king, Henry VIII received an important lesson in kingship. Chivalry might be the founding principle of the Knights of the Garter, but politics was a murkier business – and the successful ruler needed to balance the two. While the seventeen-year-old prince had enjoyed a lengthier education in the demands of kingship than his father – who had leaped onto the throne after fourteen years of exile – Henry's royal apprenticeship was still not complete. Until he was eleven years old he had received the education of a princely younger son, and only after the death of his brother Arthur was it adapted into something suitable for a future king. Education was fundamentally utilitarian in 1509: a person was educated to a level appropriate to the future expected of them – and not generally beyond that. For everyone, education demanded an introduction to the basics of religion, proper behaviour and the necessary skills to make a living or keep house independently. But since the demands of that future living, and the degree of expected deference, varied widely across social rank as well as gender, education was adaptable to the individual in question. There was no expectation of a universal level of learning.

It was generally recognized that successful kingship had a three-fold basis: protection of the church, defence of the realm and the giving of justice. By the time of his succession, Henry had received enough education to be competent, if not yet accomplished, in all three. Protection of the church was easiest for a king's education to incorporate, for all education began with religion. The language of the church was also that of education and literacy so to be 'literate' (*literatus*) in 1509 meant to be able to read Latin, not English. Thus, the first 'books' a child would pore over if they were to learn to read were primers or Books of Hours, in which the divine offices of the day, various psalms and the litany of the mass were laid out in Latin. Sometimes primers were available in the vernacular, or with English prayers, but in general the language of learning was Latin. The daughters of Alice and John Middleton, Helen and little Alice, would have begun their lessons at a prayer table with their mother, primers open, repeating prayers and learning to construct words from the letters written there. This image of maternal education appeared in the very books that they were reading, where pictures of the Virgin Mary teaching Jesus with a prayer book sat alongside depictions of the Virgin's own education by her mother

St Anne. The first words any child was likely to see and learn were those in the primer before them: the prayers of *Pater Noster* and *Ave Maria*: Our Father, Hail Mary. Thus did children imbibe the beliefs that were the foundation of contemporary religion.

While the words of education were Latin, the written material of daily life could well be in English, so the ability to read at all was a valuable skill. By 1500 the guilds of the Goldsmiths, Scriveners and Skinners in London all had rules that apprentices must be able to write and read before entering their apprenticeship and some provided schooling to ensure it. The lawyer Thomas More noted that 'far more than four parts of all the whole [realm] divided into ten could never read English yet', which suggests that over half of the king's subjects could read something of their own language, even if they did not understand Latin.* It was therefore possible to be functionally literate, while remaining technically *illiteratus*.[2]

Like many of his subjects, Prince Henry had learned to read in the company of his mother and sisters. As the duty of a parent was to produce a useful, virtuous child regardless of gender, girls needed education as well as their brothers – they just might not need as much of it. Prince Henry's sisters, Margaret and Mary, shared his tutors and schoolroom until adolescence, but not even they enjoyed the level of humanist education afforded to the

---

* There is considerable variety in historians' estimation of English literacy in the early sixteenth century. Some believe More's figure is overly optimistic, citing the evidence of signatures, which suggest that 90 per cent of men and 99 per cent of women were writing illiterate. Where literacy was noted in a number of Essex court cases, it suggested that one in seven women could read, compared to a third of men. Studies of London laymen in the late fifteenth century showed that around half were literate, in agreement with More's assessment. In reality, literacy varied greatly across social status and region: urban men were more likely to read than rural ones, and men in general more likely than women.

daughters of London lawyer Thomas More, who had Greek as well as Latin on their curriculum. Even among the wealthy, female education was marked by a greater informality – it might be had in a convent or with a tutor, but in general there was less emphasis on scholastic practice. This can be seen in the handwriting that survives, even on royal documents. Princess Margaret's writing and spelling were markedly poorer than her brother's, probably because she had not been made to practise as assiduously.

Henry's education really changed at the age of thirteen, when he was removed from the company of his female relatives to that of his father and the royal court. This removal to more focused education was another experience he shared with his subjects, albeit rather later in childhood than was common. One Venetian visitor commented that the English must be very unaffectionate because they sent their offspring away from home 'to hard service', at between seven and nine years of age, 'in order that their children might learn better manners'.[3] This opinion probably reflected the initial feelings of children suddenly separated from family and a familiar home. When the Yorkshire adolescent Dorothy Plumpton was sent to live with her relative Lady Darcy she complained repeatedly to her father Sir Robert – although she was careful to maintain the respectful, formal tone expected when children addressed their parents:

Right worshipful father, in the most humble manner that I can, I recommend me unto you, and to my lady my mother and to all my brothers and sisters...

Letting you wit [know] that I sent to you message... to send for me to come home to you, and as yet I had no answer... Therefore I beseech you to send a servant of yours to my lady and to me, and show now by your fatherly kindness that I am your child, for I have sent you diverse messages and writings, and I had never answer again.[4]

For all Sir Robert's apparent lack of interest in Dorothy's welfare, this stage of a child's life involved their guardian in considerable effort and care – whether finding an apprenticeship, work in service, a place in grammar school, or a position in a noble household, as in Dorothy's case. All required preparation, planning and expenditure. Parental concern extended even beyond the grave, with some leaving endowments for education in their wills. When Dame Katherine Hawte of Kent drew up her will in 1493, some of her eight children were less than six years old, and she stipulated that all the lands she had purchased should be sold in order to fund them through school.

For other guardians, the concern was simply to safeguard a child's future by whatever means available. When Robert Wood of Little Staughton in Bedfordshire provided in his will for his son's future, he put forward a choice for the boy's education: either his executors should send Master Wood to school, or engage him in a 'profitable craft'.[5] By the latter, Wood probably envisaged the on-the-job training available to many children of lower to middling status: becoming indentured as an apprentice. Apprenticeships usually began in a child's teens, although some trade regulations felt it necessary to specify that someone could be no younger than twelve when they entered a master's service. It was an apprentice's duty to run errands for their master, lighting fires and setting up the workplace. The wealthy tailor's widow Thomasine Percyvale continued to keep apprentices in the trade after the death of her last husband Sir John in 1503 and three of them were still in her household at her death in 1512. Among their number was a youth called Ralph Walker. No doubt throughout the working day it was

Ralph's lot to take on the less skilful and more tiresome tasks, in return for being fed, watered and clothed at Thomasine's expense. As his seven-year term of apprenticeship passed, Ralph would be trusted with more responsibility and would steadily increase his knowledge until he was able to practise the craft for himself. Apprentices were forbidden to marry or work for their own profit during their term of indenture, and could be chastised physically and verbally by their master – although only within reason. Some apprentices were so eager to set up in their own business that they failed to complete their terms and attempted to work independently before their time was served, which was expressly forbidden by the ordinances of most crafts.

While female apprenticeships were unusual in the sixteenth century, it was generally accepted that the daughters and wives of existing traders would assist in the family business. The most common trade in which women took on apprentices independently was silkwork, which, like brewing, was an industry particularly associated with women. Girls came to London to be apprenticed as silkwomen from as far afield as Yorkshire, Bristol and Norfolk and could go on to make lifelong careers in the trade. Another route into a career for women was through marriage. Thomasine Percyvale is one of a number of women who continued their husband's business after his death – Thomasine inherited businesses and apprentices from each of her three husbands. It may even have been through her status within the tailoring craft that her third husband, John Percyvale, was able to secure his own elevated position in the community. Thomasine was essentially a silent partner in the family firm. The involvement of wives in their husbands' trade is often overlooked because of the convention in documents of subsuming a woman's identity into that of her husband. Thus, in the documents recording the transfer of Stephen Piers's family tailoring business to his son John – written in the late fifteenth century and covering a period of several years – only the final indenture names the two men's wives as being involved in the business as well as their husbands.[6]

Thomasine had started out in life as a servant, moving to London from her native Cornwall. Her initial education was probably the same informal one that many children received within a working household – in which a daughter or son assisted their parents in their particular trade or profession. This too was preparation for a future career. Those intended for life as tenant farmers or in other family trades outside guild control learned 'on the job' alongside their elders, gaining a wealth of practical knowledge that did not demand literacy, and so went largely undocumented. The daughter of a household, expected to go on to set up a marital home and raise her own children, would have learned at her mother's elbow and assisted in the upbringing of siblings. Women might also undergo a period of domestic service before marriage, earning money by doing work that they would otherwise probably have been doing at home unpaid, but these positions did not generally lead to long-term careers in the same way as apprenticeships. In books of guidance that mention female education, the most important life skills girls were expected to learn were behavioural: to be pious and chaste, charitable and deferential. Arithmetic would certainly be important for balancing the household accounts – if the task was not delegated to a servant – but reading and writing were less prized skills. There was some argument about whether women should be allowed to read at all. The widely read thirteenth-century work on education by Giles of Rome suggested that only women of high birth should read and learn science – for others, their time would be better occupied quietly working with textiles. *The Book of the Knight of the Tower*, written by a French courtier in the fourteenth century and printed by William Caxton in 1483, offered advice from a father to his daughters. While admitting that writing was not overly important to women, it argued that reading was 'good and profitable to all women, for a woman that can read may better know the perils of the soul and her savement'.[7] Thomasine Percyvale seems to have shared a contemporary lack of concern about formal education for women. In her will she left bequests for a number of children she had been raising 'of alms', that is, out of her own charity. The boys were to be provided with 'meat, drink, learning and clothing' until they were assisted into a career at twenty-one, either as 'men of the Church' or in a trade. The girls, however, were to have only 'meat, drink and clothing'. It is possible that Thomasine intended them to be apprenticed in spite of this lack of education, as she asked the executors of her will to 'provide for them a good and a convenient master or mistress' when they were fourteen, with a further ten marks to be given to each of them when they were twenty-one – seven years after they entered such service. However, it is equally possible that, in an echo of her own experience, Thomasine intended the girls instead to enter domestic service and then marry.[8]

Thomasine's patronage reflects one of the only real routes to education available to working-class children. Without charitable endowment – whether via a local school, or direct sponsorship such as Thomasine's – formal education was beyond the means of most families. This was because all education involved expense, even if it was only through loss of a child's labour, or in purchasing the necessary materials and suitable clothing for school.

The lowest level of formal education, and the one most widely available to children, was the 'petty' or 'song' school. Here, between the ages of five and seven, children would learn the songs of religious liturgy as a route to literacy. Local priests, licensed by the church, taught the children without charge as a pious duty. The youngest 'petty scholars' in these schools learned their alphabet from 'horn books': thin text nailed onto a piece of wood, covered with a transparent layer of horn. They also tackled the graces (short petitions and prayers for meal times), collects, prayers and Creed. Recitation and rote learning were key; the remarkably precocious Margaret Plumpton was four years old when she was complimented on having nearly learned her psalter. To be able to memorize psalms is not the same as being able to read them, however, and even after attending song schools children may not have been functionally literate.

The next phase of formal education demanded payment – only the children of families who could pay could attend. Between the ages of around seven to twelve, scholars could learn *lectura*, the art of reading, using psalters and church books. Generally this cost around six pence a quarter. From ten or twelve years old, and for an additional two pence a quarter, the scholars could progress onto *grammatica*: the teaching of Latin grammar. The students of grammar were expected to repeat Latin texts read by the master (particularly if books were in short supply, which in most schools they must have been), with the emphasis on their inflection and fluency as much as their understanding of meaning. Both readers and grammarians might be taught in the same school by the same master, although there were schools which had specialist tutors for the different topics, like Archbishop Thomas Rotherham's foundation in his Yorkshire home town.

Rotherham's school also employed a writing master, an innovation that was becoming slightly more common by 1509, especially in urban centres where clerks, secretaries and apprentices to shippers or merchants would be in demand. Writing masters were probably teaching secretarial skills and accounting as well as simple penmanship, but their abilities were considered inferior to those of the grammar masters – their work was too obviously vocational, aimed at a lower class of scholar. Rotherham explicitly stated in 1483 that his intention in offering secretarial training was to provide 'youths endowed with the light and sharpness of ability, who do not all wish to attain the dignity and elevation of the priesthood' with the necessary skills to be 'fitted for the mechanical arts and other concerns of this world.' Robert Sherborne, who founded Rolleston school in 1524, considered writing a skill valuable only to those boys who were too dull or lazy for the grammar school curriculum. As a reflection of his inferior status, the writing master at Rotherham was paid only £5 6s. 8d., not much more than half the ten-pound wage of the grammarian.[9] Since many schools had no such specialist staff member, peripatetic tutors toured counties teaching writing in schools for a few weeks a year. In towns, scriveners' guilds carefully controlled access to the skill, sometimes making it illegal for a priest with a moderate annual salary to make money from teaching writing.

Reading and grammar schools were usually established through the endowment of a local dignitary or organization. The former often took the form of 'chantry schools', in which a private chantry chapel was endowed as an act of piety for local 'childer apt to learn at school'. (In this context, 'children' almost always meant boys.)[10] Chantry schools were run by priest-masters who combined prayer for their benefactor and family with schooling. Thomasine Percyvale endowed a chantry school in her home town of Week St Mary, Cornwall, in 1506 and appointed John Andrewe, a master of Winchester College, as priest-schoolmaster for life. His salary of twenty pounds a year was paid from the rents of local lands, in return for which he was expected to give daily lessons and ensure that his charges also attended matins, mass and evensong on holy days. Thomasine established her chantry school decades after leaving Cornwall, perhaps following the example of her late husband Sir John Percyvale, who endowed a chantry school in his home town of Macclesfield in 1503. Concern for the poor of their home town – even after years of absence – was not unique to the Percyvales. In 1486 the Bishop of Worcester endowed a school in Hull. He had been raised there, as the son of a local merchant.

These schools mirrored those established by boroughs, corporations or guilds. An unmarried schoolmaster, who was usually a priest and might – although it was rarely a requirement – have a degree, would teach from a canopied and throne-like chair, his pupils on benches before him in the single schoolroom. In one documented instance the schoolmaster was female: Elen Skolemastre of Taunton was left a bequest of a few shillings in 1494. The schoolmaster's pupils could number anything between twenty and over a hundred, depending on the size of the town or parish in which they worked. Andrewe was well paid by the standards of the time, but other priest-masters could be less fortunate, paid only five or six pounds annually. Accommodation was often provided to compensate for the low earnings. The master in Hull grammar school was even given livery to wear like a city official.

The school day was long, beginning at six or seven o'clock in the morning and ending at five or six in the evening, with breaks for breakfast and dinner. There were a few weeks' summer holidays in August, and on festival days teaching was replaced by additional religious duties. Sundays were days off for most students, but the priest – and any sponsored boys whose scholarship demanded it – had to sing divine service. Besides their six weeks of summer holiday, schools in Wotton and Newland in Gloucestershire gave their students fortnight-long holidays at Christmas and Easter, as well as a week off at Whitsun.

The expansion of schooling through charitable endowment did not necessarily broaden access to education across the classes. Even where schooling was offered *gratis* to poor children there would be a limited number of places available. Thomas Rotherham's foundation provided free food, clothing and instruction – but only to the six 'poorest [boys] in those parts'. Elizabeth and William Chamber's chantry school at Aldwincle, founded in 1489, likewise offered six places to local poor boys. Additional demands might be placed on the children receiving 'free' education that could create social tensions with their fellow students. Boys whose education was provided for by local bequest had the additional responsibility of beginning and ending each day with the priest, singing prayers. At Aldwincle chantry school, the six poor boys had to join the chaplain nightly in singing *De Profundis* in memory of their departed benefactors. St Paul's school, refounded in London in 1508–12, had only one poor scholar. Alongside his lessons he was expected to sweep the school and oversee the sale of urine on site.

Exactly how free this education was is also in question. The scholar would need to arrive at school appropriately dressed, provided with materials like pen, textbook, parchment or paper, and fed and watered during the day. A quire of paper (eight leaves) cost four pence, equivalent to a day's wages for a manual labourer, and parchment was even more expensive.[11] Edward Querton received 'free' schooling at Ewelme, Oxfordshire, in 1464–5, but since his guardian had to pay 1s. 3½ d. for his materials over a period of six months, there was still considerable financial outlay involved in his education.[12] Moreover, since long-distance travel (by animal or vehicle) was beyond the means of most labourers, a free school place had to be within walking distance for it to be practical. In reality, even schools established as charitable ventures rarely sought to expand social inclusion. Sir John Percyvale's chantry school in Macclesfield (founded in 1503) was explicitly intended to teach grammar to 'gentleman's sons and other good men's children of the town and country'. The borough school of Ipswich made clear that its aim was to educate its own – it actually offered a discount to burgesses' sons in 1477: they would be charged two pence less a quarter for learning grammar.[13]

No matter how eager to learn a child might be, and how theoretically supportive their parents, poverty must often have been a barrier to education. It certainly was in the case of William Green. In 1509 Green, the son of a Lincolnshire labourer, was learning his grammar in his village school. After two years of paying for this education, his father Stephen made him return to work as a farm labourer, occasionally manning the 'long-saw'.* As the years passed William continued to try to educate himself when finances allowed, attending school in Boston while working to pay for the privilege. Eventually he was made an acolyte by an Austin friar and was able to make his way to Cambridge, where he persisted in his studies.† However, he could only 'sometimes [go] to the colleges' as in the day he had to work 'in bearing of ale and picking of saffron' and he relied on charitable donations for his meat and drink. After years of unsuccessful efforts to complete his education, he eventually turned to forgery, producing false documents of ordination as a priest. He was caught in his lie at Norwich and put before the local court. His fate is not recorded.[14]

William had clearly hoped that he could gain education and training through the church in order to improve his circumstances.

---

* The two-man 'long saw' demanded that one sawyer toil in a pit while their partner worked the saw from above.

† An acolyte attended a priest during mass, performing lesser duties like bearing and lighting candles.

Many religious centres such as abbeys and convents contained educational establishments within them. Like learning secretarial skills in a town or being apprenticed in a trade, taking one's education in a house of religion was often intended to train a child for a career in the church. In the thirteenth century, a number of monasteries had started offering destitute children free education, food and lodging as a charitable endeavour, taking boys (or 'clerks') into the almonry. This building, used to give alms of food to the poor, was at the outer edges of the monastic compound. The boys often went on to careers as lay servants in the monastery, or even to become monks and priests. However, since free education was as enticing to the wealthy as the poor, and the wealthy tended to be better connected, over time the social rank of almonry clerks had risen. At Durham Cathedral the prior was explicitly allowed to overrule monks hoping to promote their own relatives to positions in the almonry 'at the instance of lords and magnates whom we may not offend'.[15]

As a result, by 1509 there were a number of pupils being schooled in monasteries without any expectation that they would make their life there. Generally they were drawn from the ranks of the gentry, aristocracy and civic elites. The pupils were educated in small numbers, much as they might have been at any great lay household in the realm, but with the advantage that these innocent children (generally between six and twelve years old) were segregated from the older, rowdier youths who lived in lay households. For the abbesses and priors running such establishments, education brought in a little extra money: perhaps six pence per pupil a week. Both boys and girls were schooled in convents – in the 1520s the early education of Gregory, son of the London lawyer Thomas Cromwell, was supervised by the prioress of Little Marlow, Margaret Vernon. St Mary's Abbey in Winchester had a library and a *dogmatista* (teacher) named Agnes Cox, who probably offered lessons to children from outside the convent as well as sisters within it. In addition, the novices being schooled in their duties inside the convent had their own mistress, Margaret Legh. Elsewhere in Hampshire, Romsey Abbey employed one Alice Whytingstale as Mistress of the School in 1502.[16]

Male monasteries took in only boys, and where they were highborn they often graduated from a religious house to further education at university. Richard Beere, abbot of Glastonbury Abbey, educated his nephew in-house in the 1510s, before the boy studied at Oxford and the Inns of Court. Higher education of this sort was the preserve of the wealthy, who entered into it in their mid- to late teens. Marmaduke Constable, a gentleman's son from the East Riding of Yorkshire, was a few years younger than many university students when he was sent to Cambridge at the age of twelve, and still precocious when he entered an Inn of Chancery to begin his legal training at fifteen. Seventeen or eighteen was a more usual age to enter legal instruction, which a young man would usually pursue for three years before being admitted to an Inn of Court.

At university, students like Marmaduke studied a liberal arts syllabus, comprised of the *trivium* (grammar, logic and rhetoric) and *quadrivium* (arithmetic, astronomy, geometry and music). They were expected to demonstrate their knowledge through disputation. Debate was just as important at the Inns of Court, but students were also expected to undertake some practical observation. In the courts of Westminster, gown-wearing legal students could be seen squeezed into wooden cribs, where they watched real cases and passed opinions on what they witnessed. Among their number not so many years before had been the brothers-in-law John Rastell and Thomas More, who followed family tradition by going into the legal profession. Both had forged successful careers as a result. More had become a member of parliament and successfully manoeuvred himself into the orbit of the royal court, coming into contact with internationally renowned humanist scholars like Desiderius Erasmus. Rastell had been appointed coroner for Coventry, making him the second most important civic lawyer in the city. His position entitled him to the goods of local suicides as well as granting him entry into the upper levels of civic life. But by 1509 he had given up that highly prized job to establish himself in the far less secure career of a London printer. Attending university or Inns of Court involved several years of study, and demanded considerable financial investment on the part of a student's family. Some students were forced out of education when their debts grew too great, and poorer pupils eager to improve themselves through education faced an uphill struggle.

The wealthiest members of society avoided the avenues of education offered by school and college, and instead received instruction in the households of their peers and social superiors – if possible, at the royal court. It was intended that, by being educated in such households, youths of both sexes would make contacts for their future life while learning the essentials of respectful behaviour and other courtly accomplishments. Thomas More had combined a little of both forms of schooling, for he lived in the household of John Morton, archbishop of Canterbury, at Lambeth Palace between grammar school and university. Many of the senior peers of the country were raised in royal households. The duke of Buckingham and his brother Henry grew up as wards of Margaret Beaufort. The friendships – and benefits – forged in this informal environment could last a lifetime: William Compton was a nobody from Warwickshire when he joined the household of the infant Prince Henry, but once his boyhood friend became king he was elevated beyond all imagining. He died in 1528 still one of Henry's closest companions, having built up a substantial Midlands estate off the back of royal patronage.

Prince Henry had something of a topsy-turvy education. He remained in his female-dominated household even after the death of his elder brother and mother, past an age when most aristocratic sons were removed from their sisters' company. Moreover, when he was thirteen – the age when others would leave their families, bound for university, apprenticeship or service – he was not sent away to rule as prince of Wales like his brother Arthur had been. Instead, he was brought closer to his father's side, and raised alongside him at court. The intention may well have been to ensure that the king could oversee the remainder of his son's education, while the prince would learn through example. The Spanish ambassador certainly saw the prince's transition to the court in such terms:

> It is not only from love that the king takes the prince with him; he wishes to improve him. Certainly there could be no better school in the world than the society of such a father as Henry VII.[17]

Prince Henry had not wanted for schooling even before coming to court. A number of tutors had been attending to his diverse educational needs since he was five or six – for he was to be a true renaissance prince. Alongside his grounding in history, grammar and Latin from the likes of John Skelton and the pioneering educator William Hone, Henry was also taught French and music by Giles Duwes. Even before Duwes's appointment, the prince must have been a keen musician – at seven he was given a lute by his father, and he had further musical lessons from Guillam, a 'schoolmaster at pipes'. To ensure that the martial element of his future career was not neglected – for a king still needed to be a warrior – he was also appointed a 'master at arms'. The last stage of Henry's education was in the traditional training for war among aristocrats and kings: the tournament. For at least a year before his father's death, Henry had tested his physical power and horsemanship in various tiltyards, even competing in contests before the king and court. However, in deference to the very real dangers of the joust – in which grown men in armour bearing blunt-tipped lances galloped towards each other and tried to strike their opponent – Henry had competed only in the less perilous competition of 'running at the ring'. This contest still demanded a keen eye, good reactions and skill in the saddle, but was rather less noble a venture: instead of hitting a knight, a suspended ring was speared with a lance. Such martial activities recalled the heroes of popular contemporary romance – a Spanish ambassador described jousts being done 'in imitation of Amadis and Lancelot, and other knights of olden times, of whom so much is written in books'.[18]

Nestling within royal and noble libraries were books designed to give further exempla of chivalric and honourable behaviour to Henry and his fellows in the tiltyard; carefully bound, beautifully illuminated works of chivalry, of history, of classical literature and particularly of religion. There were also, increasingly, printed works. Henry VII followed the example of his Yorkist predecessors in promoting his own printer, Richard Pynson, who worked in the shadow of St Paul's Cathedral. His mother Margaret Beaufort was a patron of the two foremost printers in England, William Caxton and Wynkyn de Worde. In 1509, Worde was working at the sign of the Sun in Fleet Street, London, and producing considerable quantities of religious texts, many of them purchased by Margaret, to add to her ever-increasing library. A pious, intelligent woman who regretted her own inferiority in Latin, Margaret was a bibliophile of eclectic and cosmopolitan tastes: she had in her collection works of poetry and fiction; a volume of Jean Froissart's histories in manuscript, covered with black velvet; a number of books by Boccaccio; John Lydgate's *Siege of Troy*; English works by John Gower and Geoffrey Chaucer; and a copy of *Magna Carta* in French. She also exchanged books with her attendants and friends, an activity shared by many noblewomen and men.

Such repositories of books were an economic impossibility for most, and libraries both aristocratic and monastic were carefully guarded, and sometimes even transported between manors with their owners. However, the arrival of printing presses made book ownership – albeit of poorer-quality, printed-paper works – possible for a much broader swathe of the population. Textbooks could be bought for a matter of pennies, primers and ABCs to learn the alphabet for even less.[19] Printing was a growing trade in England, as it was across all Europe. Since the arrival of William Caxton in 1476, printing presses had proliferated in London, their output clustered in stalls beneath the lead-roofed spire of St Paul's Cathedral, and in the university towns of Oxford and Cambridge where students and tutors bought up the work of licensed local vendors or foreign workers. By 1509 bookbinders, illuminators, printers and sellers could be found as 'stationers' (literally, stationed in a fixed location rather than peddling their works around the country) from St Albans to Hereford and Exeter to York.

When the Coventry lawyer John Rastell began his career as a printer, he followed in the footsteps of a number of provincial stationers by migrating to London to set up shop. It was easier there to come by the necessary tools of his trade: the linen-rag paper which arrived tightly bound in sheaves on ships from Genoa and Bordeaux, the dyes, panel stamps, cases and type founts to print and bind his books.* It was a cut-throat business, and like many trades, printers tended to pass their tools down the generations, or sell them on at a hefty fee. Rastell's printing work was conducted alongside a successful legal practice, and many printers found it necessary to diversify in order to make a living, since print runs in the hundreds were necessary to claw back the expense of setting up a press in the first place. Some sold pre-printed and cheaply bound continental imports of religious texts and volumes of psalters. Others turned to selling alcohol. The Westminster printer Jean Barbier was described in a lawsuit as a 'beer brewer... [and] printer'.[20] Likewise, the first printer in Norwich, Anthony de Solen, was admitted as a freeman of the city as a printer and seller of Rhenish wine.

Solen and Barbier's names suggest that they were not native Englishmen, and the presence of other foreign printers throughout the country is in keeping with the nature of this trade in printed materials, which depended so much on continental imports. Rastell went all the way to Rouen in France to buy the type founts for his press, which he purchased from Italian printers trading there. The Dutch brothers Frederick and Gerard Freez had settled in York, another major centre of the printed word. Frederick was enfranchised as a freeman of the city in 1497 and both he and his wife Joanna were admitted as members of the Corpus Christi Guild in 1500. As a printer, bookbinder and stationer he may have worked from his dwelling place at 'the Rose otherwise called the Bull', an inn on Coney Street.[21] Gerard, who went by the surname Wanesford, travelled to sell the books he had printed and imported, and died on a business trip to Norfolk in 1510. His will reveals links to

---

* A type 'fount' was a physical set of letters or other characters making up a single typeface, which would be combined to produce the words in a printed text. The font on a computer would be the modern equivalent.

other printers up and down the country. Both brothers were connected to Margaret Beaufort's printer Wynkyn de Worde. Perhaps
they had worked alongside him while learning their trade at the
presses in Mainz and Cologne.[22]

For the casual observer, much of the stock of presses and stalls
around St Paul's or in Freez's shop in York would have been of
little interest. The vast majority of works were printed in Latin,
and even those in English tended to be Latin translations. For the
true humanist, eager to self-educate with ancient biblical and classical texts in their original languages, presses were churning out
works of the Church Fathers like Augustine and Jerome or the
perennially popular classical authors Virgil and Ovid. From Italy,
specialist works in Greek and Hebrew could be imported for the
homo trilinguis, learned in the three humanist languages of Latin,
Greek and Hebrew. French works were also well represented, particularly courtly romances featuring heroes of the Trojan war and
Arthurian knights. However, it was religious works that made up
the bulk of a stationer's stocks – perhaps half of the total output
of printing presses in 1509 dealt with matters of religion. Thomas
à Kempsis's *Imitation of Christ* nestled alongside illuminated bibles
and cheap, unbound prayer books, breviaries and Books of Hours,
with their woodcut images in red and black.

Taking the books into their hands, the Freez brothers and John
Rastell could discern who had printed the work and where the
paper came from – even whose type fount had been imitated.
Paper bore watermarks, and if Rastell came across paper with
an eight-petalled flower within a double circle he would recognize the sign of the first paper mill in England. It belonged to his
fellow Coventryman John Tate, who had established it in the 1490s.
The printer Wynkyn de Worde used Tate paper for his imprints
of the *Golden Legend* and *Canterbury Tales*. Images within books,

called colophons, helped to identify the stationer, printer or paper-maker who had produced them. Often the colophon was a pun on the printer's name. The works of the printer Hugo Goes had a colophon of a large letter H and a goose. Ursyn Mylner's more intricate design featured an ass and a bear (punning on 'ursine'), supporting a tree bearing a shield with a mill on one side and a sun on the other. The mill was another punning reference to his name, while the sun was the sign of Wynkyn de Worde. By using Worde's symbol in this way, Mylner was probably asserting a connection with the prolific printer. John Rastell used a colophon that not only identified him as the printer but also expressed his philosophy: winding through a shield on which his initials J and R were entwined was a banner reading *Justicia Regat*: 'Let justice rule'.

John Rastell was a sincere and egalitarian educator: he believed knowledge was the answer to contemporary ills, and that printing could be a means to provide knowledge to the masses. Work in the printing trade was by no means a guaranteed investment, and to enter it for altruistic reasons Rastell must have been firm in his beliefs. He was emboldened to make the move to London and into printing thanks to an inheritance from his long-term sponsor, and possibly aunt, Joan Symonds, but he may also have been motivated by alarm. Coventry was a well-known centre of religious dissent, particularly of the heresy known as Lollardy. Lollards followed the teaching of John Wycliffe, eschewing church ceremony in favour of scripturally based personal religion. In order to better understand religious texts, they commissioned and disseminated illegal translations of scripture. Lollards had no respect for the veneration afforded to St George, condemning all relics, statues and images of saints as dead sticks and stones. In recent years there had been a clampdown on prominent Lollards by the bishop of Coventry and Lichfield. Had Rastell's name been among the suspected radicals on the bishop's list? He was certainly connected to one wealthy local merchant with Lollard tendencies – in 1507 he had overseen the will of Richard Cooke, among whose bequests was 'one Bible in English'. And Rastell was unafraid to take on the goods of a suicide heretic some years later in London, even though they were closely associated with Lollardy. It is possible that Rastell's educational moral endeavours were no more than orthodox religion combined with humanist principles. There was a fine line between inquiring piety and heresy. However, there is no doubt that he left behind a city with a strong Lollard community, in which literacy was a valuable commodity and religious education could have alarming consequences.

Among the Coventry Lollards was the young spicer Thomas Villers. While there were as many dissenting views as there were Lollards, as a male merchant born in Coventry to a literate family, Villers was as close to a typical Lollard as you could get. From cutlers and tailors in Kent to leather- and cloth-workers in the Midlands, Lollardy particularly appealed to artisans and tradesmen. Many were well-established members of their communities, often in their middle age, and they were more likely to be men than women. Like many Lollards, Villers denied the 'sacrament of the altar' whereby the priest transformed bread and wine into Christ's body and blood. One night in 1508, while sharing a room away from home, he entered into a fierce debate with the twenty-two-year-old mercer William Lodge about this crucial religious question. Villers insisted that the miracle of the mass was false: 'I tell you, a priest cannot make even the smallest fingernail, much less the Lord's body.' Lodge refused to be drawn into such heretical areas, insisting like a good Catholic that he 'believe[d] whatever the Church teaches'.[23] All the same, at Easter – the one festival of the year when the church demanded all its followers take the eucharist – Villers lined up to do the same. He knew that private debates were one thing, but open defiance of the church's strictures was quite another. Condemnation as a heretic could see him lashed to a stake and publicly burned to death.

Like other closet heretics, Villers no doubt recalled the past century of oppression Lollards had endured. In the early fifteenth century, Lollardy had been supported by Oxford's academic community, by the gentry and even – it was whispered – by the royal family. But in the wake of the rising tide of Lollardy, and with Lollards joining the rebellion of a Wycliffite baron called John Oldcastle in 1413–14, all religious heterodoxy had been fiercely suppressed by church and government, and translations of the Bible into English were strictly forbidden. Lollardy lived on, but its proponents kept a low profile until the last decades of the fifteenth century, when its resurgence coincided happily with an increased circulation of printed works. As a textual community who emphasized the primacy of the written word of God over the ceremonies of the church, the exchange and discussion of scriptural works was an integral part of Lollard life, and literacy a highly prized skill. Thomas Villers's family and co-religionists taught each other to read in order to spread their message.

Oddly enough, many of the works that Villers and his co-religionists read together in their gatherings were orthodox: books of lives of the saints or primers in English containing prayers and religious offices, as well as Gospels and Testaments both Old and New. The Lollards' dissenting act was the way in which they used these works. As lay people operating outside the church's control, they met together to debate theological questions for themselves and came to conclusions that undermined centuries of Catholic ritual and tradition. At Christmas 1509 the Kentish cutler Stephen Castelyn joined a gathering of Lollards at the house of his friend, where the Book of Matthew was read aloud in English. The conclusions that Castelyn and his friends came to had alarming repercussions for the Catholic Church. 'As they understood it... the sacrament of the altar, baptism, matrimony and priesthood' were all denied by this gospel. In other words, four of the most fundamental rituals of Catholicism had no grounding in scripture. 'It was pity', they felt, 'that [this fact] might not be known openly', tacitly suggesting that they intended to inform others of their realization.[24]

While Geoffrey Blyth, bishop of Coventry and Lichfield, was leading his own single-minded campaign against heresy in the first years of Henry VIII's reign, he considered the books that the Lollards used almost as dangerous as the heretics themselves. Imprisoning suspected heretics was valuable not only because it took Lollards off the streets, but also because their capture enabled him to 'get to my hands right many damnable books, which shall annoy no more by God's grace'. Other authorities tended to agree. When four Lollards were publicly punished at St Paul's Cross in London they were made to stand 'with the books of their lore hanging about them, which books were, at the time of the sermon, there burnt'. Since to be found in possession of 'books containing heresy' was in itself evidence of heresy it is little wonder that Lollards took pains to conceal their precious texts, especially during periods of heightened suspicion. One of the leading Coventry Lollards, Alice Rowley, hid her book up her sleeve when she carried it to friends' houses for readings, and when twenty-year-old Julian Young was warned to hide her books during the bishop's investigations she stashed them under the mattress of Alice's bed. Even the ability to read could be dangerous, since the lowly birth of most Lollards meant they were unlikely to be literate by orthodox routes. When Julian was examined for heresy she refused to admit that she could 'read perfectly' – as a tailor's daughter, proficiency at learning would only raise suspicions. In the end she confessed to her literacy only when a leading member of the Lollard community testified to the fact before Julian and her examiner.[25]

The word of God was the root of knowledge but Lollards did not always require the word to take physical form. Important works could be memorized and the ability to recite whole texts by heart was highly admired. Throughout the country, Lollards practised their memories to spread their message: Thomas Villers's sister Thomasina Bradeley could 'read well and can almost recite from memory the chapters of [Saint] Paul'; the Bristolian Henry Tuke had memorized the Book of Revelation; the Birmingham shoemaker John Gest was said to know by heart not only the epistle of Paul dealing with charity but also the section of the gospel in which the Devil tempts God. Most impressive of all was Elizabeth, the thirteen-year-old daughter of a London cooper, who could recite both the Gospels and Epistles by heart.[26]

Some of these Lollard communities, particularly those of the Chilterns and the Weald of Kent, had survived throughout the entire fifteenth century with multiple generations of the same families keeping the faith alive. Even in areas where Lollardy was a recent arrival, ties of kinship helped to spread and support the community. Thomas Villers had been taught his dissenting opinions at his mother's knee, and had a network of relatives and friends in Coventry who shared his thinking, including his brother-in-law Thomas Branbrooke, his sister Thomasina, her husband Richard Bradeley, and, of course, his mother. Education within families was an important means of spreading religious dissent, which Lollards used to their advantage. Agnes Grebill of Tenterden in Kent learned her 'heresy' from her husband John in the early 1480s, and both parents attempted to pass their beliefs onto their children, carrying it into the next century. Beyond the family, those who shared a household as servants could also find themselves drawn to the beliefs of their masters. Joan Gest served the Coventry tailor John Smyth and it was he 'who first attracted and drew her into heresy'. She then brought her younger husband John Gest into the fold.

Of course, not all families shared dissenting opinions. Agnes Grebill was eventually condemned to death by her own husband and children, and John Colins of Burford was so incensed by his father's instruction on the Ten Commandments that he 'said he would disclose his father's errors and make him to be burned, but his mother entreated him not to do so'.[27] While Alice Rowley was willing to hide heretical books in her clothing, her husband was no friend to Lollardy and drove the suspected Lollard Joan Warde into exile.

Beyond the local community, a network of co-religionists offered shelter and support to those, like Joan, who were forced to flee their home town because they feared persecution. Joan was approaching her fifties when she left Coventry in the early 1490s, escorted by a Lollard associate. It was an advanced age to be on the run, but she remained devoted to her faith throughout. She hid out for a few months at the home of a co-religionist leather-dresser in Northampton before making her way to London, where she was again sheltered by a Lollard ally. There, Joan met and married the shoemaker Thomas Wasshingburn, whose commitment to his faith stretched all the way back to the 1480s, and the pair lived in London for some years before eventually moving to Maidstone in Kent. They arrived at a dangerous time, for the archbishop of Canterbury was stepping up his investigations into heresy, and both Thomas and Joan fell beneath his gaze. Both were arrested, both renounced their opinions and Joan was branded on the cheek with the letter 'H' for heretic and made to abjure her faith. As Thomas was a relapsed heretic, he may well have been executed for his beliefs. Certainly, when Joan returned to Coventry as a branded woman, she was alone. Even this could not drive her from Lollardy, however, and in 1509 she was still meeting with Alice Rowley, Thomas Villers and their fellow dissenters.

The network of Lollards stretching across the country was suspected and feared by the authorities. It was evidence that learning could be dangerous – literacy was a route to sedition. By dissociating themselves from the Catholic Church, Lollards distanced themselves from their communities and the traditional bonds of loyalty – or so government saw it. In 1509 Lollards were rightly cautious but relatively safe. However, within two years there would be a brutal clampdown on their beliefs, with public penance, burnings and abjurations so common that one contemporary joked that the price of firewood rocketed.[28]

PERHAPS THESE RELIGIOUS dissidents were on the minds of Margaret Beaufort, Bishop Fox, Sir Thomas Lovell and their allies in the first forty-eight hours of Prince Henry's reign. The first year of the bellicose young Henry V's rule a century earlier had been disrupted by the revolt of John Oldcastle and his Lollard supporters, with fighting outside London and armed men mustering across the north and west of England. Given the rising tide of religious dissent and general dissatisfaction with Henry VII's rule, it was not unthinkable that another such revolt could happen again. If one of the rival court factions enlisted the support of their retinues against Prince Henry – or, far more likely, against his advisers Beaufort, Fox and Lovell – similar scenes of unrest could play out once more.

Anxieties were running high. Foreign merchants in London hid their goods for safekeeping. The stalwart Lancastrian loyalist the earl of Oxford wrote his will, spurred on by the imminent accession of a new king. In his long lifetime he had seen regimes overthrown, kings murdered and usurpers suddenly crowned. He knew that the deaths of kings heralded instability – well might he dwell in his will on 'the uncertainty and unstableness of this wretched life'.[29] After all, Henry VII had appeared from nowhere and swept to power in an extraordinary battle with only five thousand solders at his back – and most of them were French. It was his great good fortune that he had killed his opponent Richard III outright, but as the years passed, other potential rivals for power had matured to adulthood: the de la Pole brothers, the marquess of Dorset. For those rivals, Henry's remarkable success demonstrated that anything was possible with God on your side – and why should not God be on theirs in similar circumstances? For the time being, Oxford threw in his lot with his old allies Fox, Lovell and Beaufort. After being ushered into a private chamber on St George's Day and told of the king's death, he moved swiftly to secure the Tower of London to welcome Henry's son – and any potential rebels who needed restraining.

In the pardon issued by Prince Henry's caretaker government on 25 April, Dorset, the de la Poles and their known supporters were excluded. Even the duke of Buckingham's family was held suspect: on the morning of 24 April his younger brother Henry Stafford was suddenly arrested and carted off to Oxford's keeping in the Tower. Two other names were among those exempt from the royal pardon of 25 April: Sir Richard Empson and Edmund Dudley.

Empson and Dudley were Henry VII's men through and through – cautious, mercenary and suspicious – and in the last days of their king's life they too had made careful preparation for the dawning of the new reign. They took no chances, calling on loyal men to bring armed retainers 'arrayed in manner of war' to their homes. In Dudley's house on Candlewick Street, the armoury bristled with plate armour, chain mail, bows and arrows and spiked bills. The councillors knew how unpopular their activities on behalf of King Henry had been. They suspected action would be taken against them after the loss of their royal patron. But in their anxiety to protect themselves, they made a terrible miscalculation. For two ministers to muster and arm a private retinue in the heart of the city looked alarmingly like the bad old days of the Wars of the Roses. What they viewed as defensive action against dispossession their enemies saw as aggression. Were they hoping to seize the young king and use him as their puppet? Were they even plotting a coup that would deprive Prince Henry of power entirely? In their understandable paranoia, they had played into their enemies' hands. Of course, they were right to be paranoid – Fox, Lovell and Beaufort were out to bring them down – but Empson and Dudley's actions sealed their fates.

The morning after St George's Day, armed men surrounded the homes of Empson and Dudley. The lords themselves were seized and carted away to the Tower of London, their stockpiled weapons and mustered retinues never raised to action. Other 'promoters' with suspect loyalty were rounded up. The king's death was finally announced in the city and his son moved to the Tower to prepare for his coronation. As he rode through London's streets that fine April afternoon, Prince Henry, the glorious son of York and Lancaster, had already had his first practical lesson in kingship. Kings must appear infallible – their ministers could take the fall for monarchical mistakes. It was a lesson he would not forget.

IV

MAY

𝔜outh must have some dalliance

ON 8 MAY 1509, a debate that had dragged on for seven years was finally resolved. Catherine of Aragon, widowed princess of Wales and infanta of Spain, was to marry Henry VIII.

Catherine wrote to her father in delight. She had long suspected that only Henry VII's death would bring about this wished-for marriage, and so it had proven. During the many years in which their union had been planned, promised, broken and debated afresh, Catherine and Prince Henry had maintained a familial affection for one another, exchanging New Year gifts as a matter of course. Only a year earlier, Henry had given Catherine a 'fair rose of rubies set in a rose white and green' and in 1507 she had gifted him 'a goodly girdle [belt] of white satin' and a gold buckle of Spanish work.[1] Perhaps there might have been more romantic exchanges over the years if the couple had seen more of each other but Catherine was convinced that she had been kept away from the prince by Henry VII. Even when they were in the same palace, they had been denied access to one another. Now their dutiful, platonic affection could develop into something more.

Was Henry VIII doing little more than following the policy of his father in agreeing to the match, or was this an early flash of

Henrician independence? Contemporaries were fed different stories about the union. Writing to Margaret of Savoy, England's ally in the Low Countries, Henry couched the union in purely diplomatic terms, insisting he was playing the dutiful son and fulfilling his father's dying wish: he said he 'was charged by Henry VII, on his death bed… to fulfil the old treaty with Ferdinand and Isabella of Spain by taking their daughter Catherine in marriage; now that he is of full age, [he] would not disobey'. But royal councillors told the Spanish ambassador Gutierre Gomez de Fuensalida that the old king had assured his son that he was free to marry whomever he wanted. Two of Henry's closest advisers in those early days, Bishop Fox and the royal secretary Thomas Ruthall, were certainly arguing for the match. Fox reported to Fuensalida 'that he was going to advise Henry that he should make up his mind to marry Catherine quickly' as the 'king's council were currently in favour of the marriage'. Currently, he emphasized. Clearly he suspected that might change. There were inevitable voices of dissent, chief among which was that of the archbishop of Canterbury, William Warham, who was unsure of the validity of marrying one's sister-in-law. Fox had a simple solution for Fuensalida, who was equally eager to conclude the match: they should arrange the marriage 'before people started to interfere in the matter and construct obstacles'. That certainly seems to have accorded with Henry's wishes, and there is something adolescent in the sprint to settle the betrothal, which was agreed little more than a fortnight after the old king's death. For a prince ever eager to wage glorious war, there was also the added appeal that marriage to Catherine meant alliance with her family, and the potential for combined assault on the old enemy France. For all his manoeuvring behind the scenes, Bishop Fox was careful to publicly assign decision-making to Henry VIII himself. 'The king is king [now],' Fox reminded Fuensalida, 'and not prince.'[2]

The simple fact is that Henry was ready to marry. He was almost eighteen, and for years had been forced to watch from the sidelines as his companions at court engaged in their own romantic dalliances. There had been the magnificent pageantry of his two sisters' unions: Margaret, married to King James IV of Scotland five years previously; and Mary, whose betrothal to Charles of Ghent, one of the most powerful princes in Europe, had been celebrated only last Christmas. The affairs of his male friends probably had even more immediate impact on the teenage prince. His old companion in studies, William Blount, lord Mountjoy, had been pursuing his own Spanish match. In July 1509 he married Iñez de Venagas, one of Catherine's ladies-in-waiting. Mountjoy's neighbour in the aptly named Knightrider Street, London, was Charles Brandon, one of the group of young heroes of the joust known as the King's Spears. Henry had watched him compete in tournaments for years, and had probably heard something of Brandon's romantic history, which was astonishingly unscrupulous. He had 'married' Anne Browne, the daughter of the lieutenant of Calais, in a ceremony that was legally dubious enough for him to repudiate her after she gave birth to his daughter. He then promptly married Anne's aunt, who was twenty years his senior, twice widowed and wealthy. That union ended within two years, after Brandon had stripped as much from his wife's estate as possible. He then took up with Anne again, this time publicly marrying her (she was understandably taking no chances with their marriage's validity) and in 1509 they lived together with their second child. Outside of these marital confusions he also managed to sire three illegitimate children. Brandon did not fit anyone's ideal of a romantic hero, but his exploits must have made an impact on the less sexually experienced Henry.

The ethos of Henry VII's household had been one of fidelity and sexual continence, and Prince Henry may still have been a virgin at the time of his marriage. Seeking an outlet for his sexual desires within an accepted social and romantic framework, marriage with Catherine was the logical step to take. Perhaps Henry imagined himself as the hero of his own courtly romance: an honourable young knight rescuing a lady in distress from a life of penury, unhappiness and exile. As recently as March Catherine had despaired, hyperbolically contemplating suicide and pleading with her father to let her become a nun. Now she was a queen-in-waiting once more, the change in her circumstances was dramatic. She left behind the stinking lodgings over the stables in Richmond Palace and the cloistered penury of Durham House to join the royal household as it travelled up the Thames to Greenwich. This luxurious riverside palace, where she was no longer denied access to Henry, was to remain a favourite with Catherine for years afterwards, symbolizing freedom from her long-held anxieties.

The timing for this royal wooing could not have been better, for May was a month for pleasure, enjoyment and, above all, love. This period between the heavy work of ploughing, sowing and haymaking, when summer heat first rippled over the country and lengthening days left more opportunity for leisure, was the logical time to be outside enjoying oneself, and for centuries both high- and lowborn had made a point of doing so. Bone ice-skates were long since put away and the butchers who baited their bulls through winter months now turned their minds to other sports. In the great houses of the realm the gentry laid aside the dice, cards and chessboards on which they had exercised their minds and risked their purses to take up hunting instead. The grass season that brought the best hunting, after the noble hart, had not yet arrived but there were still plenty of opportunities to ride out with falcons on the wrist and bows at the hip to kill smaller prey.

These were far from idle pleasures, for exercise was known to be good for body and mind. The courtier Sir Thomas Elyot devoted pages and pages of his *Book Named the Governor* to recommended pastimes for gentlemen. Wrestling, dancing and swimming were all considered worthy activities but football was given short shrift: it was 'nothing but beastly fury and extreme violence, whereof proceedeth hurt'. Dice and card games were similarly frivolous, but he felt chess had its benefits. 'Of all games wherein is no bodily exercise,' chess was 'most to be commended, for therein is right subtle engine, whereby the wit is made more sharp and remembrance quickened.' Superior to all of these was hunting deer. By riding out to hunt, men practised their skills of horsemanship, of stalking, of shooting, of cunning – all necessary abilities for the battlefield, where gentlemen were expected eventually to test their mettle. They could even be joined in chasing after hares by hardy 'gentlewomen, who fear neither sun nor wind for impairing their beauty'.[3]

There was also a moral dimension to these diversions. As Henry VIII wrote in the song *Pastime with Good Company*, 'idleness is chief mistress of vices all'. By amusing themselves in sport and games, men and women avoided sin. After all, Henry wrote, 'youth must have some dalliance'.

As the evenings lengthened, there was more leisure time for young workers across the country. Cockfighting and feats of arms drew crowds of youths, like Thomasine Percyvale's apprentice Ralph Walker, to the fields surrounding city walls. There, men wrestled, threw stones, practised with bucklers and wasters (small shields and practice swords) or, if they could afford it, shot arrows at the butts. Young women loitered nearby to watch the activities, playing music and dancing to amuse themselves. If Ralph had been feeling particularly daring he might have headed for the Thames, where boys engaged in a form of water jousting, rowing towards one another in wherries while a companion held a long staff in his hands like a knight's lance – one or other, or both, was thereby overthrown and ducked in the water, to the amusement of everyone watching from the banks.

Workers were not totally free to entertain themselves as they liked, however. Their diversions were proscribed by law, so that 'no apprentice or agricultural worker, labourer, or servant in a craft' could play tennis, dice, cards, bowls or boardgames outside the twelve days of Christmas. Anyone found contravening these restrictions faced a day in the stocks. Shooting with a crossbow was also forbidden to anyone with lands and tenements of less than 200 marks – unless they were defending their home. Part of the motivation for these laws was to avoid disturbances of the peace through gambling or poaching, but another major concern was to force workers back to the archery butts. From the mid-fourteenth century onwards there had been anxious opining that young people were neglecting their longbows in favour of easier sport, putting national security at risk. 'Shooting with long bows is done little or not at all,' fretted parliament in 1504, 'and will probably soon be lost and utterly in decline, to the great harm and enfeebling of this realm, and to the comfort of our foreign enemies.'[4] Since 1363, Englishmen had been commanded to spend their Sundays and holidays practising archery. Slabs of turf were piled outside city walls and fenced off with rails to enable local youths to take up their bows, and local competitions added a festive edge to the action – as well as offering people the chance to win money. Despite governmental anxiety, young people were still practising their archery, albeit in lower numbers: deaths as a result of archery far outnumber those from football, wrestling or other distracting sports.[5]

The most famous English archer, Robin Hood, was to the fore in many May activities, alongside his legendary companions. May Day was a riot of celebration, when traditional norms were turned on their head. Giants processed through the streets, players dressed as Robin Hood and Little John paraded with Maid Marian while bells jangled, and lowborn youths usurped the roles of abbots, kings and ladies. Nature was brought indoors. Garlands of 'may' – hawthorn, sycamore, birch and whitethorn – were dangled over doorways, gates and churches, and a great tree trunk dragged from the woodland to stand in the market square of towns. Bonfires burned in the streets while 'morrises' of crazed postures were danced around them with drums beating.

These pastimes ought to have been curtailed by a country in mourning, but as the Spanish ambassador Gutierre Gomez de Fuensalida reported in the aftermath of Henry VII's death, his subjects were unmoved:

> They do not cry much for the dead king. In fact they show so much pleasure that it is as if everyone had been let out of prison.[6]

Whatever may have been privately felt, the royal court went through the motions of national grief. Henry VII's funeral, meticulously organized by his mother Margaret Beaufort, lasted three days. Commemorations began the afternoon after Prince Henry and Catherine's betrothal had been agreed. At three o'clock on 9 May, the king's funeral procession left Richmond Palace, his coffin lying beneath a life-size effigy of the man himself, orb, sceptre, robes and crown prominently displayed. His funeral car was drawn by eight horses draped in black, and accompanied by knights carrying his armour, sword and helmet. Presumably chosen for the height and slender frame he shared with Henry VII, the young courtier Sir Edward Howard rode in the late king's battle armour, the royal battleaxe held in his hand, its sharp head resting on his foot. As the procession reached London Bridge and entered the city, the swordbearer of London and king's messengers rode two by two at the head of a march of thousands of torchbearers.

The body lay in state at St Paul's Cathedral that night, before being escorted to Westminster Abbey for the final stages of the funeral on the morning of 11 May. As befitted a king who had won his crown in battle, Henry VII's armour, sword and helmet were laid on the altar. Then the regalia were removed from the king's coffin. Finally, as a mere man, the body of Henry VII was laid in the vault with his wife. The old regime was ended. Heralds removed their tabards, embroidered with the royal arms, and hung them on the hearse. The officers of the king's household broke their white staves of office over the vault and threw them on top of the coffin. When the vault was finally closed and covered in cloth-of-gold, the heralds replaced their tabards, symbolizing their service to a new master. 'Long live the noble king,' they cried, 'the noble king Henry VIII.'[7]

Henry did not attend the funeral, but his sister and future wife were in the abbey that day. Chief among the mourners was his grandmother Margaret Beaufort, a tiny figure in black velvet. These women had witnessed the deep affection between Henry VII and his queen Elizabeth of York in life, and as testament to that love the king had chosen to be buried beside the body of his wife. Theirs had been a political union that turned to genuine affection, reflecting the wider experience of many of their subjects. Marriage was as much pragmatic as romantic in Tudor England, for it established not only the personal happiness of the couple, but also their future social status and economic security. As such, it concerned and involved not only the bride and groom, but their family and community as well.

Since young people could not be expected to know what was best for them, the marriages of the rich were frequently arranged

– and as it could take years for a marital settlement to be agreed, the negotiations might begin before the bride and groom were out of their cradles. Church law dictated that brides must be twelve years old and grooms fourteen in order to consent to a marriage, but betrothals – and occasionally actual marriages – were made in infancy to ensure the most advantageous alliances. Catherine of Aragon and Prince Arthur were betrothed when they were toddlers and married when barely into their teens. Henry VIII's grand-mother Margaret Beaufort, as sole heir to her father's fortune, had been married three times by the age of fifteen and gave birth to the future Henry VII when she was just thirteen. In fact, the most common age for nobly born girls to marry was between thirteen and sixteen.[8] Young as this seems, Catherine and Margaret were old maids compared to some of their contemporaries. One of the key figures in the ongoing dispute over the Plumpton inheritance in Yorkshire was Margaret Plumpton, who was married at the age of five. Similarly, the orphan Agnes Barbron was heiress to a valu-able share in the Lancaster manor of Poulton. Eager to get his hands on Agnes's inheritance, her guardian did what any sensible Tudor guardian would have done and arranged Agnes's marriage to his son. The bride was only nine years old.

Margaret Plumpton and Agnes Barbron might have married as children but it is very unlikely that they consummated their marriages until they were in their teens. Fourteen seems to have been generally considered an acceptable age for girls to embark on sexual relationships. Agnes was 'very sickly in her youth', so her guardian did not make her 'accompany or lie with' her husband until five years into her marriage.[9] By allowing the marriage to remain unconsummated for so long, he was taking a risk, though, for such unions could be more easily dissolved and if that hap-pened, Agnes's estate would revert to her ownership. Margaret

Beaufort's second husband Edmund Tudor had exercised no such restraint when he married his twelve-year-old bride and the juvenile childbirth she endured as a result was deeply traumatic. It probably made her unable to bear more children. Later in life, when Margaret counselled Henry VII to delay the marriage of his own daughter until she was fourteen years old, she probably spoke as much from painful personal experience as dynastic pragmatism.

For those lower down the social scale, marriage was something to be contemplated only after establishing a secure economic future, probably when both parties were in their mid-twenties. Women waited until they had gained some money and experience in service, and men until they had set themselves up in a trade, or served out their apprenticeship. Marriage was forbidden while an apprentice was indentured to a master. In 1501 the Mercers' Guild refused to enrol an apprentice below the age of sixteen and since a ten-year term was compulsory, any budding mercers had to wait until they were in their mid-twenties to marry. Those who tried to defy this stricture could find themselves in a prison cell. The unfortunate Anthony Pontisbury of Cheapside in London was imprisoned on his wedding day. 'Having an inward love to a young woman... and the young woman having the same unto him', he tried to marry despite not having served out the term of his apprenticeship. Anthony defended himself by attacking the entire prohibition on apprentice marriage, which he said was 'contrary to the laws of God and causeth much fornication and adultery to be within the said city'.[10]

Regardless of status, economic matters were to the fore in the arranging of most marriages, from complex negotiation over money, land and manor houses all the way down to bartering of brides for farm animals. Thomas Watson of Eccleshall, Staffordshire, married his bride on the promise of money, clothes, a bed and a cow. A mutually agreeable marriage settlement demanded not only immediate profit but also the assurance of future security. As such, a reasonably equable swap was demanded: a bride's dowry in return for her share in a jointure of her husband's estate.* The dowry, or 'marriage portion' as it was sometimes known, could be money, but for the gentle and aristocratic it was usually a portion of the bride's parents' estate. Once delivered to the groom, the bride could make no further claim on her dowry. Such was the necessity for women to bring dowries to their marriage that wills proliferate with charitable bequests of money to nieces, goddaughters or poor maidens of the parish, to be used towards their marriage. But the demand for a dowry did not mean that marital bargaining was a one-way street. In return for the dowry a groom was expected to provide a jointure of his own estate to the bride, to be held by both husband and wife during marriage, then pass to the surviving partner after their spouse's death. It was also an accepted part of English common law that a widow could claim 'dower rights' to a third of her husband's estate at his death. In Welsh practice, dower and dowry both existed but could not consist of land, only of goods and property.

There were high financial stakes at play for the wealthy and it could take years to pay off a dowry. In 1518 Margaret de la Pole agreed to a dowry of three thousand marks for her daughter Ursula's marriage to the duke of Buckingham's heir. The sum was so vast it had to be paid off over a five-year period. Many parents had to offset the outgoing costs of one child's marriage against the incoming injection of funds from another's. Thus, Edward, viscount Lisle, planned to use the marriage portion he would receive

* The jointure was land held jointly by a husband and wife, giving women a legal entitlement to be involved in any decision affecting it.

for his son's marriage to pay for the dowries of his daughters. In such circumstances, securing the best possible deal for a child's marriage was no mere mercenary endeavour, but a complex balancing act in which the bride and groom's feelings came a long way down the list of concerns.

With such a focus on the financial in the run-up to a wedding, it is perhaps unsurprising that the language of marriage arrangement was more marketplace than marriage bed: parents gleefully reported how they had secured a 'bargain' or bemoaned the hard-ball tactics of their prospective in-laws. In some cases, negotiations were pressed to such an extreme that they broke down entirely. The widowed Lady Maud Parr ended eight months of discussion with Lord Scrope over the marriage of her daughter Katherine because his offer 'concerning the jointure... is so little and so far from the custom of the country and his demands is so great' that she would no longer 'meddle with the said bargain'.[11]

Where the future happiness of a couple seemed genuinely to be at stake, financial concerns could be put slightly to one side. The East Anglian gentleman John Paston worked for five months to arrange his marriage to a besotted teenage neighbour, Margery Brews, only for negotiations to disintegrate in the face of her father's fierce brinksmanship. Margery had three sisters who also needed to be provided for, and her father was all too aware of the disadvantage they would face if he let himself be talked into too generous a settlement for Margery: 'I were right loath to bestow so much upon one daughter, that the other her sisters should fare the worse.'[12] John and Margery were so in love that their mothers could not stand idly by and let the relationship crumble. Margery's mother wrote rather teasingly to tell John that 'ye have made [Margery] such advocate for you that I may never have rest night nor day, for calling and crying upon to bring the said matter to effect'. Margery entreated both sides to take less advantageous financial settlements in order to move the match forward, pleading with John to accept a lower dowry even as she made her mother play on her father's sympathies:

> My lady my mother hath laboured the matter to my father full diligently, but she can no more get than ye know of... My father will no more money part withal in that behalf but a hundred pounds and fifty mark, which is right far from the accomplishment of your desire. Wherefore, if that ye could be content with that good, and my poor person, I would be the merriest maiden on ground.

Eventually, John's mother Margaret called a meeting with Margery's parents to thrash out the final details of the marriage to 'take some way that it shall not break'. By adding one of her own manors to the Paston jointure for Margery, Margaret finally succeeded in bringing the marriage about.

Even if a couple were not as in love with each other as Margery Brews and John Paston, affection was still of some importance when making matches, and guardians were not totally unfeeling. In the same year that Margery and John struggled towards their marriage, Richard Fowler, chancellor of the duchy of Lancaster, willed that his son Richard should marry Anne Stradling if she became an heir 'in case he and she can find in their hearts to love either other by way of marriage and else not'.[13] Margaret Paston had given similar advice to her eldest son when she heard a report that he might marry a kinswoman of the queen. She told him that he should marry her only 'if ye can find in your heart to love her, so that she be such one as ye can think to have issue by, or else, by my troth, I had rather that ye never married in your life'.[14] As Margaret makes clear, part of parental concern for affection within marriage was that without it children were unlikely to result – and without children, estates could be divided or lost entirely.

However, parental indulgence of the romantic inclinations of their offspring went only so far. In 1512 the duke of Buckingham decided to break his daughter Elizabeth Stafford's betrothal to his ward Ralph Neville when a better offer for her hand came from Thomas Howard, earl of Surrey. Elizabeth was less than delighted at the news and entreated her father to uphold the original engagement, for she and Ralph 'had loved together two years'. Buckingham offered Surrey another of his daughters in place of Elizabeth, but the earl would not be swayed – he would have Elizabeth or no one. Unwilling to lose such a prestigious alliance, Buckingham forced his daughter to overcome her misgivings and marry Surrey.[15]

According to church law, the consent of bride and groom was essential for a marriage to take place but, as Elizabeth Stafford's case shows, that 'consent' could be very grudgingly given. Beyond this requirement, the necessary protocol for marriage to be undertaken was minimal, and some unions were of decidedly questionable validity. If vows were exchanged in the presence of witnesses and followed by consummation, marriage was presumed to have taken place, even if there had been no public announcement or church blessing of the union. However, if a couple declared their commitment to each other alone, the 'handfasted' marriage would not necessarily be recognized at law, even if it was later consummated. The distinction between betrothal and marriage was also rather muddy, since declaring consent to a future marriage (*per verba de futuro*) could still be a binding marriage if followed by consummation. This meant that if a man promised himself to one woman and slept with her, then changed his mind and married another by church-sanctioned public rites, it was the second marriage that was invalid and any children born to this union were illegitimate. This was the charge that had been laid against Elizabeth of York's parents in order to legitimate her uncle Richard III's claim on the throne: Richard's brother Edward IV had sworn to marry a woman called Eleanor Butler before he illicitly wed his queen, Elizabeth Woodville. Richard asserted that this made Edward and Elizabeth's marriage illegal and their children – including the unfortunate 'Princes in the Tower' – illegitimate. As the next 'legitimate' heir, Richard could claim the throne for himself.

Edward IV was following a well-trodden path in his dalliances with Eleanor and Elizabeth. A number of men imitated him and Charles Brandon by seducing women into their beds with a promise of marriage, and then going back on the offer when pressed to make it legal. The Londoner Alice Parker agreed to sleep with her suitor Richard Tenwinter only if he would marry her. When they were alone in her bedchamber Richard promised 'I will wed you as well as I can,' and they had sex. Since the only 'witness' to the vow was an eavesdropper in the hall of the house, Richard later disavowed the betrothal and Alice's attempts to enforce the marriage at law were probably futile. But protective parents were wise to this sort of behaviour and such tactics were not always successful. Piers Curtes expected that a promise of future marriage and exchange of rings would be enough to persuade the young widow Agnes Skern into his bed, but Agnes's mother refused to allow Piers to sleep with Agnes until the pair were fully married. Whether Piers was sincere or not, Agnes's mother was taking no chances.[16]

Consent of parents or guardians was not required for a marriage to be valid, but having it made the couple's lives considerably easier. Margaret Paston may have actively supported her son John's love match with Margery Brews, but she was outraged by her own daughter Margery's *mésalliance* with the family's estate manager Richard Calle. A servant at least a decade older than her, Richard was considered eminently unsuitable for the gently born Margery. Unfortunately by the time Margaret learned of their affection, the lovers had already been involved for two years and they seized the opportunity to marry before the Pastons could close ranks and prevent them. Margaret was furious: Margery's 'demeaning had sticked sore at our hearts… I charged my servants that she should not be received in mine house.' Even Margery's usually genial brother John was horrified and declared that Richard 'should never have [his] good will' for the marriage. But despite the combined efforts of the family and the bishop of Norwich, the marriage could not be broken and the couple were exiled from home. A few years later Calle was allowed back into the employ of the Pastons, but Margery's degradation in the eyes of her family was never accepted.[17]

Elena Couper of Welton in Yorkshire faced a similar reaction from her parents when she contracted herself in marriage to John Wistow. Like Margery Paston, she endured a long courtship and secret betrothal, but her lover was made of rather less stern stuff than Richard Calle. Having once promised himself to Elena, he got cold feet about going through with the marriage without familial support. Elena was more dedicated and, despite interest from other men, she took action to secure John once and for all. She brought him to a friend's house, this time with witnesses in tow, and gave him an ultimatum:

John, there is two young men about me in the town [who wish] to have me to wife. And I have loved thee this two year. And you knowest well that you and I be handfast betwixt us. And because you shall not varry nor take another and love another better than me, we will be handfast here afore these folks at they may bear record thereupon.[18]

Under pressure, John agreed to the marriage. Elena's family were less easily persuaded. When her mother learned that Elena was married she called her 'filth and harlot' and threatened physical violence: 'Why, art thou handfast with John Wistow? When thy father knows it he will ding thee and mischief thee.'

Elena was resolute, however, and went on her knees before her father. Appealing to his purse rather than his heart, she assured him, 'I desire no more of your goods but [only] your blessing.' Sometimes dowries and jointures were forgotten in the desire simply to be married according to one's own choosing.

The safest course of action for any prospective bride or groom was to marry in a public location, and perhaps it was for this reason that *al fresco* weddings seem such a feature of Tudor life. Richard Adamson married Beatrix Cuke on the high street in front of his house at Langtoft with his father (the local vicar) and two other witnesses standing by. Where churches were used for weddings, couples tended to exchange their vows in front of relatives and neighbours at the porch door, before going inside to receive the priest's blessing. If a couple were living away from home they might marry in front of their new 'family' of fellow servants and master. The details of some nuptials are decidedly curious: one fifteenth-century couple married by Beverley Gate in Hull while milking a cow.

With such informality in the contracting of marriage, it is unsurprising that there was considerable variety in practice, but a few traditions had grown over the centuries. New clothes were bought for weddings where couples could afford it, and where they could not they used textiles bequeathed to the local church for such occasions. White was becoming a more common colour for wedding clothing, particularly for brides, and had been worn by both Catherine of Aragon and Prince Arthur at their wedding in 1501. The couple would exchange vows of commitment to each other which varied from wedding to wedding, but contained certain recurring elements: a promise of commitment, for better or worse, in sickness and in health, 'till death us depart' [sic]. Women promised to be bonny 'at bed and at board', although not generally to obey.[19] Gifts or tokens of love would be exchanged between the bride and groom. The child bride Mary Trotter was given a bracelet of silk by Henry Redyng when they illicitly married – she was still wearing it some months later when the validity of their union was investigated by officials. Other common romantic gifts included finely worked sleeves, silk flowers, gloves, purses of coins – and of course rings. Elena Couper was given a silver-gilt ring as 'trothplight' by John Wistow.

Upon marrying, a woman was supposed to be 'ruled' by her husband – her surname changed to his and her possessions transferred to his control. A good wife would be deferential to her husband, and a good husband kind to his wife in order to maintain domestic peace. Mutual respect was expected, if not outright love. In plays of this period, husbands and wives address each other as 'sir' or 'dame' as well as by their Christian names, and in letters a similar deference of address is often used. Richard Calle referred to his wife Margery as 'mine own lady and mistress' and wives frequently address their 'right worshipful husband'.[20]

Of course, the ideal of marital behaviour did not always match up to reality. The courtier poet Sir Thomas Wyatt offered this sage advice to his newly married son:

Love well and agree with your wife, for where [there] is noise and debate in the house, there is unquiet dwelling. And much more where it is in one bed. Frame well yourself to love, and rule well and honestly your wife as your fellow and she shall love and reverence you as her head. [21]

However, this was very much a case of 'do as I say, not as I do', for when Wyatt wrote this he had been separated from his wife for a decade and was living with his mistress. He laid the blame for his marital troubles squarely at his wife's door: 'The fault is both in your mother and me,' he told his son, 'but chiefly in her.'

Whoever was responsible for a marriage's breakdown, it was the woman who was more likely to suffer as a result. When Thomas Wyatt stopped financially supporting his wife, she could do little but appeal to him for money through her brother. Even then, Wyatt refused. This was the unfortunate fate of a number of women whose husbands proved unwilling or unable to support them financially. Without an influential patron of their own, these women were powerless to protect themselves. Sir William Knyvett lamented that his son-in-law's 'negligence and misordered living' had brought his daughter Anne 'into great danger and poverty'. When making his will he tried to provide for her and save her from her 'poor life' with a bequest to her and her children of twenty pounds a year for clothes and other necessities. The countess of Oxford appealed all the way to the chancellor for help after three years of trying to regulate her husband's 'riotous behaviour' yielded no results. Her husband was then twenty-one and not only drinking too much, dressing extravagantly and quarrelling with his wife, but also abstaining from his sexual duties as a husband. The countess believed he was being kept from her bed by his kinsman and heir, who wished to ensure that no child would be born to take his place in the line of succession to the earldom. Unhappiness and financial control were not an aristocratic preserve. Arthur and

Anker Frechwell of Derbyshire were comparatively low born, but by the time of Arthur's death their marriage had broken down to such an extent that when he wrote his will he threatened Anker with the denial of her dower unless she returned certain jewels she had stolen from him.[22]

As a woman's goods were legally the possession of her husband, she had no power to prevent their alienation during marriage. Mary, Lady Willoughby, claimed to have lost jewels, plate and household goods worth over a thousand pounds because her husband Sir Gervais Clifton had 'wasted and destroyed' them.[23] The husband of Dame Elizabeth Bodulgate used his wife's gold collar as security for his debts, and she was still trying to claim it back from his creditors after he had died and she had remarried. As long as they were married, women could not even write wills without their husband's permission.

Women had little recourse at law for mistreatment by their husbands, whether financially or physically. A husband had the right and duty to chastise his wife in whatever manner he thought fit as long as it did not threaten her life or shed her blood. The duke of Buckingham's daughter Elizabeth Stafford lived in relative contentment with her husband the earl of Surrey – later the duke of Norfolk – for nearly twenty years, but when the marriage fell apart in the 1530s it did so in spectacular fashion. Norfolk took up with a mistress, Bess Holland, a situation that Elizabeth could not endure. She loudly and widely condemned him, alleging that in retaliation Norfolk 'locked me up in a chamber, [and] took away my jewels and apparel' then 'made his women bind me till the blood came out at my finger ends, and they... sat on my breast till I spat blood, and he never punished them, and all this was done for Bess Holland's sake'.[24] Norfolk treated Elizabeth harshly because he hoped to force her into a divorce, but she stoutly refused.

Ironically, physical cruelty was one of the few circumstances that could enable a woman to get a divorce – although only if her life was endangered or blood shed. Even then, it could be difficult for a woman to escape an abusive relationship, as it was considered trespass to receive a man's wife into one's home without her husband's permission. This meant that a woman's family could find themselves legally in the wrong when they tried to offer sanctuary. Richard Vergeons was 'slain at his own door' and his wife imprisoned for trespass when they took in his abused sister-in-law, Mrs Hyll. She had been threatened by her husband with a dagger. Vergeons had tried reasoning with Hyll, saying that although it was right for a husband to direct his wife, he ought to 'guide her and chastise her under a due manner and not to draw his dagger to her'. Where women did appeal for divorce on the grounds of cruelty, the success of their case depended on their neighbours supporting their claims. Katherine Burwell of London gained her divorce only because the local parson and two other neighbours witnessed her estranged husband threatening to cut her throat during an attempted reconciliation in the Saracen's Head tavern.[25]

Astonishingly, even when women were kidnapped into marriage it could take years to free them. In June 1509, Margaret Kebell and Ralph Egerton were finally able to marry after seven years of engagement and enforced separation. Margaret had spent the period since their betrothal in 1502 as hostage to a forced marriage. A law of 1487 had declared abduction of 'women having substances' (that is, women of means) a felony, but the complete authority of a husband over his wife's goods had made wealthy women enticing targets for unscrupulous men, and a number of forced marriages appear in the statute books during Henry VII's reign. No unwilling wife was more dogged in her attempt to free herself from such an unwanted match than Margaret Kebell.[26]

Margaret had much to attract the attention of an admirer: at twenty-five she was a childless widow, and an heiress in her own right to a substantial inheritance of Staffordshire lands. In January 1502, she and Ralph Egerton were at the home of Margaret's uncle on the edge of the Peak District, celebrating their betrothal. But at six o'clock in the morning of 2 February, before dawn had even broken, the peaceful gathering was disrupted by the arrival of over a hundred men on horseback. At their head was Roger Vernon, a rival for local authority who now staked his claim on Margaret. Throwing her possessions into a basket and confiscating a hundred pounds which she was carrying, Vernon made it clear to Margaret that she either came with his men quietly or she would be taken by force and imprisoned in the Peaks until she was more compliant. With little option, Margaret got on a horse and joined Vernon's party. The kidnappers tore across the moors at breakneck pace to reach the safety of Vernon's Derbyshire lands. By the time a rescue party with Ralph and Margaret's mother in it managed to catch up with them, it was too late to free her. She was smuggled into Vernon's territories, forcibly married in a Derby church and then hidden in the home of one of Vernon's confederates in Herefordshire.

Some women might have resigned themselves to their fates when they found themselves eighty miles from home in unknown country, surrounded by their hated husband's allies. Not so Margaret. At Easter she managed to escape Vernon's clutches and made for London, reuniting en route with a rescue party sent by her mother. For the next seven years Margaret tried every avenue possible to rid herself of her unwanted marriage and take revenge on Vernon and his accomplices, to no avail. Since she had married in a city church with no immediate menace in evidence, it was deemed that she had consented to the union. Local partisanship

ensured that the kidnappers she accused in London escaped justice
in their own county. Only a combination of direct appeal to the
king's mercy, church law and resilient opposition on Margaret's
part eventually yielded results. It must have been with considerable
relief that Margaret and Ralph finally married in June 1509.

IN THE SAME month, on 11 June, another couple who had waited
years for their wedding to arrive had their wedding day. Henry
and Catherine married at Greenwich Palace. In stark contrast to
the public pomp and pageantry of Catherine's first marriage, this
union was celebrated privately, and few details of the occasion
survive. We know that in the couple's vows, politics took primacy
over romance. Henry was asked in Latin:

> Most illustrious Prince, is it your will to fulfil the treaty of mar-
> riage concluded by your father, the late King of England, and the
> parents of the Princess of Wales, the King and Queen of Spain;
> and, as the Pope has dispensed with this marriage, to take the
> Princess who is here present for your lawful wife? [27]

He replied *Volo*, 'I will'. And when Catherine was asked the same,
so did she – one imagines with considerable eagerness. They were
words she had waited an almost unbearably long time to speak.
In the end, it had taken little more than a month to resolve the
thorny diplomatic issues that had troubled England and Spain
for seven years. England now had an intelligent and experienced
young queen to sit beside its handsome new king. Preparations
were already underway for their joint coronation.

V

MIDSUMMER

'All England is in ecstasies'

Summer had arrived and towns all across England witnessed a strange transformation. In the place of merchants' stalls stood two-storey painted canvases on wheels, adorned with winged angels. Tradesmen's shops were overshadowed by carts and scaffolds from which devils leered and souls danced. Even in bright sunlight, the rumble of thunder could be heard. At York, the city was overrun, over a dozen pageant wagons moving around the streets from dawn, and in Coventry the most famous pageants in all England were performed. Over the next month, from the day of Corpus Christi to Midsummer on 24 June, communities of guilds, fraternities, parishes and city officials gathered together across the kingdom to put on grand displays of community spirit.* In London, midsummer watches could involve processions of over two thousand, with archers, gunners, choristers and guildsmen, all in white cotton, lined up according to precedence. Alongside them paraded morris dancers, a giant and St George. Midsummer

* Corpus Christi was a movable feast, whose date varied annually in line with Easter. Fifty days after Easter came Pentecost or Whitsunday, and one week after that was Trinity Sunday. The feast of Corpus Christi (literally 'the body of Christ') was celebrated on the Thursday after Trinity Sunday.

was the traditional time to put aside old enmities and rejoice in friendship, gathering together around bonfires in towns and villages across the country. It was also the day that Henry VIII had chosen for his and Catherine's coronation.

While the rest of the country was in the grip of guild displays, London was struck by a fever of preparation for the royal event. Tailors and goldsmiths were kept desperately busy creating the magnificent clothing of the nobility and their horses. Embroiderers worked their fingers raw. Elizabeth Worship, the royal silkwoman, must have been worked off her feet.[1] The chronicler Edward Hall recorded the hive of activity around the royal court and capital:

> If I should declare what pain, labour and diligence the Tailors, Embroiderers and Goldsmiths took, both to make and devise garments for lords, ladies, knights and esquires and also for decking, trapping and adorning of coursers, jennets and palfreys* it were too long to rehearse.[2]

Between 22 and 23 June, the capital was transformed. Tapestries and cloth-of-gold glistened in windows. On Midsummer Eve, sweating in their livery, all the guilds and senior officials of London, John Middleton among them, stood in rank at Cheapside. Crosses glinted in priests' hands and the new king and queen processed through a mist of incense from the Tower of London to Westminster Abbey for their coronation.

Crowds pressed against the barriers that had been erected in the streets of London, and peered from windows all along the route to catch a glimpse of the vast royal party as it passed. Among their number, looking out from a rented room in Cheapside, was

---

* Coursers, jennets and palfreys are types of horse.

Margaret Beaufort, the matriarch of the Tudor dynasty. Beside her, Princess Mary peered out onto the crowded streets below as row upon row of men and women processed to Westminster. The beaming Queen Catherine was easy to spot: resplendent in white satin, her litter borne by two gleaming pale horses, trapped in white cloth-of-gold.* Her auburn hair hung loose on her shoulders, and over it lay a circlet studded with pearls. The duke of Buckingham made a good fist of drawing the crowd's attention to himself. As the pre-eminent nobleman in attendance, and chief steward for the day, he wore an immensely expensive ensemble that included a silver staff of office and gold chain smothered in rubies and precious stones. But even Buckingham could not out-shine the king that day. High above the crowd, the teenage Henry rode on horseback through the streets to the adoring cheers of his subjects. His red hair gleamed as brightly as the jewels on his clothes. His tall frame was swathed in a gown of velvet and ermine, the layers beneath studded with rubies, pearls and emeralds. Even the harness of his horse was made of damask and gold. He moved at the centre of a throng of choristers and crimson-clad knights. To the waiting crowds he looked like a hero resurrected from some ancient legend, framed by a backdrop of tapestry and goldwork.

Alas, for all their meticulous preparation for this occasion, even the aldermen of London could not control the weather. A burst of rain sent the crowds shrieking for cover and Queen Catherine – the canopy of her litter no match for English downpours – was forced to take shelter in a draper's shop, water dripping down her unbound hair. For Catherine and Henry, it was an irritation. For the trades-men of London, it was a financial disaster: priceless tapestries and

---

* A litter was a canopied couch, either carried at front and rear on men's shoulders or, as here, drawn by horses.

arrases had been ruined. While the king and queen rode on to their coronation and their 'solemn feast and jousts', the merchants of London fretted over how to reclaim their expenditure.

Agricultural communities had long come together at this time of year to make hay or shear their sheep, hoping for fine weather and a good harvest. Such hopes sat alongside an all-too-rational fear of the reverse. If rain washed out crops or spread disease among animals it could be disastrous, and not only for those who made their living on the land. Towns and cities relied on imported supplies of food, and especially grain. The effects of bad harvests lingered long. When harvests failed, prices rocketed and stayed unnaturally inflated for years, which meant hunger for the masses. The sixteenth century had begun with two consecutive years of poor crops, doubling the price of flour in London. Although the harvests of 1502–3 were better, it took five years for prices to return to the level they had been in the summer of 1500.

In such circumstances, the communal activities of a parish, trade or town could have important consequences for people's ability to survive the hard times – and their enjoyment of the good. The pageants of Corpus Christi, just like the midsummer celebrations in London, were organized and funded to a very large extent by local guilds. These organizations – whose name derived from the traditional payment or 'geld' given to gain membership – were quasi-religious conglomerations of local people, usually sharing a common trade. They had their origins all the way back in the twelfth century, but by the dawn of the sixteenth had become a crucial part of civic life. It was through trade guilds (sometimes also known as 'mysteries') that teenagers were indentured as apprentices, to learn the craft of their parents or aspire to better themselves with a new trade. After a minimum of seven years, apprentices were eligible to set up in business, take on apprentices of their own and become 'freemen' of the guild. Without the 'liberty' of the guild or city, it was extremely difficult to operate within the local area, as heavy fines were meted out to the unen-franchised for attempting to muscle in on guild industries. Across most of the country, the local guildhall or chapel served as a focus for guild interests, and the usual boundary of a guild's power was the city walls. However, the Goldsmiths' influence exerted itself throughout the entire realm, ensuring that no one could work gold or silver without being inspected, approved and paying the necessary fee to the guild in London. Guilds allowed women to participate in their celebrations and often to become members, but usually only alongside their husbands and never with the option of gaining a ruling position within the company. The exception to this rule was the 'men and women of the whole craft of silkwork', a trade dominated by women. Although there seems to have been no specific guild of silkworkers, artisans in the trade acted to all intents and purposes like one, with a collective identity and co-operative protection of their business in the face of outsiders.

However, even where guilds were formed primarily for the pro-tection of an industry – from the wealthy Merchants, Tailors and Butchers down to the low-paid Thatchers, Pinners or notoriously lazy Spur-makers – they also fulfilled a religious function. All were attached to a place of worship, usually connected to the patron saint of their trade (St Dunstan for Goldsmiths, St Eloy for Black-smiths) and celebrated their feast days by processing to their own chapel or church, where every guild member was obliged to light a candle. There were also guilds that were purely religious, without any affiliation to business. Among these was the Corpus Christi Guild in York, of which the Dutch printer Frederick Freez and his wife Joanna were members. On the day after Corpus Christi, early in the morning, guild members would assemble at Holy Trinity

Priory on the very edge of the city, wearing their livery coats and bearing torches. As a richly bejewelled shrine containing a piece of the consecrated host was brought out on a great bier, Frederick and Joanna joined their brothers and sisters of the guild to watch the procession. Bells pealed, priests sang, the streets were strewn with flowers and the sun rose over the spires of the city as the 'body of Christ' was paraded through the streets of York.

Like the Corpus Christi Guild procession, summer pageants were a tangible symbol of the prosperity and fellowship of religious and craft communities.* While the coronation celebrations had necessarily been planned in a matter of weeks, preparations for Corpus Christi pageants began months ahead of schedule. In York, it was Lent when the mayor supervised 'four of the most cunning, discrete and able players within this City' as they examined all the players, plays and pageants that would be involved in the celebrations. The smiths of Coventry rehearsed their pageant not long after, in Easter week, and again during Whitsun week to ensure they were prepared. Then, in the days before the feast, there was a flurry of activity. Costumes were borrowed from the clergy or local gentry; masks brought out of storage; props and pageants painted. In Lincoln, the pageant of Bethlehem demanded dyed damask cloth, a cage for doves, censers for angels, cord for the stars and 'a great head gilded, set with seven beams and seven glasses for the same and one long beam from the mouth of the said head'. The pageant wagons themselves – the wheeled stages that trundled through streets while players performed their pieces from them – entailed considerable expenditure, so were used year after year, with running repairs keeping them in service.[3]

* 'Pageant' was used to mean both the play, and the wagons on which the pieces were performed.

The image-maker Thomas Drawswerd had gained free admission to the fraternity of the Holy Trinity in York on condition that he 'make the pageant of the doom' for the Mercers, cannibalizing pieces of the old pageant to do so. The Corpus Christi celebrations of John Rastell's native Coventry featured a Doomsday pageant similar to that of the York Mercers, vividly reminding onlookers that their decisions in this life would affect their comfort in the next. In a visually literate but predominantly writing-illiterate culture, scenes needed to be visible to, and understood by, as many spectators as possible, so figurative items were used: a throne for King Herod, painted canvas to represent clouds in heaven or the cave of Jesus' sepulchre. The Lake of Gennesaret in Palestine could be represented simply by digging a hole in front of a scaffold, filling it with water and floating a boat on it. Drawswerd's Doomsday pageant probably represented a hellmouth, from which demons would leap as it rolled through the streets, to prod at and dance with the onlookers. On the day of the performance – in York, this began at half past four in the morning – refreshments were set out for those taking part, the axles of the pageant wagons greased with soap, their insides strewn with rushes, then the civic clerk checked the wagons against his register, the players leaped inside and the pageant-drivers put their shoulders to the wheel and settled to their long day's work.

The pageants were an expression of the pride of the city, its crafts and its religious fraternities. Doubtless this is why the performances were sometimes left to professionals. A team of 'players' progressed through the towns of Lincolnshire and South Yorkshire annually, performing in Grimsby, Boston, Louth, Long Sutton and Doncaster. In Chester 'players of price' (paid actors) were eschewed in favour of 'crafts men and mean men'. The most important parts tended to be paid on a sliding scale, with the starring roles – like

Noah in the mariner's pageant at Hull – paid a shilling. In this piece, God was paid the same amount as the man playing Noah's wife, but at Coventry God was clearly a more substantial role, as it was paid at three shillings and four pence. Perhaps Coventry, which was renowned for its pageants, was a more generous city altogether: a 'soul' (whether saved or damned) would earn twenty pence for his work at Corpus Christi, and a 'worm of conscience' eight pence. Some roles were evidently doubled up, as 'the man who hanged Judas' was also paid four pence 'for cock crowing'.[4]

The topics of these pageants varied from town to town and between guilds, but they were always on a religious theme. In their most theatrically advanced incarnations, as at York, Chester or Coventry, they included a full cycle of events that progressed through the city, with different guilds taking responsibility for separate pageants that could last for days. Noah was traditionally associated with shipwrights (as in York and Newcastle) or with watermen (as at Beverley and Chester), so their guilds took responsibility for his pageant. Presumably, the fact that pertinent guilds would have access to the necessary props for their pageant was part of the play-allotting process. The Last Supper, suitably enough, was often performed by the Bakers' Guild; the Disputation of Christ in the Temple by the Scriveners; the coming of the Magi by Goldsmiths, with their handy stockpile of gold (if not frankincense and myrrh); while the pageant showing the scourging of Christ was produced – with wince-inducing literal-mindedness – by the Butchers. Quite why the Tailors were associated with the fall of Lucifer in Beverley is not clear. In simpler versions, as at Newcastle, Reading and Louth, pageants were performed in a single location, usually a marketplace near a church, to ensure maximum space for a crowd to enjoy the spectacle.

The whole community was brought together by these pageants. The citizens of Coventry believed that the plays contributed to 'the wealth and worship of the whole body' of the town. From the great lords who donated the pay of minstrels, as the duke of Buckingham and earl of Northumberland did for Grimsby in 1499, to the porter John Barnes who oversaw the pageant for Lincoln Cathedral, to the boys playing female parts and the women in the crowds watching, all were involved in this ritual display of community spirit.

The coronation pageantry of the royal court might be more lavish, but at root was the same principle of community. Henry and Catherine's coronation was feted with two days of tournaments and jousts, martial celebrations that were now an expected feature of all major court occasions. Even the cash-conscious Henry VII had spent lavishly on jousts. He knew that these displays of arms were not idle spectacle, but a powerful propaganda tool, emphasizing the unity of the realm and reaffirming the warrior class's loyalty to their ruler – two essential messages to convey in the wake of a bloody civil war. Where Corpus Christi pageants demonstrated the wealth and generosity of the guilds, a court tournament advertised the magnificence and power of the king. It helped that, like civic pageants, tournaments were witnessed by hundreds of spectators, all being fed the same message.

Tournaments had originally been an elite and exclusive activity, intended to serve as training for warfare. But they had evolved far beyond their origins in the twelfth century, when teams of knights would simply arm themselves, jump on horseback and attack each other across fields and woodland. By the fifteenth century, tournaments had evolved into displays of skill and honour, with ladies acting as focal points and judges of the action. Now knights fought 'as well for their ladies as also for laud or praise to be given [to] them[selves]'.[5] Increasingly, tournaments were accompanied by pageantry for the entertainment of spectators, with viewing stands erected so they could better enjoy the sport. They had become pieces of theatre, with knights riding as symbols of chivalry or as figures from legend. While in civic pageants religious imagery dominated, the court flaunted its learning in stories laden with classical allusion.

Most tournaments – like that in 1509 – extended over several days, punctuated by pomp and theatricality, with multiple forms of combat on display. The joust is the most immediately recognizable of these contests, and was probably the most thrilling for the spectators watching. In this contest, two knights, separated by a wooden barrier called a 'tilt', charged at each other on horseback and tried to strike their opponent with a long, blunt-tipped lance. Points were awarded if a knight broke his lance on his opponent's helm, his *targe* (a small jousting shield) or other places above the waist. If they struck these points but failed to break their lance it was called an *attaint*, and would still count towards their score. In rare cases, unhorsing an opponent would also score points, although this dangerous practice was not as popular in England as it was on the Continent. Points could be lost – and even fines given – for dishonourable behaviour like striking an opponent on the back or killing his horse. The two other most common contests in a tournament were the tourney and the foot combat. In the tourney the mounted knights fought one another with swords rather than lances, while the foot combat or mêlée was fought across a barrier by unmounted knights. In this contest the knight wielded axe, sword or short spear. Occasionally, tournaments might also include 'running at large' where knights jousted without the tilt between them. An additional display of arms was available for less experienced competitors, who could 'tilt at the quintain' or 'run at the ring', both of which involved striking a target with a lance while on horseback. Henry VIII had demonstrated his ability in such lesser challenges when he was prince, but had never participated in the full joust. Even now, a crowned king and only days from his eighteenth birthday, he still acted as spectator and judge rather than joining his peers in the lists.

But if he had to be a spectator, there were certainly worse ways to do it. For the coronation jousts, Henry's army of joiners, carpenters and painters had erected an astonishing royal viewing stand. The new king and queen sat enthroned in a gallery designed to look like a great turreted castle, wreathed all over with golden vines. Inside green and white painted lozenges, symbols of the king and queen were entwined: their initials, the Tudor rose, the Spanish pomegranate. From the mouths of the castle's gargoyles flowed red, white and claret wine.* From this position, Henry watched the spectacle unfold before him. The first stage of a joust was the entry of the combatants from pageant wagons. But these were far from the soap-greased, patchwork-repair jobs of his subjects. Tournament pageants displayed high levels of technical ingenuity. In previous tournaments, the combatants had made their entrance in structures that imitated fully rigged ships, guns firing as they moved; a fortress, 'with proper turrets and pinnacles of curious work'; a 'great mountain of green', surmounted by a maiden clad 'in her hair'; and even a dragon led by a giant with a tree in its hand.⁶

The pageants of 1509 were tied together with the action to tell a flattering story of the new king's wisdom and honour. On the first day of the tournament, the 'scholars of Pallas Athena' (the

---

* Claret (from the French clairet) was, until about 1600, distinct from red and white wines. It had a yellowish or light red colour.

goddess of wisdom) arrived bearing a crystal shield and wearing glistening plate armour. Pallas Athena herself rode atop a turret wrought in cloth-of-gold, down which more roses and pomegranates cascaded. From this elevated position she addressed the king, asking that her scholars would act as defenders against any and all challengers during the tournament. On cue, the challengers, sixty horsemen in cloth-of-gold and -silver, surged into the yard to the martial accompaniment of drums and fife. They came, they declared, 'to do feats of arms for the love of ladies' and were headed by a figure in blue velvet bearing a golden spear: Cupid himself. Cupid presented his spear to the queen and sought her permission to enter the fray. In a crowd-pleasing speech to bait his opponents, Cupid wondered whether Pallas Athena's scholars were there to teach feats of arms or to learn them?

On the second day of the jousts, Henry's eighteenth birthday, the challengers came disguised as huntsmen in green satin, heralded by horns blowing and a pageant 'made like a park'. When the gates of this pageant were opened, deer fled out, pursued by hunting hounds. A forester beheaded one of the deer and presented it to the queen and her ladies in the name of the chaste goddess of the hunt, Diana. Would the ladies permit his fellow huntsmen to take up the challenge of Pallas's knights? The queen dutifully demurred to the king, who permitted the challenge of a tourney, but 'conceiving that there was some grudge and displeasure between them', limited the contest to a certain number of strokes. Either Henry was right that there was a grudge between the fighters, or they were just over-eager to display their martial skill, because the knights refused to stop at the approved number of blows. When the marshals stepped in to prise them apart, the knights kept fighting. Even Charles Brandon's horse was feeling unusually combative, fighting 'with his teeth and feet like a serpent'. Eventually, the king had to command his royal guards to intervene and break up the mêlée. It was an unfortunately chaotic end to the chivalric demonstration.[7]

Had the tournament knights been performing in a town pageant, they would have been heavily fined for such a poor display. The pride of the community was invested in their performances and the local officials would not put up with anyone embarrassing themselves – and their town – in the way that Brandon and his colleagues had done. When Beverley's pageants descended into chaos the alderman of the painters had to hand over a two-shilling fine. He was condemned for allowing his craft's production of *The Three Kings of Cologne* to be 'badly and confusedly played, in contempt of the whole community, before many strangers'.[8]

Like the royal jousts, civic pageants told stories to their crowds of spectators. These tales were intended not only to entertain but also to remind the onlookers of their duties to the local community. In York, Thomas Drawswerd's Doomsday pageant warned that admittance to heaven was dependent on charitable acts of mercy, and this reflected the reality of civic activity on the part of the pageant's sponsor, the Mercers. They, like all guilds, functioned in part as a support structure for their members in a time when the safety net of a welfare system was conspicuously absent. In this sense, the entry fees paid into a guild were a form of insurance policy, used not only to provide for their pageant displays and feast-day celebrations, but also to support members who fell into poverty or ill health. The Guild of the Smiths of Chesterfield granted any brother who fell sick a halfpenny a day from the common fund until they were recovered. If one of their members fell into poverty he could call at any of his brother guild members' homes, 'where each shall be courteously received, and there shall be given to him, as if he were the master of the house, whatever he wants of meat, drink and clothing; and he shall have a halfpenny like those who are sick'.

Loans were even granted by the guild, to be repaid under threat of suspension within the agreed terms. The Smiths of Chesterfield were only one among many guilds who promised to help their members when they had brushes with the law. The Palmers' Guild of Ludlow agreed to 'use every means in their power' to free imprisoned members and the Guild of St Leonard in Lynn visited its imprisoned brothers and sisters to offer them comfort.

Even those outside the guild could benefit from their charity. Corpus Christi Guild in York provided eight beds for impoverished 'strangers' and the Guild of the Holy Cross in Birmingham provided almshouses as well as food, clothing and rent-free tenements for the local poor. The guild-merchant of Coventry kept a lodging house of thirteen beds for passing pilgrims, and the very highways and bridges over which the pilgrims passed might have been funded by the guilds whose hospitality they sought.[9]

Not all experiences of the guild system were so positive. Records from the guild courts reveal instances of mistreated apprentices, long-drawn-out legal disputes and sexual misconduct. The ironmonger Richard Dobbes of London called his ex-apprentice William Gomon before the Ironmongers' Hall after Gomon departed his service early, carrying off twenty marks' worth of Dobbes's goods. Although they came to a mutual agreement, Dobbes was still pursuing the case after Gomon's death. Runaway apprentices often justified their broken indentures by claiming their masters had mistreated them. John Saunders said he fled his apprenticeship to the apothecary Richard Smyth in Cambridge because he was 'neglected and ill-treated'. Thomas May, who was apprenticed to the London haberdasher John Hill, was not even given the chance to run away. While indentured to Hill, 'a very unreasonable man', he was given no training, but instead forced to work in the kitchen and undertake any other menial tasks Hill demanded. After four years of such treatment, May complained that he was not being taught a proper trade as he had expected, so Hill accused his apprentice of stealing and had him arrested. Without any local friends to act as surety for him, May languished in prison while his father appealed through the law courts for his release.[10]

There were also cases of young apprentices being sexually exploited by their masters and mistresses. Thirteen-year-old Joan Hammond was apprenticed in London to a woman named Alison Boston, who sold Joan 'to divers persons for divers sums of money to execute and exercise with them the horrible vice of lechery'. Similarly, the ten-year-old Mary Trotter was placed in the house-hold of Mrs Tonkey to train as a silkwoman, but with her mistress's collusion was abducted by Tonkey's brother Henry Redyng and taken to Hastings. There, he 'did ravish the said Mary, she not being above the age of eleven years, and to cloak the said detest-able demeanour the said Henry Redyng has married her'. Mary's parents appealed to Star Chamber to have Tonkey and Redyng punished and the marriage dissolved.[11]

MIDSUMMER WAS A season for the laying aside of differences and disputes. On Midsummer Eve, bonfires were lit as part of the com-munal summer celebrations and these 'friendship fires' were often accompanied by food, drink and garlands of flowers, intended to bring together neighbours and mend any local rifts with collective merry-making. Perhaps Henry had been dwelling on the meaning of these bonfires, for as he prepared for his coronation he had also begun a process of reconciliation with the nobility, particularly with those Yorkists who had been suppressed during his father's reign. Henry VIII, after all, had the blood of both Lancaster and York flowing in his veins. The Tudor rose combining the Yorkist white rose with the Lancastrian red could just as well have been Henry himself. As the poet John Skelton, Henry's old tutor, expressed it in his work celebrating the coronation: 'The rose both white and red, in one rose now doth grow.'[12]

The lawyer Thomas More was even more carried away by this theme, and in his own coronation poem he located the 'twin roses' of Henry's forebears in the 'colour in his cheeks'. More dubbed Henry 'the everlasting glory of our time'. 'This day is the limit of our slavery,' he wrote, 'the beginning of our freedom, the end of sadness, the source of joy.'[13]

More and his fellow humanist Lord Mountjoy saw Henry VIII's accession as the beginning of a 'golden age'. 'All England is in ecstasies,' Lord Mountjoy wrote to their friend Erasmus.[14] But for all this hyperbolic optimism, Henry VIII was not exactly profligate. He might be more even-handed than his father, but his behaviour towards his relatives at the start of his reign could best be described as cautiously benevolent. Margaret Pole, the cousin of Henry's mother Queen Elizabeth of York, was placed in a position of honour in the household of Catherine of Aragon and attended the coronation clothed at Catherine's expense, but she was still addressed only as 'Dame Margaret Pole', not by her confiscated title of countess of Salisbury. Titles and positions determined someone's status at court in a very real way, and to be denied either was a legitimate cause of frustration. Another royal cousin would have shared Dame Margaret's dissatisfaction. The duke of Buckingham had a hereditary right to serve in the position of constable of England, a right he was regranted by Henry – for the day before the coronation only. Since Buckingham's brother was still imprisoned in the Tower, the family must have had rather more mixed feelings about the young prince's accession than Mountjoy, Skelton and More.

One Yorkist who did have cause to celebrate was Thomas Grey, marquess of Dorset. Dorset had been one of the heroes of the joust during Henry VII's reign. On numerous occasions he had fought for the king in the tournaments proclaiming loyalty to the Tudors, but by autumn 1508 Dorset was arrested on suspicion of conspiring against the crown and imprisoned in Calais Castle. At Prince Henry's accession his cousin Dorset was explicitly exempted from the general pardon. So when, shortly after the coronation, the royal councillor Sir Thomas Lovell landed in Calais, Dorset had every reason to fear bad news. But Lovell did not arrive with a warrant for Dorset's imminent execution – instead, he came to escort him back to England as a free man. Dorset was not officially pardoned until August, but by that time he had already returned to court and been restored to royal favour. In the early years of Henry VIII's reign he became once again a fixture of the royal joust.

As the sun set on Henry's eighteenth birthday, the tournaments celebrating his coronation came to a close. As Henry and his queen handed out prizes to the knights and enterprisers of his celebratory jousts – Pallas Athena's crystal shield, Cupid's golden spear, Diana's hunting dogs and the scholars' swords – was it with a twinge of jealousy? For Henry had never been permitted to play anything but the role of spectator and judge of these contests. It was a part that his father had been content with, but the energetic young king was of a more active bent. Did Henry's hand itch to take up a lance for himself? He had an ideal athletic physique – all the visitors to court commented on how tall and well built he was. Henry's family and advisers counselled caution. There was good reason to keep him away from the joust. For all it was only a pale imitation of real battle, it still involved an alarming array of very real dangers. Thomas More laid them out for the king:

All the tournaments kings have held until now have been marked by some sad mishap or by disaster thrust among the festivities by ill luck. Sometimes the ground has been drenched with the life-blood of a stricken knight; sometimes commoners have been struck by lances or have been trampled by the pounding hoofs of the maddened steeds; sometimes a scaffolding has collapsed and crushed the wretched spectators.[15]

More's rhetoric did not exaggerate. A knight called Sir James Parker had been killed in a joust before the king in 1492. It had been one thing for Henry to run at the ring when his father was alive, but now that he ruled in his own right, there was a far greater need to keep him safe. If he fell in the tiltyard, who would take the throne? With all the royal blood swilling in the veins of the court there could be dozens of claimants: Buckingham, Pole, Dorset and de la Pole were only the foremost among them. Civil war would be the inevitable outcome. Perhaps it was for this reason that even during the celebratory banquet that evening, Henry's grandmother Margaret Beaufort had warned that 'some adversity would follow'.[16]

As it transpired, she was right. For the next morning, on 29 June, the woman who had given the Tudor dynasty its claim to the throne and steered it safely through the tempests of civil war died at the age of sixty-six. One of Margaret's attendants claimed that she had fallen ill after eating a cygnet at the banquet the night before. For Henry VIII, one of the most important authority figures of his life was now gone. The day after his eighteenth birthday he found himself a king and husband, responsible for his own family and the entire kingdom, with no parents or grandparents to guide him. A young man who had been 'kept secluded like a girl' for much of his childhood now had to lead an entire country.[17] For all the celebratory verses of scholars like Skelton, More and Mountjoy, it was a heavy burden, even for Henry's broad shoulders.

VI

LAMMAS

𝕲𝖔𝖔𝖉 𝖆𝖓𝖉 𝖇𝖆𝖉 𝖑𝖔𝖗𝖉𝖘𝖍𝖎𝖕

THE FIRST OF August, known as Lammas, saw a migration of animals throughout the country. It was the customary time for beasts to be driven from workers' own exhausted farmland to the common land of their community. Pigs' noses were ringed to stop them rooting up crops, while cattle and new-shorn sheep were herded into fresh fields and poultry pecked at the earth. Animals were valuable commodities in 1509, relied upon for everything from a little extra income through sales of eggs and milk, to a national trade in wool. Perhaps unsurprisingly, they feature frequently in labourers' wills; in 1505 the Lincolnshire farmer Thomas Rawsby bequeathed ewe sheep to his servants and colts to his sons.

That summer, Henry VIII was responsible for another mass migration. On 8 July the king appointed commissions to investigate abuses against the liberties of England, reversing the perceived injustice of his father's financial constraints. Henry VII's will of 31 March 1509 had established a committee to investigate complaints, for people of whatever degree, but now the work was seen as his son's – a popular action to begin the reign of Henry VIII. Scapegoats for the avarice of his father's regime were also needed, so finally, three months after their arrests, the councillors

Dudley and Empson were brought to court, to face charges not merely of financial wrongdoing but also of treason. On 12 July Dudley was hauled before judges at London's Guildhall, while Empson faced the same charges a few weeks later in his native Northampton. Their attempt to surround themselves with armed men as Henry VII lay dying was interpreted as an attempt on the crown itself – a scheme to use Prince Henry as their puppet. After three days, Dudley was found guilty of conspiring 'to seize the [future] king and his council by force and to govern according to his will'.[1] Empson defended himself at the bar, but the outcome was the same for him as for Dudley: both were declared guilty of treason and were condemned to public execution. No date was set for their deaths, so the lords clung to hope of a royal pardon. But during those hot summer days, both were far from the king's mind.

Throughout the summer months, while his commissioners circled the kingdom and Dudley and Empson fretted in their cells, Henry focused on enjoying himself. The 'grass season' between August and October was the traditional time for the royal progress, when the king showed himself to his subjects and allowed the court to disport itself in hunting. Before Henry and Catherine had even left London, ripples of activity had spread outwards from the court. Royal servants called harbingers, consulting the *gests* that outlined the planned royal itinerary, rode out to ensure that the towns through which the court would pass were free from sickness. In the close confines of the royal household, plague could spread like wildfire and any courtier who suspected he might be sick had to stay away for three days. Once sure of the safety of the route, the clerk of the market was sent 'to warn the [local] people to bake, to brew and to make ready other victual' for the royal party.[2] The officers of the king's works moved into the royal houses on the route, opening doors and windows to air the musty rooms, clearing chimneys and filling storerooms, laying down fresh rushes and perfuming the royal apartments. Transporting the rich furnishings and clothes of the royal party was a job in itself, and was entrusted to the staff of the wardrobe – men like part-time thespian and full-time yeoman tailor Richard Gibson. The opulent fabrics had to be packed in linen trussing sheets or laid between firm pieces of buckram to protect them during transport. Then they were loaded into ironbound, leather-covered coffers and placed in painted carts pulled by half-a-dozen horses. The royal apothecary Richard Babham provided perfume to keep clothes sweet-smelling, and both men and women carried scented pomanders to ward off foul odours. Many of the fabrics in their clothing were too delicate to be intensively cleaned, so scenting was a useful means of overcoming any ingrained smells.

The king and queen did not travel alone. A display of magnificence was expected of a monarch, and the myriad servants around them provided that lustre while also fulfilling crucial support roles behind the scenes. Henry's boyhood friend William Compton had been elevated to the role of groom of the stool and was responsible for ensuring that the king's apartments were clean and comfortable on arrival. In his new position of trust he also had responsibility for the twenty-four locks kept in store at Woking Palace when they visited. Unlike some royal palaces, this riverside retreat did not have locks permanently attached to its doors. The vast household encircling Catherine and Henry trundled and trotted across the countryside as it moved between Surrey manors, spilling out over the edges of roads onto the verges. Along with the hundreds of human servants, the court also had an animal presence. Under the canvas covers of one great wagon snuffled the buck hounds, a vital part of the household during the hunting season. Many royal manors were located in or alongside royal parks and forests, allowing easy access to deer.

The roads over which this rolling royal circus travelled tended to be of good quality, allowing the court to move at a stately fifteen to twenty miles a day. Beyond the royal highways, though, transport was a challenge, and the presence of well-constructed bridges, hard-wearing road surfaces and safe causeways could not be taken for granted. Quicksand was a danger near the coast; rivers were liable to flood and prevent passage; the hills and craggy peaks of the north made travel by any means of transport difficult; even in relatively prosperous towns, streets could be unpaved, leaving mud in the streets to be churned beneath travellers' feet. Local people might help themselves to stones and earth from walls and roads, thereby creating hazards for passers-by. In 1499 a miller from Aylesbury dug an enormous clay pit on the road into town, which drowned an unwary glove-merchant. When John Rastell and his family travelled from Coventry to London it was a three-day journey. In some places it was easier to travel by water than by land: ferries plied the stretch of the River Lindis (now called the River Witham) between Lincoln and Boston, the Severn allowed small vessels to travel as far up as Tewkesbury and London was a wherryman's paradise. The Thames was the most important water route in England, accessible all the way to Lechlade in the Cotswolds – although weirs, mills and bridges jammed the upper reaches.

Since building materials were too heavy to be transported over long distances by land, as people moved from one region of the country to another they would notice a visible change in the local buildings. Dorset, sitting on a belt of limestone, was pocked with stone-walled and stone-roofed constructions; in the southeast, brick and tile were displacing thatch and timber as the fashionable choices in architecture; in East Anglia, flint predominated; while in the heavily wooded Midlands, timber and plaster were the order of the day. If these building materials had to be moved, water transport was the best way of doing so.

Travelling by water was the royal court's preferred option too, and wherever King Henry went, he went in style. The king's barge was covered in cloth of green and white, the royal colours, and hung with gleaming arras, sweet-smelling herbs perfuming the cushioned seats. But when moving en masse away from the greater palaces of Richmond and Greenwich (an easy barge journey from London), the royal household relied instead on carts and wagons to carry their possessions, and horses to carry themselves. The queen and her ladies, or older members of the court like the sexagenarian earl of Oxford, might choose to make the journey in a litter, a seat swinging beneath a round, wooden-vaulted canopy. Two poles supported this structure, which was carried by either men or horses, like a particularly elaborate sedan chair. The litter would rock as it moved, and was suitable only for leisurely journeys. Female courtiers might prefer to travel by chariot or coach. This long, barrel-shaped structure of wood and iron was suspended by chains between enormous ironclad wheels and pulled by a team of horses. It was effectively a palace on wheels, brightly painted on the outside, while within, behind windows veiled by silk curtains, there were seats, beds, tapestries, rugs and cushions. If they chose to travel on horseback, the women of the court would either ride pillion behind a groom or side-saddle, in a chair-like apparatus that hung sideways over the horse's body. Either way, the groom had control of the reins and responsibility for keeping the palfrey moving. These side-saddles could be very impressive items – the tailor Thomasine Percyvale had two of them, both covered in blue velvet with matching harness.

From their comfortable perches, the royal court might glance at other travellers sharing the roads. Labourers walking in search of employment at the Lammas fair, traders moving their wares, and those whose appearance marked them out as migrants with a loftier purpose. These men and women in large-brimmed hats carried tall, red staffs, and might be struggling only as far as the local church. Others, dust-shrouded, were making their way east to Walsingham, or south to Canterbury and the ports beyond. They were pilgrims, walking to shrines domestic and international, to pray for remittance of their sins and healing from sickness. Their travel was serious business, for a vow of pilgrimage was no small matter. A promised pilgrimage to the major international shrines of Rome, Santiago de Compostela and Jerusalem could be revoked only by the pope. Once a vow was made the pilgrim had to adhere to it, even from beyond the grave if necessary. As she died, Margaret East of St Martin in the Bailey, Norwich, wrote instructions in her will for her 'right trusty and well beloved cousin Thomas Thurkell, shoemaker in Beer Street' to visit the local shrine of 'the Holy St Wandred', as well as those at Canterbury Cathedral and Chertsey Abbey, 'so by his pilgrimages I may be released of my vow'.[3]

Guilds and hospitals had been established over the years to support these pilgrims. The Guild of the Resurrection of Our Lord in Lincoln gathered together when any of its brothers or sisters took up pilgrimage to the Holy Land, Rome or Santiago and gave them at least a halfpenny each, flocking to the city gates to see them on their way. While travelling, pilgrims could hope for charity from the various hospitals that had been established to support this infrastructure of wandering religious. In York, the hospital of St Thomas of Canterbury without Micklegate Bar had been established to support pilgrims as they passed through the city. In Coventry, the guild-merchant kept a lodging house with thirteen beds for pilgrims, and even provided a woman to wash their feet. Where such charity was not forthcoming, pilgrims were forced to rely on a rented bed in a private home or tavern. They would spend the night clutching their few possessions, for theft was rife in roadside inns.

Among the more prolific pilgrims of the fifteenth century was Margery Kempe, a Norfolk mystic and ex-brewer in her forties, who waved farewell to her husband and fourteen children to undertake a pilgrimage to Jerusalem. She crossed the North Sea from Yarmouth and headed south through mainland Europe as far as Venice, where she took ship to the Holy Land. On her return journey she went to Rome, wearing white robes to symbolize her spiritual purity. The journey to and from Jerusalem took well over a year, but Margery did not hang up her red staff when she got home. In the following years she visited York, Hailes, Santiago de Compostela and in her sixties she was still undertaking pilgrimages, visiting the Holy Blood of Wilsnack in Brandenburg.[*]

While the Holy Land was the most sacred of sites for Christian pilgrimage, it entailed considerable effort, expense and time to reach – not to mention the potential dangers of drowning or being captured by corsairs en route. Many pilgrims restricted their perambulations to the British Isles, for there was a wealth of potential shrines within the king's realm. The cathedral in Coventry held the head of the martyred virgin St Osburg in a case of copper and gilt. At Hailes Abbey in Gloucestershire visitors could see a phial containing the blood of Jesus Christ himself. But the most famous site of pilgrimage in England, which drew visitors from all over Europe, was the shrine of the murdered archbishop St Thomas Becket in Canterbury Cathedral. A Venetian visitor described the shrine there:

---

[*] Margery recounted her experiences in the earliest surviving autobiography to be written in English, which was written in the 1430s.

[It] surpasses all belief. This, notwithstanding its great size [,] is entirely covered over with plates of pure gold; but the gold is scarcely visible from the variety of precious stones with which it is studded, such as sapphires, diamonds, rubies, balas-rubies, and emeralds; and on every side that the eye turns, something more beautiful than the other appears. The church is rather dark, and particularly so where the shrine is placed... yet I saw that ruby as well as if I had it in my hand.[4]

Relics of dead saints could be found in all the altars in the country as well as in specially designed reliquaries for the veneration of the devoted. As well as St Thomas, Canterbury Cathedral could also boast the tooth of John the Baptist, a finger of St Urban, the lip of a murdered Innocent, and three thorns from the crown Jesus Christ had worn while being crucified. It was reported that a number of monasteries held 'unicorn's horns, of an extraordinary size'. A Bohemian squire travelling in the retinue of the wealthy pilgrim Leo of Rozmital reported that there were so many relics in London's churches that it would take two full-time scribes at least a fortnight to properly describe them.[5]

The royal family shared their subjects' pious attention to shrines – Elizabeth of York had paid a man to pray for her at Our Lady of Woolpit in Suffolk and Our Lady of Walsingham in Norfolk was to enjoy considerable attention from Henry and Catherine in the years ahead. In August 1509, however, their minds were focused on rather more temporal matters. On arrival at the next manor on their progress, the palfreys being ridden or sumpter horses bearing loads would be stabled and exchanged as soon as possible for gleaming coursers for the hunt. Henry, like his father and many of his royal forebears, adored hunting. The scholar Richard Pace described how Henry rose, 'daily, except on holy days, at four or five o'clock, and hunts till nine or ten at night. He spares no pains to convert the sport of hunting into a martyrdom.'[6]

Perhaps the king's subjects caught a glimpse of him and his men as they rode out to hunt that summer: a flash of men clad in green wool and long boots as they dashed through grassland to chase down deer, horns blowing, dogs and hunting boys running alongside. Or perhaps they caught sight of the more stately progress as the court moved between royal households, taking in Woking, Farnham and Hanworth. At best it was likely to be a fleeting glimpse of the young king – that is if they even paused in their work to look up.

For Henry's subjects, this was the most energetic, prolonged period of work in the year. The air was filled with the sound of threshing, dust rising from cereal crops as they were reaped, gathered and laid out to dry before being beaten in bundles to separate the edible grains from the chaff. This was hard work, but better than the alternative: a poor harvest that left few crops, little fodder and sickly animals. Famine was always at a poor man's back, and later in Henry VIII's reign scarcity was to lead to raids on corn deliveries, attacks on French ambassadors as their bread was baked and deaths throughout the country from lack of food. A king could try to lessen economic troubles, but he could not stop the rain from flooding the fields or the sun from drying out the crops.

All possible labour was called in during harvest, and tenant farmers had to tend their own lands as well as providing service for their lords in return for meals of ale and bread. Day labourers were hired to fill the gap, earning two to four pence a day. Women made up easily half of the workforce during harvest, doing the same jobs as their husbands, sons and fathers – often for the same wages. They made hay, reaped barley and peas, gathered and bound grains, and returned to do the same tasks every year. This was a change from the usual run of things, when male and female activities were divided, with women tending to work in lower-paid industries. On the estate of the gentleman Humphrey Newton in Cheshire, his distant relative Ellen Newton brewed and made cheese – two typically female industries. Spinning the wool that was sheared earlier in the summer was also traditionally considered 'women's work', and the unmarried women who undertook it gave their name to the state of 'spinster'.

Lammas was one of the key times of year for hiring workers, with local fairs acting as recruitment markets. Humphrey Newton gave his workers contracts of up to a year, although some preferred to specify that 'they may be loose at any quarter'. These workers might be relatively local, the tenants or neighbours of their employer (certainly, this was Newton's preferred means of recruitment) but they also travelled from further afield. People often turned to migration in order to pursue the best employment opportunities, flocking to cities and towns at some distance from their own families. Thomasine Percyvale had begun life as Mistress Bonaventure of Week St Mary in Cornwall before making her living and her life in London. In the silk trade, girls came from as far afield as Bristol, Norfolk and Yorkshire to be apprenticed to London silkwomen. Ten or twenty miles was a more common distance for workers to travel, but regional centres like Exeter might draw as much as half of their migrant workers from greater distances. Even in villages this migratory impulse was in evidence. The same families did not settle in one location and stay there for centuries – in the early sixteenth century as few as one in ten families might have a connection to a village that went back five generations (around 150 years) and the turnover of many village families was considerably quicker.[7]

For some families, this migration was not just a question of economic opportunity but of freedom. In 1509 the ancient form of slavery known as serfdom still technically existed. Serfs or 'bondmen of blood' were tied to a parcel of land and expected to render service to their lord as payment for their tenancy. Their status was heritable, chaining multiple generations to the same patch of earth. In the century and a half since the Black Death, most manors had stopped recording tenancies on such terms, allowing old bonds of service to be forgotten, but where lords insisted on their serfs buying their freedom it could be a prohibitively expensive business. It was far easier just to move away from the lands they were bound to and seek economic opportunity in an area where their status was unknown. The serf George Underhill of Hampton Lovett in Worcestershire did exactly that in 1479, moving five miles away to the small town of Hartlebury, where he held land and sold food and drink to make his living. His son Richard migrated even further, going all the way to Tewkesbury, twenty miles off, to work as a tanner, but in 1503 he rejoined his father at Hartlebury.

Unfortunately not all lords were prepared to let their serfs go quietly. The duke of Buckingham, ever mindful of his own rights and prerogatives, relentlessly pursued any tenant that he believed owed him 'bond service' as a serf. During one of the many commissions sent out to inquire into the tenancies and fines owed by those on his lands, Buckingham's under-steward in Wiltshire investigated the Pynchon family 'as he heareth say [they] be bondmen to my lord's grace'. When initial questioning yielded no results the under-steward promised 'to inquire further of their fathers and grandfathers'. As far as Buckingham was concerned, once a serf family, always a serf family. But the duke was hindered in this pursuit by the unwillingness of those on his estates either to acknowledge their own inherited serfdom or inform on their neighbours. In Buckingham's lands in Wales and Gloucestershire, careful inquiry was made for serfs but 'the tenants say there be none such [here]'. One family, the Mors of Rumney, went on trial three times and even sued the duchess of Buckingham rather than submit to their alleged serfdom.[8]

The nobility and gentry were expected to keep a close watch on the administration of their estates, but Buckingham took things to extremes. Equally energetic, if less obnoxious, were the efforts of Humphrey Newton in Cheshire. He oversaw his estate of several hundred acres directly and within the first six years of ownership he had rebuilt a corn mill, constructed a fishery and new fulling mill for working wool, and marled the soil. His efforts increased the profitability of his land by almost twenty per cent.[9] Improving the quality of one's soil, using dung, seaweed, sand or 'marl' clay like Newton was essential to ensure a better harvest, especially in areas notorious for their poor earth. Between May and August chalky, claggy marl was dug out of the earth from great pits, then left on fallow ground to melt in the sun 'like molten lead over all the face of the earth,' enriching the soil. Limestone or 'stone marl' was quarried for the same purpose, and along the coast sea sand and weeds were fetched in sacks to be carried miles inland so that the fields would provide better grains and grass.[10]

In the farmland that surrounded villages, there were few fences dividing properties, and neighbours had to trust one another not to overstep the boundaries of their crops when they harvested, and to keep their crop-crushing and grain-munching livestock off each other's land. The main form of farming was the 'open-field system' centred around a village, with three huge fields divided into long strips. Lots were drawn to allocate land and each of these three fields rotated its crops annually, so that one had white crops (wheat and barley) planted before winter; another had soil-improving peas or beans planted in spring; and one was left fallow. Since the random nature of lot-drawing meant that lands could be spread out over vast distances, some farmers swapped their allotted fields to create parcels of land closer together. Such enclosure was even more useful when farming animals rather than crops and in the uplands of the West Country, Lancashire and the Weald of Kent grazing land had long been enclosed with thick old hedges.

Innocent as this impulse to enclose might seem among tenant farmers, it could spell disaster when carried out on a large scale, and by 1509 it had become a serious concern. Arable lands for grain were slowly being transformed into pasture, with sheep farming particularly prosperous at a time when cloth-working and export were the backbone of the English economy. For the lord – and it very often was a lord – doing the enclosing, there could be considerable financial gain from farming lucrative livestock rather than abundant, and therefore unprofitable, cereals. But for the surrounding community, such enclosure could be disastrous. When Sir Miles Willesthorpe of Yorkshire converted ploughland into pasture and enclosed local common land to create a deer park he was accused of destroying the entire town of Willesthorpe by his actions. Thomas Pigot's enclosure of fields in Doddershall, Buckinghamshire, caused twenty-four houses in the village to fall into ruin, and forced 120 locals to leave the area 'tearfully'. A settlement of dozens – even hundreds – of labourers farming open land was reduced by enclosure to a ragged assortment of fenced-off pastures where sheep and cattle were herded by a handful of employees.[11]

The right to land was the most important issue for almost everyone in Tudor England, one way or another. It was an investment for their future and that of their family. It was where crops were planted and what was used to feed livestock, where homes and perhaps also workshops were built. It might include water to fish in. For the wealthy, it was a symbol of honour and importance and provided them with economic support. Those who had parks and hunting lands pursued hunting for their own amusement, but also to gain high-status venison to eat and send as gifts to whichever allies they were courting. Land was power and money.

As well as making more money from pasturing livestock, lords were often motivated to enclose by a desire for good parkland in which to hunt. The inhabitants of Stoke Gifford in Gloucestershire complained bitterly when their local lord, Sir John Rodney, created Stoke Park. To do so, he enclosed forest that had been used to keep local livestock, fenced off common pasture lands, stopped off a common right of way and 'without colour or title of right but only of his extort power and might contrary to all laws and good conscience' he ejected three locals, two of them widows, and pulled down their houses.[12] Adding insult to injury, he insisted that his three ex-tenants continue to pay rent for their destroyed homes. Deer caused other problems for the inhabitants of Stoke Gifford. Agile creatures, they were easily capable of escaping their parks and wandering into neighbouring fields, devouring the crops or fodder they found in their way. Since harming the animals could be interpreted as poaching, there was little that local farmers could do to save their crops. When the people of Stoke Gifford used their dogs to try to drive away Sir John's errant deer, the hounds were killed by Sir John's servants.

Deer parks were not only a source of discontent between lords and their tenants. They were also at the root of lawsuits among the wealthy. One of King Henry's hunting companions in the summer of 1509 was probably Sir John Seymour, a bullish Wiltshire man who was fiercely protective of his hunting rights. He brought litigation against the bishop of Salisbury for killing deer in his forest of Savernake – the bishop vehemently denied it – and was accused by the widowed Lady Barnardiston of hunting 'with riotous company' in her park at Grafton. When she protested, Sir John Seymour forcibly seized her lands and impounded her cattle.[13]

The local response to such actions was frequently violent: knocking down the hated fences that denied labourers access to their common lands, forcibly reclaiming buildings, lands or goods that were seen as 'rightfully' their own property. But labourers were becoming adept at uniting to combat such privations by appealing to the law. The petitioners who complained against Sir John Rodney were legion: inhabitants of the towns of Stoke Giffard and Draycott, Sir John's tenants past and present as well as those of the local noblewoman Lady Lisle, and of the prior of the Hospital of St John of Jerusalem. Peaceful process through the lawcourts did not always cool tempers, of course. Sir John Rodney was attacked with a pike when he tried to break up an assembly of locals beating down his enclosure. It was only because one of the rioters stopped the man striking at Rodney, crying 'he is our master' that his life was saved. The tenants had been driven to such extremes in the first place by Rodney's threats that if they failed to work on his fields and buildings (unpaid) he would 'hang, beat and mayhem them'.[14]

With Henry VII's death, certain lords took it upon themselves to overturn previous rulings regarding enclosures. John Mulsho of Thingden Manor, Northamptonshire, had been ordered by Henry VII to tear down the enclosures he had erected in 1494 when his tenants and neighbours protested that they had been placed on 'common ground and pasture lying in the fields'. However, by 1509 he was up to his old tricks, enclosing and dyking Thingden fields again and – even worse for local farmers – letting rabbits prolif-erate on what had been common lands, destroying their crops. Again the inhabitants appealed to the law, but this time they were not as successful. Mulsho was allowed to keep his enclosures, and although local inhabitants had their 'accustomed' rights to food and footpath on the lands restored, they were afforded no rights to pasture their livestock.[15]

In the haze of dust and heat as they harvested, such concerns may have slipped briefly from workers' minds. For as summer gave way to autumn, the king's subjects could breathe a collective sigh of relief. The harvest had been successful. Famine would not grip England that year.

VII

ALL SAINTS AND
ALL SOULS

'We are but dust, and die we must'[1]

THE THIRTY-FIRST OF October, the eve of All Saints' Day. In the enveloping darkness of farmland and heath, small flares of light were burning. The flickering flames cast weird shadows over the faces of the men, women and children gathered around them, murmuring their prayers. Death was in the air – in the smoke of bonfires and the hot breath of prayer. On this night, and on the two that followed, dusk did not bring quiet retirement. In London, John Rastell walked through milling streets; the night air of Thomas Drawswerd's York echoed to chorusing voices and pealing church bells. In the muffled rural world of Lincolnshire farmer Stephen Green, candles and torches guttered in the night air in a chill procession. Evensong burst from church quires. Bells rang until midnight. Priests could be heard in chantry chapels around the country, praying for the souls of their benefactors. In Macclesfield, mass was said for Thomasine Percyvale's late husband John. These prayers needed to reach all the way to purgatory, to comfort the dead with hopes of heaven. Even the usually vibrant royal court wore deepest mourning black, the sword borne before the king as he travelled from chapel to chamber a lone bright flash in the gloom. The sword's velvet scabbard, the chapel carpet, the royal throne and the canopy above it were all gleaming azure blue.

The first of November was All Saints' Day or All Hallows, the day to remember the good works of saints and martyrs, and appeal for their intercession. Would they add their own worthy pleas on behalf of the dead? Would they petition God to comfort suffering souls in purgatory, the limbo world between heaven and hell? On All Souls', the following day, it was up to the living to make their own appeals, and to comfort the dead with the sound of church bells.

For the mercer's wife Alice Middleton these days, with their grim reminders of mortality, had a tragic significance in 1509. Between 4 October when he wrote his will and mid-November when it was given probate, her husband John died. Whatever the malady that struck him down, he left Alice with a significant burden to bear: she had two young daughters and was possibly pregnant with another child. Even for the irrepressible Alice, this must have been a hard festival to bear. The merchant John Dalton's will echoed many when it claimed, 'there is nothing more certain than death and nothing more uncertain than the hour of death'.[2]

The uncertainty of survival was at the forefront of many minds in 1509. As Edward Hall's *Chronicle* lamented, in that year 'the plague was great, and reigned in diverse parts of the realm'.[3] Those with trade interests in Calais, like the Middletons, had a doubly anxious time. The pestilence was rife there, and so many had died that the king sent 300 extra soldiers to defend the weakened fort. Plague was a recurrent danger. While no epidemic of recent memory had reached the terrifying death toll of the mid-fourteenth-century Black Death, which killed a third of the English population, plague had broken out with alarming regularity in the century and half since. And it was not just this illness that represented a danger to Tudor lives: typhus, leprosy, tuberculosis and measles were all serious medical dangers, masquerading under broad titles like 'the pestilence' and 'the sickness'. Worst of all, the last reign had coincided with the emergence of two more life-threatening diseases: syphilis and the sweating sickness. Syphilis, or 'French pox' as it was known to everyone except the French, had broken out during a war over Naples in the 1490s, and ravaged the French troops who unsuspectingly carried the infection back into their home territories. The first sign of illness was a genital sore, hinting at the fact that this sickness was sexually transmitted. Weeks later, ulcers, rashes and lesions spread across the body and in the most serious cases a person's entire appearance could be ruined, leaving them disfigured with large fleshy nodules called gummata.

The sweating sickness, on the other hand, was a disease that swept through communities in a matter of hours, and it was the speed with which it struck that shocked contemporaries. It first surfaced in England in 1485 and in a matter of days killed two lord mayors and several aldermen in London. Thomas Forestier, a Norman physician, was in the city when the sweating sickness first struck and claimed that 15,000 people died from it. The suddenness with which it killed clearly left an impact on him:

Many died unshriven, without respite, whilst walking in the streets... We saw two priests standing together and speaking together, and we saw both of them die suddenly... We see the wife of a tailor taken and suddenly died. Another young man walking by the street fell down suddenly. Also another gentleman riding out of the city.

'The sweat' was so named because of the intense bodily heat that came over its victims:

This sickness cometh with a great sweating and stinking, with
redness of the face and of all the body, and a continual thirst, with
a great heat and headache because of the fumes and venoms.[4]

The medical knowledge of 1509 was no match for epidemics. Tudor
'physick' had its roots in the works of classical authors like the
Greeks Hippocrates and Galen.[5] Tudors believed that the body,
like Nature itself, was made up of four constituent parts, and that
it was when these four 'humours' were unbalanced that sickness
entered the body. While the natural world was made up of earth,
wind, fire and water, the body was comprised of black bile, blood,
yellow bile (choler) and phlegm. These humours were composed
of varying levels of dryness, cold, heat and moisture and people
would always have some humoural unbalance due to their sex, and
the date and location of their birth. Women were believed to incline
to an excess of phlegm thanks to their naturally more wet and cold
complexions, while men were deemed hotter and drier, thus more
likely to be choleric or sanguine. According to similar logic, those
born in summer inclined to choler because it was the season of dry
heat, and winter babies tended towards the phlegmatic.[6]

Against this backdrop of medical understanding, the best way
to escape the plague was simply to run away from it. A 'Litil Boke'
for 'the pestilence', printed in English in 1510, advised its readers 'to
flee from such persons as be infect' during times of sickness. If they
had to tend to sickbeds, as Alice would have tended to John, they
should 'stand far from the patient holding their face toward the
door or window'.[7] No doubt Alice followed the same advice given
in works like the 'Litil Boke', lighting every fire in the Middleton
household, scattering rosewater on the floor rushes and fumigating their chambers with juniper and bay leaves. Windows were
shut against the south wind – a particularly pestilential direction

of air travel – and not only Alice's hands but her eyes and face were washed in vinegar and rose water. Since corrupt air was believed to spread disease, in times of pestilence those who had to venture out into plague-stricken streets carried vinegar-soaked sponges or even pieces of bread held over the mouth and nose.

We do not know what caused John's death, but it seems likely that he received the best available medical attention from his physicians, since he could afford to pay for it. There were three degrees of medical practitioner, of which the physician was the highest ranking and most expensive. Henry VIII's physician Thomas Linacre received an annual salary of fifty pounds, and because, like most physicians, he was also a cleric, Linacre supplemented this income with religious benefices from Easton-in-Gordano in Somerset to South Newbold in Yorkshire.* A good physician like Linacre would have been educated on the Continent, studying not only medicine but also classical works, philosophy, astrology, mathematics, geometry and music.

When John was examined by his physician he would have been asked not only about the physical symptoms of his ague but also about his diet, exercise regime, star sign, the phase of the moon at his birth and his moral behaviour. His urine might also have been inspected. The practice of uroscopy was a staple of jokes about medical practitioners and in contemporary images no doctor was complete without a bulb-shaped jordan full of urine.† A thorough

---

* By comparison, the queen's apothecary Thomas Pierson received twenty marks (thirteen pounds) salary in 1509, and the royal surgeon William Altofte an annuity of forty marks. Pierson's wages in real terms were higher, since he did not have to pay for any of his own supplies. In the 1530s, the royal apothecary's bill for supplies came to sixty pounds a year.

† A jordan was a vessel used by physicians for samples, and a colloquial term for a chamber pot.

medical investigation would not usually include a physical exam-
ination, although it might demand the consultation of a horoscope
showing the disposition of the heavens both when John was born
and when he fell ill. Based on all of these diagnostic efforts, the
physician could then recommend a *regimen sanitas* (a health regime)
in the hope of restoring John to health.

If nothing else, the physician would recommend a course of
moral improvement: John should have honest conversation, good
company, not eat or drink too much and avoid the company of
loose women. 'Penance and confession [were] to be preferred [to]
all other medicines,' according to the 'Litil Boke'.[8] The holistic
nature of Tudor medicine should not be underestimated. The
physician Andrew Boorde considered enjoyment of music, laughter and song to be greatly beneficial to an individual's physical
wellbeing:

> Laudable mirth is one man or one neighbour to be merry with
> another, with honesty and virtue, without swearing and slander-
> ing and ribaldry speaking. Mirth is in musical instruments, and
> ghostly and godly singing... Mirth is one of the chiefest things
> of Physick... Mirth and rejoicing doth lengthen a man's life and
> doth expel sickness.[9]

The importance of mirth to good health in part explains the
presence of artificial and natural fools in royal and noble households. Today, we would characterize natural fools or 'innocents'
as people with learning disabilities. They usually lived as part of
a household in the care of 'keepers' who took responsibility for
their wages and clothing, and provided 'honest mirth' for their
employers.[10] Artificial fools, on the other hand, were jokers and
tumblers affecting 'foolishness', and their wages and rewards were

SO GREAT A PRINCE

paid directly. Henry VII and his family maintained a number of fools over the years, both innocent and artificial. The most famous of the king's fools, Peche or Patch, was probably an artificial fool as he received his own wages and had no keeper, whereas Dik the fool was clothed by the royal wardrobe, cared for by a keeper and did not receive direct payments of rewards or wages. Henry VIII had grown up with his own fool called John Goose, and Goose may still have been in his service in 1509 – there was certainly one fool being maintained by the keeper of the fools John Devers in 1514. There were also fools in a number of noble households. During the last decades of the previous century Edward of Middleham and the duke of Norfolk both retained fools, and the duke of Buckingham kept them during Henry VIII's reign.

The Middletons had no fool, but the straight-talking Alice no doubt provided John with wit and 'honest conversation'. She is also likely to have provided herbal assistance to him, for many women who headed households had knowledge of domestic medical care. If more complex or hard-to-come-by herbal remedies were demanded, Alice would have enlisted the services of an apothecary, the second type of medical practitioner. Even in the highest levels of society, the connection between the domestic and medicinal remained – Henry VIII's apothecary, who had attended his coronation earlier in the year, was Richard Babham. He was also the king's confectioner. Babham not only provided the royal family with herbal medicines, he also kept their lodgings smelling sweet with flower waters; royal breath was freshened with anise or fennel comfits and gargles; and royal bodies perfumed with scented baths, jellies and candies.

If a physician decided that John Middleton suffered from an excess of one particular humour he was likely to prescribe a 'purge', which would demand the services of the lowest-ranking doctor: the surgeon. For excess blood, phlebotomy (blood-letting) was prescribed. If he had too much bile or choler, it would mean taking either an emetic to make him sick or an enema to flush out his bowels. Because surgeons were involved in this messy, hands-on area of human treatment, they were considered to be lower down the pecking order than physicians and apothecaries, but they were actually more likely to have practical experience of treatment, since a number of them served as battlefield or navy surgeons before taking up quieter practice.

But even this combination of medical experience, training and practice could not always cheat death. The 'Litil Boke' observed that one patient would die and another survive because some were 'more disposed to die than another'.[11] In fact, some believed that involving the medical profession was more likely to worsen a patient's condition than improve their health – perhaps not unreasonably, given the harm that could be done by over-zealous purges and blood-letting. Agnes Paston of Norfolk warned her son in the city to take care: 'For God's sake beware what medicines ye take of any physicians of London. I shall never trust them.'[12]

Agnes believed her husband and uncle had died after excessive medical intervention from London physicians, so she had good reason to caution her son. Perhaps it was better to trust in the divine, by making a pilgrimage or praying to the relevant saint. There were patron saints for all manner of ailments. St Apollonia was called on for the toothache – since she had been tortured by the Romans with tooth-extraction before her martyrdom, presumably she was considered duly sympathetic. For similar reasons, St Margaret of Antioch, who had burst out of the belly of a dragon, was invoked during childbirth. No doubt during this plague year, the patron saint of pestilence St Roch received more attention than usual.

When prayer, pilgrimage and physicians' best efforts failed, all that was left was to prepare for the inevitable. John Middleton ensured that his will dealt with debtors and creditors, then divided up his property and money as clearly as possible, leaving dowries for his daughters, a home for his wife and detailed instructions in case 'it fortune Alice my wife to be with child the day of my decease'. The affection that the spouses shared is evident in his endowment of 'the residue of all my goods... unto the said Alice my wife she therewith to do her free will and pleasure'.[13] In return, Alice was to oversee John's burial. He wished to be laid to rest in front of the high altar in St Katherine Coleman church in London – a position of considerable importance, in the heart of the quire, which reflected his wealth and status as a successful mercer. Burial expenses existed on a sliding scale, depending on where someone wished to be interred. At St Margaret's, Westminster, it cost only two pence to be buried in the churchyard while burial within the church was considerably more: six shillings and eight pence. At Hull, burial within the parish church demanded a payment of one to two pounds and was reserved for local dignitaries and their families: ex-mayors, sheriffs, aldermen and chamberlains. Location in death was thus a reflection of one's activities in life. Rectors and vicars were often buried in the chancel of the church where they had served, chantry priests before the altar where they held mass, and a number of laypeople chose to be buried where they had prayed in life. John Brode of Faversham requested burial in his local church, 'before the image of St Anne in the south aisle there, under the pew where I sit'. At other times, husbands sought burial near the pew where their widow would continue to sit after they were gone.[14]

Choice of burial location was influenced by something more than just reflection of status. It was driven by the same impulse that directed alms to be given at funerals, charity to be bestowed on the local parish, mass to be said on the anniversary of a death. It was part of a vast economy of bartering for prayer. After burial location and the discharging of debts, John's next concern – listed several lines before any bequests of property or money – was for prayers to be said for 'my soul, the soul of my father and mother, my children's soul… [and] all persons' souls'. The religious mindset of 1509 was a reciprocal one, in which charity was given not only to win God's salvation by the act itself, but also to ensure future reward through the grateful prayers of those who were helped. As John put it, he gave charity to his local parish 'to the intent that the parishioners there pray specially for my soul'. These prayers could shorten a person's time in the miseries of purgatory before reaching heaven.[15]

With this in mind, John gave bequests to five different churches and five houses of London friars. Highways were to be mended with his money, poor maidens' marriages arranged, poor house-holders assisted, and a month after his death twelve poor men were to receive new black gowns, in memory of Jesus' twelve apostles. Implicitly – and sometimes explicitly – this was done to win the worthy prayers of all these people for himself and his family. The prayers of the religious, the infirm and the poor were all considered particularly valuable.

By choosing burial in the quire of a church, in its very heart, John also left a reminder of himself for future priests and churchgoers. Perhaps when they walked over his grave marker they would think of him and cast a prayer heavenwards. For this reason, burials lined the path of the churchyard and ran along the central aisle within the church – the very places someone's surviving family, friends and colleagues would walk whenever they attended services. As Gilbert Carleton, the vicar of Farningham in Kent, wrote in his will: 'Every creature coming in at the [porch] door may tread upon my burial.' Children who died young seem often to have been buried near the font, making an implicit connection between their innocence and rebirth in the afterlife with the holy water that had baptized them.[16]

Some people set the wheels in motion for their spiritual well-being long before their death. Alongside arranging the same elaborate ritual of charitable donations as John Middleton, the tailor's widow Thomasine Percyvale was also raising five poor children as an act of charity. Years before she made her will, she had already established her chantry chapel and school in Week St Mary, Cornwall. Chantries, at their simplest, were altars where priests prayed for the soul of their donor. At their most elaborate, they were miniature chapels within a larger church: beautifully sculpted spiritual spaces with painted panels inside and sweeping pinnacles above, drawing the eye heavenwards.

Thomasine, unlike John, had no children or spouse to provide for, which is perhaps why she left such considerable donations to hospitals and 'lazarhouses' (leper hospitals). With no welfare support from government, the poor, infirm and dying relied on such bequests to pay for medical attention, just as poor children depended on chantry schools for their education. By 1509, it was established that almshouses provided for the infirm and elderly, and hospitals for the poor, for children, for single mothers, for pilgrims, for the mad and the leprous. All were funded by pious bequests from the charitable wealthy. There was no assumption of a communal responsibility for the nation's weak and sickly, and medical care was almost never free. One of the largest English hospitals was St Leonard's in York, which could hold over a hundred patients, but most catered to little more than a handful. The Hospital of St John the Baptist, Coventry, maintained only twenty beds for 'the sick poor and wayfarers'.[17]

Hospitals had their origins in the monastic tradition of offering hospitality to those in need, and most distributed alms of food at their gates as well as providing medical care. St Bartholomew's Hospital in Smithfield, London, provided relief to 'poor pilgrims, soldiers, sailors and others of all nations'.[18] Over the course of the fifteenth century, trade and civic guilds had started to get involved in medical care, providing a form of health insurance for those guild members who fell into sickness or poverty. The Ludlow Palmers' Guild promised that:

> If any of our poorer brothers or sisters fall into grievous sickness, they shall be helped, both as to their bodily needs and other wants, out of the common fund of the guild, until their health is renewed as it was before. But if anyone becomes a leper, or blind, or maimed in limb, or smitten with any other incurable disorder (which God forbid) we wish that the goods of the guild shall be largely bestowed on him.[19]

Some guilds established hospitals and almshouses to provide for their elderly or impoverished members. In 1506 the wealthy Coventry draper Thomas Bond established a hospital at Bablake for ten poor men, to be chosen from the members of the Trinity Guild or, if none of that fraternity had need, then from one of the brothers of the city's Corpus Christi Guild. Trinity Hospital in Bristol, a century older than Bond's foundation, gave accommodation to six poor men and six poor women.

Since those who survived infancy could expect to live, on average, only until their mid-thirties, there were relatively few elderly and infirm people to take care of.[20] Those who did make it to a more advanced age – and some lived into their sixties and seventies – relied on their families to support them. Where family

provision was lacking, they turned to the church and civic authorities. Some contemporaries were highly suspicious of those taking
up the offer of charitable provision, fearing lest 'sturdy beggars'
should live off the fat of such alms. When a merchant made his
will in 1479 he specifically excluded from his bequest to the poor of
London 'common beggars going about all the daylight and lying in
[hospitals] the night time'.[21]

As always, those with independent finances were more likely
to find comfortable accommodation. The moneyed sick might be
offered semi-permanent accommodation at a hospital in return
for rent or a bequest on their death. For the poor, who could not
afford such arrangements, medical care had to be paid for with
prayer rather than coin. Benefactors of almshouses and hospitals
expected the residents to remember them in their prayers and
many hospital infirmaries were laid out in the naves of churches,
not only because they were large enough to hold multiple beds
but also to enable the bedridden patients to participate in services.
Thomas Bond of Coventry required that the ten men using his
hospital at Bablake attended daily at matins, mass and evensong to
'pray for the souls of the founder and his ancestors, and all Christian souls, more especially the brothers and sisters of the Trinity
Guild'. Additionally, they were to go to church after supper every
day and say fifteen Our Fathers, the same number of Hail Marys
and three Creeds.[22]

The location of a hospital could determine its function. St Bartholomew's and St Thomas's in London were located near the
'stews' where prostitutes plied their trade, and both provided care
for unmarried mothers. The London mayor Richard Whittington
provided a maternity wing for single women at St Thomas's in
his will of 1421, on the proviso that the women's presence there
should be kept secret so that they could go on to make respectable

marriages.* If a woman died in childbirth in St Bartholomew's, her baby would be raised and educated in the hospital alongside the babies the brethren had rescued from Newgate Prison. Radiating out along the roads of London could be found half-a-dozen hospitals specifically intended to care for lepers, since the lepers themselves had been banned from entering the city since 1472. The situation of these hospitals on the main roads meant that they could beg alms from passing travellers. It was for these 'lazarhouses' that Thomasine Percyvale left such substantial bequests.

The care available in these charitable organizations varied. Patients were expected to provide their own linen and blankets, which were kept after their death and used for those who had no bedding to bring. St Mary's Bishopsgate in London had 180 beds with lamps for its patients to see by and sisters who tended to the sick, but with money dwindling they did not have enough food, clothing or money for repairs. Amid the 'multitude of miserable persons of both sexes... who are so alienated in mind and possessed of unclean spirits that they must be restrained with chains and fetters' at St Mary's Bethlehem in London (also known as 'Bedlam'), pigs freely roamed and the deputy warden ran an alehouse.[23]

The royal family had not neglected their own charitable duties. Henry VII had a long-term project for a hospital to be dedicated to Jesus, the Virgin Mary and St John the Baptist, which would be founded on the site of the old Savoy Palace in London. Although he founded the hospital in 1505 little had been achieved by the time of his death, and he left a bequest of 10,000 marks for the hospital to be completed in his son's reign. The king's intention was that a

---

* This is the same 'Dick Whittington' of legend, who rose from humble origins to become mayor of London.

hundred poor men would be cared for in an innovative structure where every inmate had his own bed inside an individual cubicle. A matron and twelve unmarried nurses cared for the physical needs of the patients, visiting them twice daily and providing baths, food and even delousing their clothes in an oven before tucking them between their three sheets and two blankets. Every bed had a counterpane with a Tudor rose, lest the patients forget who had provided them with such comfort. For the men's spiritual needs, four chaplains and two priests were on hand, while a physician, surgeon and apothecary kept on top of any medical necessities. The king's executors were at work ensuring everything would be carried out as the king wished – including, of course, provision for the poor to pray for Henry VII at evensong.

The old king must have been on his son's mind as he walked the corridors of Greenwich Palace, surrounded by deepest mourning black. Perhaps Henry VIII contemplated the others he had lost in the past decade too: his eldest brother dead at fifteen, four infant brothers and sisters likewise entombed, his parents, his ever-watchful grandmother. The passing of that last voice of calm rationality must have been keenly felt. Still only eighteen years old, Henry VIII stood isolated from some of the most important influences of his youth. But amid all this thought of death there was one bright spark of new life. On 1 November 1509, Catherine and Henry celebrated a momentous event for the new reign – the quickening of their child.* Henry wrote to his father-in-law Ferdinand of Aragon to tell him the good news: 'The queen is

---

* Since the due dates of babies were difficult to establish in Tudor England, the 'quickening' of a child was the first certain indication of pregnancy. This was the point, at around four months into a pregnancy, when the baby could be felt moving inside its mother's womb.

pregnant, and the child in her womb is alive… He and his kingdom rejoice at this good news.'[24]

Now there was a line tethering the king and queen into a future not only for themselves, but for the entire Tudor dynasty.

VIII

CHRISTMAS

𝔣east and fast

ON THE MORNING of 1 December 1509, a clerk of Lincoln Cathedral made a careful addition to the pages of his accounts book. An annuity of twenty shillings was to be paid to the cathedral's porter, John Barnes, for his 'labour and care carried out every year'.[1] Barnes was a jack of all trades. In addition to his duties as porter, he also maintained the cathedral clock, operated a mechanical dove that was displayed at Pentecost, and on Christmas morning it was he who winched the cords that made a gilded star move inside the body of the cathedral, revealing to the shepherds in the nativity play the location of the Virgin Mary and infant Jesus. The cathedral was justly proud of its nativity play, a high point in its religious calendar. However, it was far from alone in sponsoring such entertainment. Across the country, December saw accounts balanced and preparations made for the arrival of travelling players, dancing bears, waits and minstrels. On 25 December, the season of feasting and misrule would begin. It was just the month before then that presented a challenge.

As the clerk of Lincoln Cathedral, John Barnes the porter, and most of the rest of the country could attest, the first day of December was grim: sharp frost in the air, ice-rimed dirt on the roads, and a month of rumbling stomachs and fish in prospect. The four weeks before Christmas made up the season of Advent, when no flesh or fat could be consumed. At the heart of the pious self-denial of Advent and its counterpart, the pre-Easter Lenten fast, was very good common sense. Martinmas on 11 November was the traditional time to butcher meat, preparing provisions to last the winter. From then onwards, supplies of food would have to come 'from stock' rather than be eaten fresh, and they had to last until they could be replenished in the following year. It was the true beginning of a long, lean winter. Lent, on the other hand, fell just as spring arrived and one might imagine that it was a season of plenty. In fact, in the month before Easter, surviving winter stocks would have dwindled to their lowest levels and very little produce was ready to eat. This was the time of year when crops were sown, not reaped. Newborn animals needed to be grazed and fattened before they could make it to table.

During Advent, most of the country would have been mournfully occupied with the absence of good food. One contemporary song on the theme of Advent expresses these feelings all too clearly:

> We ate no puddings nor no sauce,
> But stinking fish not worth a louse…
> There was no fresh fish far nor near,
> Salt fish and salmon was too dear…
> Our bread was brown, our ale was thin,
> Our bread was musty in the bin.[2]

Lent and Advent were the longest sustained periods of self-denial, but the entire year was an ebbing and flowing tide of fasting and feasting. People were also supposed to abstain from meat on Fridays, Saturdays and Wednesdays, on 'ember days' and on the vigils of important saints' days.* Some even added their own idiosyncratic patterns of pious fasting into the mix, like the Lady Fast. If following this diet, someone noted the day of the week on which Lady Day (25 March) fell and made that day a weekly fast for the entire year. Even without such additions, there were over a hundred days a year on which people were obliged to fast. Some exceptions were made to these rules: pregnant women, the elderly, sickly and very young were generally allowed to abstain from the rigours of fasting.

What could someone actually eat on a fast day in 1509? Although eggs and milk were forbidden during Advent and Lent – almond milk was the usual substitute – outside these seasons the restrictions on fast days were more relaxed. On Wednesdays, meat was often served at court, suggesting that this was seen as a lesser fast day. In great houses, piscine feasts were dished up: fresh salmon and cod, dog-fish, tench, bream, whiting, plaice – even eels and porpoise. But for those living further inland or who could not afford to buy fresh, salted and cured fish were the main foodstuffs, particularly the unappetizing stockfish. These revolting dried fish were cheap (half the price of salt fish) but needed to be hammered and soaked for hours to make them palatable. Self-denial might be expected but starvation was not, so to avoid vast swathes of the population dying of hunger when fish supplies were low, certain acceptable 'fast-day foods' were suspiciously non-piscine. Chief among these was the barnacle goose, a dish encountered in the fifteenth century by the Bohemian traveller Gabriel Tetzel. 'It was supposed to be a fish,' he reported sceptically, having tried barnacle goose during Lent, 'because it begins like a worm in the sea, and

---

* 'Ember days' were the Fridays, Wednesdays and Saturdays following the feasts of St Lucy (13 December), Holy Cross Day (14 September) and the movable feasts of Whit Sunday and Ash Wednesday.

only later assumes the shape of a duck... But in my mouth it was flesh.'[3] The barnacle goose was believed to start life as a 'barnacle' hanging from trees near the water's edge. After falling into the water it would hatch into a bird, but since its home was the sea or a river, it could still be eaten as 'fish'. Similar logic dictated that puffin flesh and seal could be consumed during Advent and Lent. In fact, for many, the food eaten in these fasting seasons would have been fairly similar to their diet during the rest of the year: peas, beans and cereals in some manner of pudding or stew made up their two meals a day. Breakfast, if taken at all, was a small meal of bread and ale, and the main meal of the day was dinner, which was served at around ten or eleven in the morning. The lighter meal of supper was eaten in the late afternoon, at around four o'clock.

Lent and Advent fell during seasons when food was scarce but it was never forgotten that the fasting was intended as religious devotion. Self-denial was a crucial spiritual exercise in Christianity. For some though, this holy hunger was also motivated by a desire for control in a world where they felt they lacked power. Catherine of Aragon was criticized by no less an authority than the pope for taking the 'fervour of her devotion' in 'fasting, abstinence and pilgrimage' to extremes, to such an extent that it could 'stand in the way of the procreation of children'. The Spanish ambassador Luis Caroz observed that 'irregularity in her eating and the food which she takes cause her some indisposition, the consequence of which is that she not does menstruate well'. Catherine's eating habits became most erratic during periods of intense anxiety and stress, and it is likely that this supposedly devotional fasting was actually an attempt, perhaps subconscious, to regain control when she had none. The letter from Pope Julius II arrived during her prolonged and miserable widowhood and Caroz made his observations after she had lost her first child. For women in general, operating within a patriarchal system where husbands, fathers, sons, priests and the entirely male ruling elite of local government were all entitled to pass judgement on their behaviour, dietary control could be the only means of self-command available. The fifteenth-century mystic Margery Kempe was unable to prevent her husband from demanding his 'marital debt' of sex with her, but she could choose to fast and thereby have authority over her body that way.[4]

The Tudor world was one in which equilibrium was key, and self-denial, whatever its cause, was rewarded by an ensuing orgy of religiously licensed gorging. Vigils of saints' days preceded a feast-day celebration; Lent was followed by the Easter weekend and a week-long knees-up called 'Hocktide'; and after Advent came the twelve days of Christmas. This unadorned title does little to convey the boundary-breaking, gluttonous festivity of the season. For tenants and those in employment, there was usually a contribution of food from masters at this time, meaning it might be one of the rare occasions throughout the year when poverty was no bar to participation in the festivities on offer.

Christmas Eve was the last fast day of Advent and as people across the country gathered holly and ivy to bring into their homes and hang from their doorframes, they might have not have cared so much that the cold bit through their thin-soled leather shoes and woollen gloves. On Christmas morning, in a final nod to piety, mass was heard and then an eruption of festivity burst out across the country. The misery of Advent was over, as this festive song crowed:

> Farewell Advent
> Christmas is come
> Farewell from us both all and some.
> With patience thou hast us fed,

And made us go hungry to bed,
For lack of meat we were nigh dead,
Farewell from (us both all and some).[5]

The twelve days of Christmas contained several different religious festivals. After Christmas Day itself there were the feast days of Saints Stephen (26th), John the Evangelist (27th) and Thomas Becket (29th). Sandwiched between them came Childermas or Holy Innocents Day on 28 December. 31 December was the feast day of St Silvester and 1 January the feast of the Circumcision. Although the turning year was formally dated from Lady Day on 25 March, 1 January was also known as New Year's Day. In ancient Rome, the Kalends of January had seen gifts presented to the emperor and, in imitation of this display of fealty, New Year's Day was still the traditional time for masters and servants to exchange gifts. Henry VII and Elizabeth of York had received their gifts early on New Year's morning in their separate chambers – once they had put on their shoes, according to household ordinances – with trumpet blasts heralding the arrival of the presents. Later in Henry VIII's reign, the presentation of gifts became a more public affair, with servants of great lords conveying messages from their masters as they handed over their gifts in the king's presence chamber. The king received them with a word or two of thanks, if he pleased, while details of the gifts and their givers were carefully noted down. Henry and Catherine reciprocated the gifts of cup, gold plate, embellished clothing or money that they received, usually basing their own presents on a sliding scale according to the importance of the recipient. The senior courtiers received the heaviest goblets or largest purses, while the 'divers poor men, women and children that bought capons, hens, eggs, books of wax and other trifles' to the king were rewarded with small donations of money.[6]

Gifts were also exchanged within the royal family – Henry VII had commanded in his household ordinances that the queen's should be the first gift presented to him on New Year's morning.

The last day of Christmas was Twelfth Night, or Epiphany, and was the excuse for the most elaborate feasting and display. At the royal court, Henry and Catherine sat enthroned beneath magnificent canopies, wearing ermine-furred robes and bejewelled crowns. Since this was the day that the three kings had presented gifts to Jesus, the king and queen gave offerings of 'gold, silver and cense' (frankincense) to the chapel.[7] In the greater houses of the land, lords and ladies likewise sat in state before their households, entertained with music, theatre, dancing and the traditional wassail.

While the royal court and nobility enjoyed feast after feast, for the lower levels of society Christmas meals were likely to have been, at best, some boiled meat and winter vegetables, enlivened with herbs, onions and garlic from their own garden. Wages had increased and meat was available to a broader section of society but for some this season of 'feast' might bring little relief from hunger. Vast numbers of peasant families would have barely enough to sustain them through the summer, never mind the winter. Cereals were the main foodstuff, with milk, cheese, bacon and eggs added to the pot when they could be acquired and when religion permitted. Many relatively poor households would have kept animals in pens and maintained vegetable gardens to supply cabbage and onion. The main peasant cooking vessels were brass pots and pans, in which cereal-based pottages and puddings were stewed. Few labourerers' households had an oven, although some villages kept one for communal use. The type of bread being baked would also depend on the available supplies, and it was not always made from wheat: in the northern counties of England, oats were the main cereal crop, while in Norfolk and Worcestershire it was rye. The peasant diet was affected by the changing seasons, but in general must have been monotonous in the extreme.

On the other hand, the diet of the wealthy was not necessarily much healthier than that of their social inferiors. The consumption of dairy products and fresh fruit and vegetables was minimal among the upper classes. Sugar was also beginning to work its way into the aristocratic diet, rotting teeth and fattening bellies, whereas honey was the healthier sweetener available to the lower levels of society. Among the rich, red meat was a huge part of daily diet and between a third and a half of all household expenditure went on meat and fish. At Christmas time, this mania for meat was even greater. It was expected that on the greater feast days of Christmas, New Year and Twelfth Night, lords would hold 'open house' for their neighbours, servants and tenants, at which enormous quantities of food would be on offer. In 1507, only recently removed to his family seat of Thornbury in Gloucestershire, the duke of Buckingham held lavish Christmas feasts to impress his wealthy neighbours and to inspire loyalty in his tenants and servants.* Buckingham invited almost 300 guests to supper on Christmas Day and his banquet at Twelfth Night hosted 459 diners. Roping in two additional cooks from Bristol to assist in his kitchens, the duke served an incredible feast of swans, peacocks, suckling pigs, herons, quails 'from the store' and a veritable flock of small feathered birds, including twenty-three widgeons, eighteen teals and three dozen larks. The party got through almost 700 loaves of bread.[8]

Swans also featured on the Christmas menu of Buckingham's brother-in-law, Henry Percy, earl of Northumberland, who served

---

* One of these neighbours was the same Sir John Rodney of Stoke Gifford who was causing his own tenants such grief with errant deer and legally dubious enclosures.

venison alongside them. Venison was a high-status food, often exchanged between friends and allies. Since deer had to be hunted from one's own parkland, its presence on the dining table said a lot about the wealth of the giver and the importance of the recipient. In other great households, and in Oxford colleges, boar's head was served, and already this impressive dish was becoming associated with Christmas meals in popular song:

> The boars head in hand I bring
> With garlands gay and birds singing [9]

These 'birds singing' were probably live animals garnishing the great plate of boar meat. Food was a form of theatre, with sugar sculpted into allegorical or fantastical shapes, and jellies set to look like animals and castles. At a feast to entertain foreign dignitaries, Henry VIII presented a meal in which 'all the viands placed before [him] were borne by an elephant, or by lions, or panthers, or other animals, marvellously designed'. These were not, in all probability, real animals but 'marvellously designed' costumes or pageant wagons. [10]

Certain foods and drinks were considered particularly festive. The wassail cake, and a wassail cup made of precious metal, were paraded into great halls on Twelfth Night, accompanied by a collective call and response from the company. This wassail played a central role in the ritual surrounding the earl of Northumberland's celebrations at Wressle Castle in Yorkshire. After evensong on Twelfth Night, the whole household processed from the chapel to the earl's candlelit great hall, the children of the chapel singing as they led the way. There, the earl and countess sat while everyone else took their 'standings' to enjoy an evening of feasting and entertainment. A play was performed by the young noblemen of the household, interrupted by players and minstrels in disguise, who called forward young ladies to dance. Once the playing and dancing was over, two wassail cakes were carried into the hall, one each for the earl and countess, surrounded by high-ranking servants bearing candles. The fruit-sweetened cake was carved before the crowd. This was only the first of three courses of food, during which the steward of the household would cry out 'wassail', a call that equates to 'your good health'. The chapel choir responded in song. Throughout the meal, minstrels and trumpeters played, and the evening ended with another grand procession accompanied by the choir, out of the hall, up the great staircase and all the way to the doors of the earl and countess's bedchamber.

This celebration marked the conclusion of the earl's twelve days of Christmas, but throughout there had been music, dances, pageants, plays, singing and gambling. The earl even had his bear-ward (bear-keeper) bring 'his lordship's beasts for making of his lordship's pastime'.[11] Our image of these great feasts might be of bone-flinging drunkards crammed into a dirty hall, but in fact those eating from the trestle tables in the earl of Northumberland's great hall would have been expected to demonstrate proper dining etiquette. There were even specific servants called gentlemen ushers who had responsibility for ensuring protocol was followed within greater households. Modelled on the royal court, rules called ordinances were drawn up for the earl's household, advising these gentlemen ushers how to ensure the smooth running of such ceremonial occasions. The gentlemen ushers had to see that carpet was laid in the upper end of the hall, that the tables were dressed with cloth and that the chamber was hung with tapestries.

The guests at Northumberland's table would also be expected to demonstrate their manners, bringing their own knife and spoon with them, and to arrive with clean hands and nails. Linen napkins would be provided, not to be thrown into the lap, but instead to rest over the left arm or shoulder, there to protect expensive clothing from any spatters of food, and also to enable diners to delicately wipe their primary eating implements: the hands. Evidently there were some rogue elements even at the royal court, since instructions had to be given for servants eating in hall not to wipe their hands on the tapestries.[12] Among the noble and gentle classes, the carving of meat was an essential life skill, taught to the young men living in greater households as part of their education. Different animals naturally demanded different techniques, so if a man could demonstrate his carving skills at the table, he would be off to a good start. However, if someone else was carving, he needed only to worry about his own plate. Communal dishes called 'messes' were placed on the table, and using thumb and fingers, people would take a piece of meat from the mess and place it on their plate. Taking too much was considered greedy, so some restraint was advisable. Then the meat would be pinned in place with two fingers while it was cut into bite-sized pieces with a knife. Fingers were also used to carry the food to the mouth – eating with a knife was a sign of incivility. Forks were not unknown in 1509, but they were not widely used. Henry VIII kept his for when he was helping himself to candied fruit at the end of a meal.

While seated at table, diners should be upright and still, their hands in their lap if not occupied with food, and their gaze steady. Fidgeting about in a seat would give the impression that they were constantly passing wind, and craning their necks around to stare at what was going on was also considered the height of boorishness. If a person had to burp, cough or sneeze they should do it quietly, turning away from their eating companions, who would be closely pressed in around them. Just as sharing a bed was commonplace among all levels of society, so eating was generally done in close quarters to others: diners would probably be squeezed on to a bench alongside their companions at dinner. For this reason, spreading legs wide and leaning elbows on the table, invading others' space, were understandably considered antisocial. Since halls were still generally used for both eating and sleeping, the benches and trestle tables were designed to be easy to put away. Any leftover food or pieces of meat that proved too hard to swallow should not be thrown on the floor or tablecloth, since they would just have to be cleaned away by the lower servants before they rolled out their mattresses to sleep there for the night.

Meals consisted of two or three courses, with multiple dishes in each course. The first course was likely to be made up of boiled meats, the second of the more impressive roasted dishes, and finally – if it was a really grand occasion – a *voidee* (or parting dish) of spiced and candied fruits with wine. People would sample a little of whichever dishes took their fancy but they were not expected to gorge themselves, as the leftovers were intended to be passed on down the food chain, first offered to lower servants before being given in alms to the poor at the gates. Anything really inedible to humans might be thrown to the hounds, but in general dogs were intended to work, so their diets were carefully monitored. The odd pampered lapdog might be permitted to eat with its master or mistress, but most animals were kept away from places of food preparation, service and consumption.

Christmas banquets were not merely an opportunity for eating and drinking, of course – they were also a chance for entertainment. Once food was finished and dishes cleared away, the tabletops could be turned over for 'board games' to be played. Scratched and painted into the undersides of trestle tables were outlines for games like nine men's morris and backgammon (also known as 'tables'), exercises in cunning and a good excuse for gambling. Henry VII had been a keen gambler, once losing thirteen shillings and four pence at a single game of chess. Such games were all well and good, but at Christmas livelier entertainments were sought. Music, plays, singing, dancing, even exotic animals – all were called on to display the host's generosity and impress his guests. In Thornbury, the duke of Buckingham welcomed visiting companies of 'players' from all over his estates, some even travelling from as far away as Essex. On Twelfth Night, men danced a morris in his red and black livery, adorned with bells. Throughout the twelve days of Christmas 1507–8, forty-one musicians took part in the duke's revels. The earl of Northumberland also had a range of musicians he could call on to provide accompaniment for his guests: three minstrels, five trumpeters and sixteen choristers.

Music was an important part of the Christmas festivities, and a number of cities maintained musicians or 'waits' to perform during the twelve days for their amusement. Lincoln had waits from the 1420s onwards, while Newcastle upon Tyne paid locally sponsored waits and two minstrels, William and Thomas Carr, to entertain the citizens. The waits may have provided an accompaniment for carols, these being a hybrid of dance, poetry and popular song intended to involve the whole company in attendance. In greater houses, carols tended to provide a diversion between courses of food, perhaps taking the form of a song sung by the household choir while guests remained in their seats. In its liveliest incarnation, the carol could be a circle-dance, with the whole company joining hands to dance around the parish bonfire or through a lord's great hall. While carols were often on religious themes, they were not written to be piously recited in church – some of them were downright rude. They were social songs, intended originally to provide a rhythm for communal dances, and they were not confined to Christmas, but enjoyed throughout the year.

Alongside the waits keeping the residents of Newcastle amused were animal entertainers, another common feature of Christmas revelry. During the twelve days of 1509–10, the city was visited by the bearward of the earl of Northumberland, who made a little extra money 'with his lordship's beasts'.[13] The locals clearly enjoyed their ursine activities; over the years, Newcastle also played host to the bears of the king and of Lord Darcy. But Newcastle was not alone in its enthusiasm, for animals appeared in Christmas revels all over the country. A bearward called Edward Lytster was rewarded with sixteen pence for his work at Grimsby and another, John Grene, took his dancing bears everywhere from Dover and Sandwich to Beverley. For those inclined to more violent amusements, Oxford had both a bear pit and bullring. In 1495 a student described how 'all the young folks almost of this town did run yesterday to the castle to see a bear baited with fierce dogs within the walls. It was greatly to be wondered [at]'.[14]

Account books of the London Inns of Court include some intriguing references to animal-handling Christmas jobs. A 'keeper of the lions' received eight pence in 1497, and in 1494, twenty years after the first reference to a lion-keeper, Furnival's Inn was entertained with 'lions, the waits, the harper and other particulars' at Christmas. Even more enigmatic are the payments to the 'keeper of the marmoset and jennet' in 1480 and 'the keeper of the baboon' in 1485.* Since these are one-off payments, perhaps these apes and wild cats were not real but costumed players involved in a form of dumb show.[15]

As the case of the bearward John Grene shows, entertainers travelled all over the country to make their living, but there were also

---

* A marmoset is a type of monkey. The jennet could have been a small horse, or (given the other exotic animals who appeared) the spotted-coated genet, a relative of the mongoose.

an increasing number of performers attached to specific house-holds. A number of lords had their own 'players' who were loaned out to perform at other great houses. The Howard earls of Surrey and dukes of Norfolk had maintained players since the 1480s and were still putting on pageants and 'disguisings' under Henry VII. The royal court was also entertained by players from the house-holds of the earls of Oxford, Northumberland and Wiltshire, and of the duke of Buckingham. As well as patronizing their own actors, the king and his lords also paid for outside players to come and perform for them. These players seem to have been sponsored by religious or civic organizations. During his reign, Henry VII's accounts show payments to players from London, St Albans, Wimborne Minster in Dorset and from France. Outside the royal court, many towns incorporated actors into their civic celebrations: Bristol, Lavenham and Chelmsford to name but three. In Oxford, plays were both written and performed in the colleges – Thomas More wrote a piece that was performed at Magdalen College in 1495 – and in local parishes. St Peter's church in Oxford rented out costumes for players.

The royal court was particularly keen on its dramatic displays. For his first Christmas as king, Henry VIII had players perform in the hall at Richmond Palace on 27 and 30 December, and both the Gentlemen of the Chapel Royal and the King's Players per-formed at Twelfth Night. Henry's father, Henry VII, had been the first English king to maintain his own troupe of actors, as well as patronizing his subjects' players. At one time or another during Henry VII's reign there had been four in-house groups of actors at the royal court: the King's Players, the Players of the Chapel Royal, the Queen's Players and the Prince's Players. Strictly speaking none were professional, as all had employment in other parts of the royal household. The leader of the five Players of the Chapel Royal

Henry VII, the first king of the Tudor dynasty, ended his reign resented and unpopular. 'It is as if everyone had been let out of prison,' reported one ambassador after his death.

Henry VIII was kept cloistered 'like a girl' before he came to the throne. But he soon started to stretch his political muscles and came into conflict with both his queen and council.

Henry VII's deathbed by the Garter King of Arms, Sir Thomas Wriothesley. The king's death was kept secret for two days while a coup unfolded at the heart of court.

'They think he is a fox, and such is his name' – Bishop Richard Fox oversaw the transition from one Tudor king to another, but eventually he and the council lost control over the young Henry.

The shadowy figures of Sir Richard Empson and Edmund Dudley whisper in Henry VII's ear. At the heart of the old king's web of financial manipulation, the pair proved useful scapegoats for the new regime.

Bluff and proud, the confrontational Duke of Buckingham expected to be a natural adviser to the new king.

Thomas Lovell, stalwart supporter of the Tudor family. At his death, a portrait of his master Henry VII was the only painting he owned.

The rose and pomegranate combined: a woodcut of Henry VIII and Catherine of Aragon enthroned at their joint coronation. Even a fierce rain shower failed to put a damper on this day of celebration.

Anxious and occasionally inclined to melodrama, after she arrived in England Catherine of Aragon endured the loss of a husband, her mother, her wealth and – some said – her looks.

Margaret Beaufort: indefatigable protector of the Tudor line. A child bride and teenage mother in the Wars of the Roses, she survived to witness both her son, Henry VII, and grandson, Henry VIII, crowned king.

Henry VIII sits crowned before his parliament. The first parliament of Henry's reign considered everything from fishing statutes to fashion.

Pageantry and chivalry walk hand in hand at the young king's court:
above, the impressive Knights of the Garter parade on St George's Day;
below, the pomp of the joust, when knights sallied forth 'to do feats of
arms for the love of ladies'.

A dyer works colour into the delicate cloth in his vat. Woollen cloth was the backbone of the English economy, and coloured fabrics were the height of fashion.

A winter scene: access to warmth and light – the ability to keep nature at bay – were a sign of wealth as well as a source of comfort in 1509.

As spring gives way to summer, love is in the air. For the idle wealthy, this was the season of pleasure. For those toiling in the fields, romance had to be tempered with the demands of work – as in the case of this spinster depicted on the far left.

At harvest time every worker available was called to the fields.
A poor harvest could spell famine and sickness for years to come.

Salvation through pious works, rendered as simple cause and effect:
by giving to the poor and paying for prayers, dying men would hope to be
drawn up from purgatory to heaven more quickly.

Fortune's wheel delivers a king to his throne, while grinding a fallen man
beneath. Recent history had proven that even monarchs had an uncertain future.

was William Cornish, who was usually to be found writing and directing the choral performances of the Children of the Chapel Royal. By 1509, Cornish was an old hand at performing before the court. Perhaps his most unusual role had come when he played St George in one of Henry VII's 'revels' of 1494, declaiming verse, singing an anthem and facing down a fire-breathing dragon. The gentlemen and boys of the Chapel Royal took on similarly fantastical roles in court performances, playing mariners, ladies and even, on one occasion, mermaids. Cornish's work with the Players of the Chapel Royal was not rewarded with wages or livery, although he was paid cash bonuses for his performances. At Twelfth Night 1509 the Players received the not inconsiderable sum of fifty-three shillings and four pence – not bad for a spot of moonlighting.

The King's Players were no more specialized than those of the Chapel Royal. The head player was Richard Gibson, who usually worked as porter and yeoman tailor of the great wardrobe. Another member of the five-strong troupe, John English, had worked as a joiner on the pageants of Christmas 1508. Gibson and English therefore not only had access to good-quality materials, but also personal skill as craftsmen, which they could combine to stage elaborate productions as players. Clearly, like John Barnes in Lincoln Cathedral, in this period it paid to have more than one string to a dramatic bow. The King's Players were slightly more of a fixture at the royal court, having been around since 1494. They received an annual salary of twenty marks, household livery and bonuses for their performances.

Overseeing the Christmas entertainment at the royal court was the Lord, or occasionally Abbot, of Misrule. In 1509 William Wynnsbury served as Lord of Misrule for at least the second year running – in earlier years, the role was not always accompanied by a name in royal documents – and was rewarded with the princely sum of a hundred shillings. It was his job to ensure that the twelve days were full of nonsense, chaos and carnival. Throughout the country, Christmas saw social norms turned on their head and misrule holding sway. At Christmas people could behave in a manner not allowed during the rest of the year so that, like a pressure valve being released, a brief period of chaos and transgression issued forth, to be swiftly stopped up again on 7 January. Thus servants, labourers and apprentices were allowed to gamble or play at dice, board games and cards only at Christmas. There were also many instances of inversion, where a lowly servant or citizen, like Wynnsbury, was elevated to a position of authority. Merton College, Oxford, elected a King of the Bean who ruled over his colleagues from St Edmund's Eve on 19 November until Candlemas (2 February). His 'election' may simply have consisted of him finding a dried bean in a piece of cake. This *Rex Fabarum* sat in state in the college hall and dispensed 'justice' throughout his reign, beating those whose service displeased him. In York, St Thomas's Day (29 December) saw 'Yule and his wife' riding through the streets in a 'barbarous' manner, while in fifteenth-century Norwich the 'King of Christmas' paraded in tinsel, accompanied by disguised attendants.

Henry VIII was following family tradition by patronizing a Lord of Misrule. His father appointed a Lord or Abbot of Misrule every Christmas during his reign from 1491 onwards and even his pious grandmother Margaret Beaufort saw nothing wrong with the custom, keeping a Lord of Misrule herself. Following royal example, Lords of Misrule can also be found in the households of the earl of Northumberland, the duke of Buckingham, the lord mayor and sheriffs of London as well as various university colleges and even in the homes of wealthy citizens. The Coventry vintner Henry Rogers had one of his sergeants serve as Lord of Misrule while he kept open house for his neighbours at Christmas 1518.

The London seats of legal education, the Inns of Court, had some of the most elaborate incarnations of Christmas misrule. Lincoln's Inn had at least three Lords of Misrule: a King of Christmas who ruled on Christmas Day; the King of the Cockneys who took over on Holy Innocents; and a marshal who was appointed king on New Year's Day. The Inner Temple gave its Lord of Misrule a fantastic court on St Stephen's Day (26 December), when animals were hunted around the hall. Gray's Inn had a Christmas King chosen by 'clerks of the third table', who expected to receive homage from his subjects in solemn and ceremonial fashion. Whenever he rose from his seat at the high table in the hall he was to be hailed with a shout of 'Long live the king!' To oversee all this ceremony and celebration the Inns annually appointed a master of the revels. Clearly not everyone wanted either the responsibility or the financial burden, as in 1509 John Newdigate took up his membership of Lincoln's Inn only on the condition that he would never have to serve as master of the revels.

The most innocent inversions took place, suitably enough, on Holy Innocents Day (28 December), when 'boy bishops' or 'girl abbesses' took over the duties of their religious superiors. A chorister or scholar was selected from within a religious community to don mitre, robes and staff and process around the local area, gathering money or reciting sermons. Sometimes this celebration took place on St Nicholas's Day (6 December) as a brief interlude in Advent. Both St Nicholas's and Holy Innocents were associated with children in a rather morbid fashion: St Nicholas had saved young women from a life of prostitution by giving them dowries, and had raised a group of beheaded boys from the dead; Holy Innocents was the anniversary of Herod's massacre of children under the age of two. While girl abbesses are less widely documented, boy bishops appear everywhere from Exeter to York and Norwich to Gloucester. In Oxford, four colleges sponsored a boy bishop in the fifteenth century and in 1508 Lincoln College, Oxford, paid six pence to 'St Nicholas clerk'. This sum seems to have been fairly commonplace, and in Louth, Lincolnshire, the boy bishop received the same wage for his service on Holy Innocents Day. For visiting the earl of Northumberland's home and delivering a sermon, the 'bairn bishop' of either Beverley or York received the rather more generous twenty shillings. At St Paul's Cathedral, London, the boy bishop was given supper and entertainment on the eve of Holy Innocents Day and loaned magnificent jewel-studded robes in which to deliver a sermon.

Inevitably, sometimes the misrule went too far. The high-jinks of the London lawyers at Lincoln's Inn led to the breaking down of doors by the anti-king 'Jack Straw' in 1517, so his appearance was forbidden in subsequent celebrations. There was also some unease about the use of false identities during Christmas, particularly among the lower orders. In 1511 an act of parliament forbade performers disguised with masks from visiting great houses because of the disorders they caused. Even the sale of masks was made illegal. This distrust of those who disguised their identity had a long history: as far back as 1334 the city of London had forbidden people from walking the streets masked or in costume. Bristol and Chester instituted similar prohibitions.

But at the royal court, where wealth and title allowed latitude in the law, disguising remained a favourite pastime and weeks after Christmas 1509 was over, Henry VIII was still playing games of misrule. On 18 January, he led a band of courtiers disguised 'like outlaws or Robin Hood's men' to the queen's private chambers.[16] Henry and his 'merry men' donned green hose and hood, armed themselves with bow, arrows, sword and buckler, and burst into the queen's presence. The king was fortunate to have one of the most impressive dressing-up boxes in the country, for his costumes were provided by Richard Gibson from the great wardrobe and his weapons by the master of the armoury. Perhaps the men's disguises were a little too authentic, because the women 'were abashed' and the men took their leave after a few dances. In hindsight, perhaps Henry realized that charging into his pregnant wife's room with a pack of armed men was not the wisest of activities.

This was only one occasion when the king's enthusiasm ran away with his common sense and it demonstrated that Henry would not be content with the role his father had played: benefactor of entertainments, patron of the arts, but above all a spectator. After a prolonged childhood of cosseting and care, the vibrant young Henry VIII was determined to play an active role in court celebration, and in one feast of entertainment more than any other: the joust. When the king heard that a secret contest at Richmond was being planned by some of his courtiers, he resolved that his days of watching from the sidelines were over. Henry had played his part in some of the last tournaments of his father's reign, but only in the lesser feats of arms like running at the ring, never in dangerous sports like the joust. What he really wanted was to test his mettle against the men he had watched in his father's jousts for years: knights like the strongly built Knights of the Spear Charles Brandon and Sir Edward Neville. Fortunately, Henry's old friend William Compton had a solution – for Compton, now allowed private access to the king as his groom of the stool, was slowly manoeuvring himself into the position of a royal fixer. Compton and Henry would disguise themselves as 'stranger knights' and enter the Richmond joust 'unknown to all persons and unlooked for'.

On 12 January, the king and Compton made their way to Richmond Park, where 'there were broken many staves [of lances], and great praise given to the two strangers'. But when one of the stranger knights was pitted against Sir Edward Neville, disaster struck. Neville had height and build to rival even Henry's, and with the added benefit of years more experience in the tiltyard. During the course of the contest, the stranger knight was struck by Neville and injured so badly that he seemed 'likely to die'. Seeing one of the stranger knights wounded, a voice cried out in alarm 'God save the king!' Henry's cover had been blown. In the ensuing panic, the jousters rushed to the stranger knight's side, fearing that the king himself had been mortally injured. At this, the second stranger removed his disguise. It was Henry. 'To the comfort of all people' the jousters realized that it was Compton and not their sovereign who had been wounded.

Compton recovered from his injuries, but this was not the last brush with death that Henry VIII would suffer in pursuit of glory in the tiltyard, and it was an early indication that the king was no longer willing to bow to dynastic pragmatism at the expense of his own enjoyment. He was probably emboldened to risk his neck in the joust by the knowledge of the child growing in Catherine's belly, but as his more experienced councillors Bishop Fox and Sir Thomas Lovell could have told him, a pregnant queen was no substitute for a living king. Many mothers miscarried, and many children died young. For all Henry might imagine his future was secured, they could not be so sure. If the king were killed in the joust, civil war would almost certainly follow, and as Compton had just learned in a painful lesson, jousting killed and maimed without discrimination.

Despite the anxious conclusion to his first foray into the world of jousting, Henry had clearly caught the bug. The year 1510 would see, after Henry's lean adolescence, devoid of the thrill of the joust, the king fighting in a glut of tournaments. Virtually every month saw a fresh tournament of arms. The Spanish ambassador reported that 'there are many young men who excel in this kind of warfare, but the most conspicuous amongst them all, the most assiduous, and the most interested in the combats is the king himself'.[17]

However, Henry would have to wait a little longer for his next court entertainment. For January demanded that the king finally set his mind to business. On the twenty-first day of that month, the first parliament of the reign of Henry VIII opened.

IX

PLOUGH DAY

'Fear God, honour the king'

AT ST PAUL'S Cross in London stood a sorry group of individuals. A gaggle of heretics clutched bundles of faggots in their arms, a woman in a long white gown standing alongside them with a thin taper in her hands. Beneath the lead canopy of the pulpit, a priest delivered a sermon condemning heresy, but the heretics received the disapproval of both priest and crowd in silence. They were lucky to be standing within the bounds of St Paul's churchyard and not outside the city walls at Smithfield, lashed to a stake with fire under their feet. Travellers arriving in London might pass by Smithfield, the tang of smoke on the air rising up to greet them. Or perhaps they would ride by Tyburn, where condemned forgers and traitors alike drooped from a hangman's noose. Such scenes of public punishment were visible up and down the country. Marketplaces had wooden cages and pillories, where prostitutes rubbed shoulders with corrupt brewers and vagrants – those for whom a fine was not punishment enough, but death was too harsh a penalty. The lords and gentlemen returning to London for the opening of parliament were so used to the sight they probably barely noticed them.

In January 1510 the new king called a parliament. The earl of Northumberland and Richard Fox, bishop of Winchester, were among the lords of church and state who travelled to London to sit in the House of Lords. Northumberland had been sent on his way by the senior officials of York, feasted and feted in the city's castle with dishes of fish, fine white bread and gallons of Gascon wine 'in consideration that he may be good and tender lord unto this city at the parliament'.[1] York also sent two of its citizens to fill the ranks of the Commons: the alderman William Nelson and city recorder Brian Palms.

Outside the city walls, Nelson and Palms passed curious processions of labourers, playing pipes, singing, dancing and gathering donations while a plough was carried above their heads. These 'Plough Day' rituals signalled the return to work after the festivities of the twelve days of Christmas. Since not all families could afford their own ploughs, many were communal, kept in the parish church and loaned to locals as required. On the coast, where the sea was the source of food and prosperity, instead of a plough borne by farmers the parishioners would parade a ship carried by fishermen. In Grimsby the bridges around town had to be strengthened to allow the ship to pass. There and in Boston the ship was a realistic miniature, drawn along like a cart. There are payments in the accounts of Boston's Guild of The Blessed Virgin Mary for 'various costs of repair for Noah's little ship', including work on the rigging, new wheels, 'cart clouts', canvas and cord.[2] When the Plough Day rituals were over, the plough or ship was returned to its home in the local church, and the real tools of the workers' trade were wearily taken up once more.

It took rather longer for the members of parliament to get back to work. It was six years since the last parliament had been called and while William Nelson had been elected to represent York back in 1504, Brian Palms was elected for the first time. It must have been with a thrill of anticipation that he stood in his scarlet parliamentary robes, in the crush of the Great Chamber at Westminster as parliament opened on 21 January. Once all the members were assembled the king arrived from the nearby chapel, at the head of a great procession of lords and bishops. Wearing his scarlet and ermine robes and carrying the royal sceptre, he made his way slowly through the press of people in the chamber until he reached the steps and canopy of his throne. There, he donned the 'cap of estate', taking it from the hands of the duke of Buckingham. The archbishop of Canterbury, William Warham, then opened proceedings by addressing the gathered throng in a sermon. Warham must have chosen his topic carefully, aware of the gravitas of this moment: the first parliament of a new reign; an opportunity to right the wrongs of the previous king. He spoke of justice, 'showing how necessary good laws are for the right government of any kingdom'. 'To the great applause of his audience' he said that 'under [Henry VIII's] leadership things badly done in previous times should now be reformed, unjust laws be abolished, harsh or rigorous ones should be tempered or mitigated.'[3]

He acknowledged what many there would have been thinking: the later years of Henry VII's reign had cast a shadow of avarice and paranoia over government. But now the new young king had a chance to right those wrongs. Warham's sermon had a simple message about how the people of England could ensure this reign did not descend into the injustices of the last. They should follow two precepts: 'Fear God. Honour the King.'

The king was the fount of all justice, and one of the three pillars of good kingship was the justice system. The other two were defence of the realm and protection of the church. These principles were enshrined in the oath taken at Henry's coronation only seven months before, when he had promised to confirm the ancient laws and customs of the country and the liberties of the church. In other words, he had sworn to maintain the Common Law of England, a system of legal precedents stretching all the way back to the Saxon monarchs who ruled before the Norman Conquest. The Common Law came directly from the king, dispensed by his appointed judges, and since the twelfth century royal justices had circled the realm, taking the same law from the seat of power in Westminster to the furthest corners of the kingdom. Unlike continental legal codes, which tended to be based on Roman law and determined by the will of the monarch, English Common Law was based on precedent. And it was 'common' to all the people of England because whether someone lived in Carlisle or Cornwall, Norwich or Gloucester, their judgement would be based on the same ancient principles.

So far, so simple. But this fiercely protected ideal of Common Law masks a legal procedure of mind-boggling complexity. For a start, the Tudor legal system divided the king's subjects between the lay and the religious. Only church courts could pass judgement on the religious – the state could not intervene – but they also oversaw the morality of laypeople, dealing with the odd 'witch' healer (usually male), with drunkenness or defamation and a vast array of sexual 'offences' from adultery to incest. Moreover, within the lands technically under the government of the king were territories that operated to all intents and purposes independently, most particularly the Marcher lordships of Wales. While the Principality of North and West Wales had the same administration and legal process as England, the Marcher lands that made up the rest of the country were virtually independent feudal territories under the power of their lords – men like the duke of Buckingham. There, courts were administered according to a combination of statute law, customary law and Welsh law. During Henry VII's reign almost a third of these Marcher lordships had been absorbed into the royal demesne through inheritance, purchase and forfeiture, but there was still a sizeable territory in which the king of England had little power to impose his own system of justice.

Even in England there were many tiers to the justice system, concerned with different aspects of the law. At a local level, manor or borough courts dealt with most disputes, although there were some other small courts concerned with settling local quarrels, like the 'piepowder' courts that resolved issues between traders and customers on market days.* If a case was serious enough, it would be referred from these local courts to the higher authority of the assizes and quarter sessions. Quarter sessions, whose name derived from the fact that they sat four times a year, were presided over by justices of the peace, men of standing in the local area. Assizes were held only twice a year, and their cases were settled – if a conclusion could be reached – by local juries, with the assistance of judges sent out from the central courts. If a criminal or civil case was beyond the capacity or jurisdiction of these lawgivers, it was sent to the highest courts at Westminster. Nudging against each other in the confines of Westminster Hall and its environs were a whole range of law courts: there were the royal courts of King's Bench and Common Pleas, which heard appeals from the lesser courts; the Exchequer, which dealt with financial concerns connected to the crown; the equity Court of Chancery; the royal court of Star Chamber, and many more besides. There were even private admiralty courts whose chief duty was to decide who owned the whales, dolphins and sturgeon that washed up along the English coast.

The foundation of all these courts, and of the English justice system in general, was the notion of collective responsibility. If an individual within a community did wrong then it was the duty of

---

* Piepowder courts got their name from the old French, *pié poudrous*, meaning both a 'dusty-footed' itinerant salesperson, and also someone who ran away without paying for their goods.

that community to report it and to deliver them to local authorities for trial and punishment. Constables sent out to arrest suspected criminals were often accompanied by neighbours of the victim or accused. The origins of this system lay in the 'frankpledge', which demanded that every free man between the ages of twelve and sixty swore to uphold the law in his local area and at regular intervals to present suspected miscreants for judgement. Since trial by peers had been an essential part of the English Common Law for centuries, juries of twelve men were gathered from the locality to 'present' wrongdoers and also to sit in judgement on them. From lowly jurors all the way up to justices of the peace, communal responsibility was at the heart of the legal system.

While both civil and criminal cases could be sent to Westminster or heard before royally appointed justices, people preferred, where possible, to keep dispute resolution to themselves. Many guild ordinances demanded that members take their quarrels to the guild court before having recourse to outside seats of law, and borough courts settled issues arising among the freemen of the city. Foreign merchants trading and living in England followed this principle, reporting their vexations to their consuls in London and Southampton. But, eventually, even the most fiercely independent local law enforcer might have to seek the assistance of a higher power, and the highest court in the land was parliament. Its name deriving from the French *parlement*, a meeting or discussion, parliament was the only court that could amend English law. After an intensive process of presenting petitions, debating them and sending them back for redrafting and clarification, if the lords, bishops, common members of parliament and the king agreed to a change in the law it passed into statute.

While peers like the earl of Northumberland had an automatic right to attend parliament, York's common members of parliament, William Nelson and Brian Palms, had been elected to their positions, which would last only until parliament was closed. They would have to be re-elected to office when next the king called for a parliament. Parliament had been divided in this manner into 'Lords' and 'Commons' since the early fourteenth century. The Commons were elected by men with a freehold (that is, property) worth more than forty shillings. As a borough, York could send two representatives and, like most common MPs, Nelson and Palms had a solid grounding in local government. William Nelson had been a sheriff during Henry VII's reign and for the better part of a decade he had served as an alderman in York. Despite his respectable position, he was an explosive character. Only a few years earlier he had been fined for threatening the mayor of York during a property dispute, and on more than one occasion he was taken to task for failing to keep the peace during elections.

The more restrained Brian Palms was one of a new generation of men trained in the law at the Inns of Court in London. Relatively few law students actually stayed on to become lawyers in London, and Palms and his brother Guy followed the trend by returning to York after their studies at Middle Temple to take up roles in the government of the city. Education at the Inns of Court was becoming a respectable alternative to studying at Oxford or Cambridge for the gently and nobly born and, since most highborn students would ultimately have some role in local government, this legal training was a more useful preparation for their future lives. Palms's background in the law is probably what earned him the position of recorder in York. As recorder, he was expected to have extensive knowledge of the customs and court proceedings of the city, which would be recited before courts as oral evidence. Since 1496, Palms had also been a justice of the peace, a role that had changed considerably during Henry VII's reign and was now superseding that of sheriffs like William Nelson. The justice of the peace had to be everything from financial inspector to law enforcer. It was his duty to investigate accusations of extortion against his fellow law-enforcers and tax-collectors. He was also expected to call suspected rioters to trial and commit them to gaol, grant bail to suspects if the law permitted and to take recognizances of money to keep the peace.* And all of this without a salary to support him.

Palms would have noticed other changes in the process of law during his lifetime, perhaps chief among them the move away from the often uncompromising Common Law courts towards the more adaptable equity courts of Westminster. The major failing of the Common Law was that it was inflexible – bills had to be presented in one of a limited range of Latin formulae and due process had to be followed even when one party kept maliciously disrupting it. If one side in a lawsuit repeatedly failed to appear for court hearings or to follow court rulings, the Common Law was often incapable of forcing them. For this reason, cases could go unresolved for years. Sir Robert Plumpton of Yorkshire was embroiled in disputes over various contested inheritances – first his own, then his wife Isabel's – for the best part of thirty years. As a result, in 1510 both he and Isabel ended up imprisoned in London for debt.

Increasingly, those seeking legal redress were turning to the equity courts: the Court of Star Chamber, where royal councillors and judges sat in a painted room, beneath a royal blue ceiling and twinkling gold stars; and the Court of Chancery, which despite

---

* A recognizance was a sum of money that would be held forfeit if certain conditions were not met, for instance if someone failed to appear for trial when called, or failed to keep the peace having promised to do so. It often demanded that the person involved provide allies to act as 'pledges' for the debt.

being crammed into a corner of Westminster Hall had an aura of considerable authority, since the lord chancellor who headed it was one of the king's chief ministers. In 1509, the lord chancellor was the highest churchman in the country, the archbishop of Canterbury William Warham. There were a number of benefits to pursuing a case through equity courts rather than the traditional routes. For a start, people could present bills in English rather than tortuously twisting them to fit the Latin formulae of the Common Law. The attendance of both parties during the process was assured, as a heavy fine was meted out for non-attendance. Perhaps most importantly, these courts were seen as fairer than others, as they were inclined to turn to arbitrators in order to settle disputes quickly. As a result, both parties were more likely to feel that justice had been served. Since Chancery and Star Chamber represented the authority of the most powerful politicians in the country, they also presented a more fearsome prospect for anyone tempted to defy their judgement.

In fact, the equity courts were a victim of their own success, and by the early sixteenth century they were being swamped with cases that should really have been beyond their remit. Common Law courts were supposed to settle contested titles to land, but more than half of all the suits in the equity Courts of Star Chamber and Chancery dealt with such cases.[4] Litigants tweaked their bills to ensure that what was really a dispute about land ownership appeared to fit the equity courts' concern with the perversion of justice or the unjust retention of deeds of ownership.

This disproportionate concern with land should not be surprising, as not only was land a source and symbol of wealth and influence, but the law of landownership was so exceptionally complicated that even experienced lawyers found it hard to work out who actually owned a contested estate. To make matters worse, in 1509 possession really was nine-tenths of the law – the best evidence that someone was the rightful landowner was if they were seen to be exercising their rights as landowner, with the result that physical control over land and its tenants could be taken as proof of rightful ownership in the first place. With such an incentive to take control of a contested estate, it is hardly surprising that those wealthy or powerful enough to do so took the law into their own hands and seized properties or land by force.

George and Alianore Stanley found this out to their cost. Alianore inherited the manor of Thorpe in Balne, Yorkshire, from her first marriage, and when she married George, the two of them moved there together. Unfortunately for the Stanleys, their neighbour Sir William Gascoigne contested Alianore's right to the manor and after a fruitless attempt to challenge it through the courts, he finally sent thirty of his servants 'with force and arms and in riotous wise' to seize Thorpe in Balne for himself. According to Alianore and George, Sir William also evicted all their tenants and farmers. The Stanleys appealed to Star Chamber, insisting that the question of who owned Thorpe in Balne had been resolved in their family's favour as long ago as the reign of Edward III a century and a half earlier. Gascoigne mounted his own legal defence, insisting that since he was the property's rightful owner he could not be seen to have forcibly entered – he had records from Edward II's time to prove it. Gascoigne's 'great power and might' seems to have won the day as one of his descendants was still in control of Thorpe in Balne decades later.[5]

Such 'riotous entries' into contested estates show that the arrival of the Tudor dynasty did not eradicate the violent lawlessness of the fifteenth century. In 1448 the East Anglian matriarch Margaret Paston was driven from her home by local rival Lord Moleyns, despite a valiant attempt at resistance by herself and Paston servants wielding crossbows. The records of Star Chamber in the reign of Henry VIII are still littered with references to violent usurpations of estates by rival families, and Margaret Paston was far from the last woman to hold out in the face of outside aggression. During a dispute over her inheritance of Babthorpe manor in Yorkshire, Isabel Plumpton faced down 140 men in armour as they laid siege to her home. Eventually, her rival for the manor forced his way in and pulled Isabel down the stairs and out of the house. In the first year of Henry VIII's reign a similar dispute broke out between Giles Curwen and Robert Bellingham over the manor of Poulton in Lancashire. Each party claimed to have the better right to the property and the case dragged on for decades. In 1509–10 'by perjured inquest' (at least according to his rival), Curwen persuaded the local courts that Bellingham's occupancy was illegal. He enlisted twenty allies to march with him for Poulton, seized Bellingham and, for good measure, threw him in prison in Lancaster Castle. Even then, Bellingham's wife refused to surrender her home and she was eventually dragged out only by violence. 'The said Giles and other ill disposed persons so cruelly pulled and logged the wife of [Bellingham] by the fingers of her hands that the blood burst out of her fingers ends.'[6]

According to the letter of the law, Bellingham was imprisoned not because he had illegally occupied Poulton, but because he could not find the required sureties to be granted bail. 'Sureties' were trusted friends or neighbours willing to pay bonds for a prisoner's good behaviour and given that Bellingham's home was currently under siege and his wife bolted up inside it, one imagines that none of his potential sureties were willing to risk their purse on the promise that he would not immediately return to Poulton on being freed and escalate the conflict still further. As it was, like all those whose reputation or funds were too low to secure bail, Bellingham had to sit and wait. Alongside Bellingham in the cells of Lancaster Castle would have been suspected criminals and debtors, likewise awaiting their day in court. The law allowed that, once arrested, suspected wrongdoers were to be kept confined by the local sheriff or justice of the peace, even if they did not know the cause of their imprisonment. They were given no legal counsel and their treatment would depend to a large extent on their wealth, as they would have been reliant on the willingness of friends to pay to provide them with changes of clothing, comfortable bedding – and even food and fuel. A London tailor called Thomas Clerk was imprisoned in Newgate Prison, London, for days and 'cruelly treated' without knowing the reason. Despite investigation and pleading on the part of his friends they could not discern why he was imprisoned nor gain him 'liberty upon surety'. Clerk suspected the ire of the London mayor Sir William Capell was behind his miserable treatment and petitioned Chancery for relief.[7]

Sometimes prisoners did not find out what crime they were accused of until they were brought before a jury for indictment.* If the jury then decided that there was not enough evidence to pursue the case, the prisoner was released, but if the jury judged there to be sufficient evidence and the indictment was 'endorsed', the prisoner was returned to their gaol cell until the trial began. Even after being tried at the assizes or quarter sessions, the case still might not be closed – it could be too complex for local resolution and have to go to the central law courts, in which case the prisoner would be moved under guard to one of the London prisons such as the Marshalsea or Newgate. There, conditions

---

* Indictment was the process by which a suspected criminal was presented before a jury and the alleged crime revealed by a 'bill of indictment'. The jury would then determine whether there was enough evidence to make a legal case against the suspect.

were grim. Newgate in particular drew complaints from its occupants about its 'noxious air', but all the prisons were cold and dark unless inmates could afford to buy their own candles or firewood, and keepers were over-eager to shackle their prisoners with heavy irons, from which they had to pay to be released.

Robert Bellingham escaped the privations of the London prisons, but the fact that his incarceration in Lancaster Castle prevented him from helping his wife in her defence of their manor suggests something more than due process of law may have been involved. It was not unknown for people to be imprisoned for purely malicious reasons: to derail a lawsuit they had filed; because they had refused the advances of a powerful figure; or as retaliation for some perceived slight. Time and again, petitions from prisoners repeat the same pleas: their accuser is powerful, their keeper is unscrupulous, they are imprisoned against the law 'to their utter undoing'. Alice Strekelond of London claimed to have been imprisoned twice in the late fifteenth century, despite gaining surety, because she refused the advances of a man named Edward Malery. The butcher Thomas Cessell found himself imprisoned in Newgate in Bristol as revenge for launching a suit against William Jonys, who had sold him diseased sheep. Cessell complained to the Court of Chancery that Jonys had 'such fame within the said town and is a man of [such] great substance and small conscience' that he was 'like to be undone and die in prison'. His only hope was for Chancery to allow his case to be presented to them, in the hope that it would be dismissed as baseless and he could be released.[8] In the cases of Cessell, Strekelond and Bellingham, as in so many others, prolonged imprisonment was used as a means of wearing down the resistance of the prisoner.

It was hard for prisoners awaiting trial not to despair, and once they finally arrived at court they could not necessarily look forward to a happier future. If they were found guilty of murder or the theft of goods worth more than a shilling, they would face the hangman's noose. If they were condemned for treason (conspiring in a plot against the king or his family) or even petty treason (plotting against their superiors, whether servant against master or wife against husband) their execution would be even more protracted. For men, it meant hanging, drawing and quartering. They would be dragged through filthy streets to the place of execution on a litter, attached to a horse's tail. At the gallows they would be permitted a few brief words of penance before being jolted into the air with a noose around their neck. Before they choked to death, they were cut down and their body eviscerated, then butchered into quarters. The body parts and head of the traitor were then displayed prominently, perhaps on the spikes of London Bridge or in the market square of their home town – maybe even both. Female traitors or petty traitors were not hanged, drawn and quartered; they were burned at the stake according to the punishment of the law. Condemned pirates and coin counterfeiters could expect execution as well. In London 'seathieves' were 'hanged upon a tree in [the] Thames a little from Wapping' and kept there so that every high tide the water flowed over their corpses. For 'making of false money', coiners could expect to be hanged, drawn and quartered. The coiner John Stafford of Cheshire was discovered in York with coining irons and a hundred crowns made from mixed metal ready to be gilded. For meddling in the king's currency, he was condemned to be executed in the marketplace of York.[9]

Mercifully, there were ways to avoid these capital punishments. For men, the simplest was to claim 'benefit of clergy', which permitted anyone in holy orders to be tried in an ecclesiastical court. Since the church was not permitted to shed blood, a person could not be killed for a crime that demanded a capital sentence in a lay court. The 'proof' that someone was a man of the cloth was literacy, usually a reading of the 'neck verse' of Psalm 51, which began suitably enough with the words 'have mercy on me, O God'.* However, as this system was clearly open to abuse – some laymen were also literate and even the illiterate could learn the necessary verse off by heart – in recent years the rules for benefit of clergy had been tightened up. In 1489 Henry VII made claiming the benefit through literacy a one-time-only deal, and to ensure it wasn't misused those released to the church on a first offence would be branded on their left thumb, with the letter 'M' if they had committed murder or with a 'T' if they were convicted of a felony. If someone claiming to be in holy orders requested benefit of clergy a second time the neck verse would not suffice. They had to present letters of ordination to prove their status, otherwise they would be tried as a layperson.

Women could not claim benefit of clergy as they could not be ordained as a bishop, priest or deacon. They could however claim mercy by 'pleading their belly' – that is, being pregnant. Presumably some women who were definitely not pregnant tried to plead that they were when condemned to die, so anyone who did so was inspected by up to twelve 'matrons or discreet women' to ensure they were telling the truth. Some women who entered gaol without a child may have got pregnant – by having sex with a visitor or gaoler – while waiting for their trial, in order to save themselves from the noose.

One of the worst punishments of all was reserved for those who would not plead guilty or innocent in the first place. Felons and

---

* The 'neck verse' was so called because reciting it could literally save the neck of the accused.

petty traitors who would not plead faced being crushed to death beneath great weights. *Peine forte et dure* awaited anyone refusing to plead and thereby preventing a proper trial from proceeding. Why would someone endure such an awful death when they could just face trial? The answer, as always, was land. Those condemned through the courts forfeited their lands and chattels to the crown, whereas those who endured *peine forte et dure* had the meagre comfort of knowing that their estate would descend entirely to their own family.

It is hardly surprising, with so many gruesome potential punishments, that the legal records of this period reveal so many attempted – and, indeed, successful – prison breaks. Even the disgraced minister Edmund Dudley contemplated such desperate action. During the uncertain weeks while he waited to hear whether parliament would attaint him for treason, depriving future generations of his family of any rights on his estate, he plotted a futile attempt to break out of the Tower of London. At first he was able to use his servants to put his plan into action, but as soon as they realized what he was up to they 'did but their duty... [and] refused to assist my escape'. Without outside assistance, Dudley was forced to abandon the plan.[10]

Those condemned to death, like Dudley, had nothing to lose in attempting an escape. In fact, any prisoner who escaped prison had a very real chance of saving their life, for if they made it to a churchyard or to one of several other specially appointed regions of sanctuary they could 'abjure the realm' and flee into exile. Banishment from England must have seemed far more appealing than a prolonged and grisly death.

There was even the possibility of permanent sanctuary in certain ecclesiastical areas. While every parish church and yard would allow sanctuary to be claimed for forty days – with local men bound to guard the site during that period – at the end of that time, unless a fugitive confessed to the crime and abjured the realm, they could be retaken and imprisoned by force. But vast swathes of England were independent of royal justice thanks to their status as county palatines or rights to ecclesiastical liberties, and could therefore shelter fugitives indefinitely. These areas included Westminster, Glastonbury, Colchester, Lancashire, Durham, Cheshire, the Marcher lordships of Wales, and the liberties of the archbishop of York. York's liberties alone covered ninety square miles of territory.

Henry VII was one among many who resented these areas of legal defiance, and in the first year of his reign he successfully set a precedent by removing the Yorkist rebel Humphrey Stafford from sanctuary at Culham church.* Henry insisted that sanctuaries must be able to show a royal grant specifying all the crimes for which asylum was to be permitted and since the charter for Culham did not expressly cover treason, the unfortunate Stafford was dragged out and executed.[11] Londoners put up a spirited attack on the right to permanent sanctuary at St Martin's le Grand and at Westminster, which were inconveniently close to the city's prisons and allegedly provided hideouts for ne'er-do-wells and errant apprentices to launch raids on their neighbours. Prisoners had even escaped into sanctuary after being rescued en route from their prison cell to trial. However, petitions to parliament and forcible entry into sanctuary to retake fugitives had not yet yielded any long-term benefits and the privilege of these permanent sanctuaries would not be suppressed for years to come.

As well as his attack on sanctuaries, Henry VII had also tried to prevent prison escapes by passing a Statute of Escapes in 1504. He

---

* Stafford had already taken sanctuary once; he had been hiding at Colchester since defeat at the Battle of Bosworth, and emerged in spring 1486 in a thwarted attempt to raise Worcestershire against Henry VII.

did not want a repeat of the events of 1470, when all ninety-nine prisoners in the Marshalsea absconded. By happy coincidence, this statute also enabled Henry to make a little extra money, for it set a sliding scale of fines to be paid by the keeper of prisoners if their charges escaped. Since a hundred-mark fine for the escape of a prisoner convicted of high treason was beyond the means of most keepers, any who failed to pay their fines were condemned to be imprisoned in the very institutions over which they had previously held control. This was the fate of John Bray, the keeper of Ludgate, when he failed to pay the damages owed for his escaped prisoners. The statute cannot be considered particularly successful, though, as at Christmas 1504 there was another breakout at the Marshalsea and 'many or the more part of the prisoners' escaped. This particular jailbreak did not have an entirely happy ending for the absconding prisoners, for 'shortly after many of them were taken and put in execution for that deed'.[12]

For most condemned men and women, the punishments endured were, mercifully, less terminal: fines, pillory and penance were the penalties for a wide range of offences. Food and drink vendors who traded in poor-quality goods or illegally inflated prices were punished with fines or public penance, like the London cooper John Gamelyn who was set on the pillory for 'brewing and melding of old and corrupt wine with new'. Document counterfeiters and spreaders of sedition were also clasped in the pillory's embrace. The pillory restrained its prisoner by the hands and head and was generally located in a very visible and public place, near a church or in a marketplace. Usually someone would be placed in the pillory on multiple occasions, 'for three market days' or the equivalent, in order to ensure maximum public humiliation. The fact that over half of those sentenced to public penance in London chose to evade it with charitable donation attests to the fact that such public loss of face to friends and neighbours really was considered a serious punishment. Sexual misconduct was treated similarly. Prostitutes and pimps (known as bawds) faced banishment after an all-too-public shaming in the local pillory. Adulterers might be paraded before their neighbours' houses on an open cart, or made to stand in a white sheet in church while a sermon was read denouncing their wrongdoing. A 'bawd of the stews named Thomas Togood' was set in the pillory in London in 1496 for enticing two Bankside women into prostitution.[13]

There were some other inventive forms of social mortification handed out to miscreants. 'Scolding' was a criminal offence in 1509 and those women – or, rarely, men – who engaged in verbal abuse or disturbance of the peace were usually shamed by having a 'mortar' displayed at their front door.* When Christine Knightsby of Sandwich was condemned as 'a scold, a curser, a maker of debates and strifes' she was warned that any future offence would see her punished by having 'the mortar to be hanged over her door'. This mortar seems to have been a wooden weight, presumably designed to be distinctive to onlookers and difficult for the scold to carry. Being paraded through the town wearing or carrying the mortar and loudly accompanied by pipers was a further extension of this punishment, although it was threatened more often than it was used.[14]

There were more extreme punishments for those convicted of moral laxity: imprisonment in a specially designed cage, for instance, or in a 'cucking' or 'shelving stool'. This chair-like equipment confined its (usually female) occupant, who was publicly

---

* William Clark was presented as a scold in Fordwich, Kent, in 1517. The clerk who recorded the court's proceedings was so used to scolds being female that he accidentally described Clark as *garrulatrix* (Latin for a female scold) not *garrulator* (the male equivalent).

shamed by being exhibited in the chair in front of their home, in a market square, or even transported around on the back of a cart. Occasionally the stool was attached to a long plank and used to dunk offenders in water. There was a strong association in popular imagination between female verbal abuse and female sexual incontinence, and the cucking stool was a potential punishment for both. In 1490/1, four pence was paid for a cucking stool to be built in New Romney, Kent. Perhaps the local authorities were keen to see it in service, for when three local women were banished shortly afterwards for sexual offences they were all told that if they returned within a year and a day they would 'be brought to the shelving stool and there... remain till their buttocks be three times ducked in the water'. A servant in Sandwich called Agnes Sampson, convicted of harlotry and the theft of silver spoons, was sentenced to be ducked three times in water using the cucking stool. Canterbury had a 'cage standing beside the pillory' intended for 'scolds and other malefactors', in which several female sexual offenders and a number of scolds were imprisoned.[15]

Some would have considered these women fortunate, for the male equivalent of repeated small-scale criminality was mutilation. When the London baker William Smyth was convicted of stealing a shirt in Sandwich he was condemned to

go about [the town] with a shirt the which he hath stolen and then to be set at the pillory the space of two hours and after that to be had down and his ear nailed to the pillory and there to stand to the time he doth loose himself [i.e. cut or tear himself free] and after to avoid the town forever.[16]

Smyth's mocking procession with his stolen shirt mirrors a number of similar ritual punishments. In 1516, Elizabeth Chekyn of London was convicted of being a 'common harlot and strumpet, and also was now lately taken strolling and walking by the streets of this city in a priest's array and clothing'. Among Elizabeth's clientele were a number of the priests whose clothing she was wearing – when she was arrested, she was in bed with two of them. Elizabeth's punishment was to walk through the streets of London carrying the white rod of a penitent prostitute, a letter 'H' for harlot pinned to her chest. On her left shoulder she was to display an elaborate image made of woollen cloth, showing herself in the priests' clothing.[17]

Like Chekyn and Smyth, the heretics at St Paul's Cross had to process through the streets to the place of their penance, and the candles and faggots of wood they carried were a reminder to all onlookers that the punishment for heretics was burning at the stake. Penitential processions were usually undertaken in what amounted to underwear – pale, ankle-length shifts. Because heretics were considered to have fractured their relationship with their neighbours by breaking away from the 'universal' church of Rome, their penance might also involve a public sign of their incorporation back into their religious community. While standing at St Paul's Cross, they had to be seen to listen to the priest's sermon, and they might also be commanded to stand or kneel before their fellow parishioners in church, or make offerings to local shrines. They could be forced to recite the key passages of Catholic belief in Latin: *Pater Noster, Ave Maria, Credo* (Our Father, Hail Mary, the Creed).

The symbol of heresy was the faggot, a cluster of kindling. The faggot was a potent reminder not only of the law's fiercest weapon in the war against heresy (burning to death) but also of the eternal fire that the church said awaited sinners in hell. Heretics like the Lollard Margery Goyte of Derbyshire or James Brewster, a carpenter of Colchester, were forced to publicly abjure their sins, processing through town in underclothes, with naked legs and feet, ahead of a cross-bearer.[18] In 1506, Brewster was commanded to wear a badge representing a faggot on his clothing for the rest of his life. The other sign of an abjured heretic was a branded 'H', burned onto either their cheek or hand.

It was sometimes the condition of a heretic's penance that they must watch their friends or relatives be burned at the stake. Alice Rowley had to clutch a faggot in her arms while watching her friend, the sixty-year-old Joan Warde, die at the stake in Coventry in 1512. Worse awaited the families of some condemned heretics, who were given a terrifying warning against following their parents' faith: when William Tylsworth was burned to death at Amersham in 1506, his own daughter Joan Clerk was forced to light the fire as a condition of her penance.[19]

Certain burnings would have had particular impact, even on those to whom the heretic was unknown. In 1494, the octogenarian Joan Boughton was burned to death at Smithfield with faggots and reeds for being 'a disciple' of the heretic John Wycliffe. Her ashes were gathered by co-religionists and collected in an earthenware pot as a relic of her suffering. James Brewster, having removed his badge of faggots and continued to express his beliefs even after being once punished, was burned in a single fire with his friend William Sweeting at Smithfield in 1511.

Burning at the stake was, mercifully, an uncommon punishment. When a community of heretics in Kent was investigated early in Henry VIII's reign by the archbishop of Canterbury, only one man was executed. Among the many other punishments handed out by the archbishop, thirty-three heretics were made to carry a faggot in public procession, thirty-one confined to their parish, nine forced into abstinence or fasting, seven imprisoned and one ordered simply to treat his wife well.[20] Whatever the punishment, the message was clear: disobedience in matters of religion would not be permitted.

If someone had pleaded innocent but been found guilty of a capital offence, and if all attempts to secure either benefit of clergy or plead the belly, or to escape from prison, had come to nothing, then there was one last hope remaining: a royal pardon. The king could release a prisoner condemned to die, and sometimes pardons were granted on the very steps of the scaffold. In February 1496, the condemned rebels Thomas Cressener and Thomas Astwood were dragged from their cells in Newgate Prison, lashed to hurdles and drawn through the filthy streets of London to Tower Hill. On the scaffold, they watched their co-conspirators fall, one after another, to the executioner's axe until it was their turn to die. Only then, standing in the blood of their allies and expecting the blade to sever their own heads at any moment, did they receive their pardon from Henry VII. Contrary to the popular image that execution sites were crammed with ghoulish mobs baying for blood, Cressener and Astwood's sudden pardon caused 'the rejoicing of much people, for they were both young men'.[21] Indeed, when capital punishment was the only possible recourse for lawgivers, they tended to be reluctant to impose it. In the fifteenth century, jurors on the Midlands circuit acquitted seventy per cent of those presented to them for trial. They were probably following a similar principle to that expressed by one judge of King Henry VIII when he addressed a jury: 'If you be in doubt [of a suspect's guilt] lean rather towards life than death'. It was better to release the guilty than kill the innocent.[22]

Having already been condemned to die, and with all thoughts of escape now abandoned, Empson and Dudley's only hope for survival was the clemency of the king. For a while it seemed as though such hopes were not misplaced. The chronicler Edward

Hall reported that for 'many seasons the fame ran that the queen had purchased [their] pardon'.[23] Queens often acted in this way, pleading for mercy when popular opinion was in favour of a prisoner being put to death. Their appeals enabled a king to reverse his decisions – like, for instance, condemning Dudley and Empson as traitors – without losing face. After all, how could he resist the entreaty of a beloved and compassionate wife?

But as parliament trundled through its business and ploughs tilled the fields to ready them for spring sowing, the queen was in no state to think of pardoning anyone. Early on the morning of 31 January in Westminster Palace, only a stone's throw from where parliament sat, Catherine miscarried a daughter. The only warning had been a slight pain in her knee the night before. Crippled by grief and uncertainty, Catherine and Henry kept the miscarriage secret. The only other people who knew were, of necessity, a physician; two of Catherine's Spanish women who were probably in attendance when she miscarried; and Catherine's trusted chancellor Fray Diego Fernandez. At such a time the couple must have sorely missed the calm authority and experience of Henry's grandmother Margaret Beaufort. Fernandez had been Catherine's support through the purgatorial years of widowhood, but as a friar he was unlikely to have much in the way of practical experience of pregnancy to offer. The family members who would ordinarily offer guidance were either hundreds of miles away or dead. But before Henry and Catherine revealed the fact of the miscarriage, they received a glimmer of hope. Their physician believed that Catherine was still pregnant. Her daughter had been one of two infants, he claimed, and the twin still lived. As if to confirm the story, Catherine's belly kept swelling.

The king and queen had suffered a loss, and had a terrible fright, but now it seemed all would be well. The half-dozen people who knew of the miscarriage kept their secret. By mid-February congratulations on the royal pregnancy were delivered to the king by the Venetian ambassador, one of many international embassies to offer their best wishes. Parliament carried on with its business, passing twenty statutes before closing with another lavish procession in scarlet robes. Then William Nelson and Brian Palms joined the mass exodus of MPs leaving London, to return to their business in the north. To the outside world it appeared that justice had been done and order had been restored. In the clamour of it all, Empson and Dudley were forgotten.

X

SHROVE

Contrition and suspicion

On Shrove Sunday* a banquet was held in the Parliament Chamber at Westminster. To welcome foreign ambassadors, Henry, Catherine and their court put on a display of magnificence and cosmopolitanism, celebrating the last opportunity for feasting and frivolity before the abstinence of Lent. While the queen rested beneath a great canopy of estate, her husband led a peculiar procession of courtiers around the chamber. Henry himself was 'apparelled after Turkey fashion', scimitar at his hip, wearing a sumptuously embroidered golden gown with a crimson velvet turban on his head. His courtiers had also adopted the fashions of foreign realms: some wore feathered hats and silver chains in the manner of Prussia; others imitated 'the fashion of Russia' in long gowns of yellow satin and furred hats, hatchets in their hand; ladies paraded in golden dresses like ancient Romans; and the king's sister Mary was among a party dressed as Egyptians, their arms bare from the elbow down; their hands, neck, face and arms painted so they 'seemed to be... black Mores'.[1]

* Shrove Sunday was the seventh Sunday before Easter. Shrovetide (which usually fell during February) was the last opportunity for fun before Lent began on Ash Wednesday.

Africa, Asia and Europe – the three continents of the Old World – were represented in the costumes of that chamber. Conspicuously absent, though, was any symbol of the great landmass that had been discovered barely two decades earlier: a continent that was known in England in 1509 as 'the New Found Land' but which would come to be called America. During Henry's short lifetime the map of the known world had been redrawn. The English court had already received visitors from this foreign shore: men who ate raw flesh and wore animal hides as clothing; exotic birds, from regal hawks to bright popinjays;* and 'cats of the mountain' to join the lions in the king's menagerie at the Tower of London.

While Henry's kingdom might rest on an island, it was still inextricably linked with the wider world, from the luxurious foods consumed and the exotic clothing worn at the Shrove banquet in Westminster, to the imported Spanish salt that preserved Icelandic stockfish for the masses to eat during the coming days of Lent. Beer – supposedly the most English of beverages – was in fact a continental import that, by 1509, was slowly coming to supplant home-brewed English ale,† and a number of European brewers were now resident in London. Export of English wool and cloth was essential to the national economy, but so too was an import of knowledge and skills in the form of Italian mariners, German merchants, French miners and Dutch glaziers and printers.

The royal court also contained its fair share of immigrants, for the Spanish queen had arrived in England with a large household of her compatriots, many of whom still served her. Among their

* A popinjay is a parrot.

† Hops were introduced to England in the late thirteenth century from the Low Countries but beer really gained in popularity only in the fifteenth century. By 1441 brewing with hops was so widespread that royal supervisors were appointed for the beer trade.

number was the enslaved Moor Catalina, 'whose duty it was to make the bed and attend to other secret services of Her Highness' chamber'.[2] Catalina came from Motril in Granada and probably entered royal service as a result of the *Reconquista* of 1492, when Catherine of Aragon's parents Ferdinand and Isabella (*Los Reyes Católicos*) had seized the emirate of Granada from the Muslim ruler Boabdil. When Catherine entered London in 1501, she had made a virtue of her heritage, dressing in Spanish fashions while her attendants wore their own native dress. Catalina could have been one of the 'undersized, barefoot pygmy Ethiopians' that Thomas More reported seeing that day, with more rhetorical flourish than cultural sensitivity.* Catalina was probably of a similar age to Catherine, so rather than being a 'pygmy' she was still an adolescent, and her Granadan dress might have included unfamiliar slippers or sandals that made her appear 'barefoot' to foreign eyes. A more restrained spectator described the clothing of Catherine's attendants as 'busteous† and marvellous' although he did note that 'they were not the fairest [palest] women of the company'.[3]

Catherine may also have been the first patron of John Blanke, a trumpeter of African origin who by 1507 had entered Henry VII's service. John's surname might have derived from an ironic pun on his skin colour – *blanco* meant white in Spanish – but his position within the royal household was one of considerable respect. John earned twenty shillings a month as one of eight royal trumpeters and served at both Henry VII's funeral and Henry VIII's

---

* The English tended to use 'Ethiopian', 'Blackamore', 'Barbarian' and 'Moore' indiscriminately, with little sensitivity to the actual ethnicity of those they were describing.

† Probably meaning that the clothing was in a rustic style or unusually bulky. Since Catherine's attendants wore native Spanish fashions, including the hoop-skirted farthingale, either context could be intended here.

coronation. He appears in a tournament roll for a royal joust at Westminster in February 1511, sitting on horseback, flanked by a pair of his colleagues. The trio of trumpeters wear yellow and grey livery, but John is unique in covering his head with a golden turban.

Catalina and John were far from the earliest black presences in England. Indeed, Africans had arrived before the Anglo-Saxons, for a 'division of Moors' from North Africa served in the Roman Army at Hadrian's Wall in the third century AD. More recently, an African called Pedro Alvarez had been granted freedom from Portuguese slavery by Henry VII, a manumission that was upheld when Alvarez returned to Portugal. Black men and women had an even greater presence north of the border in the Scottish court, where Henry VIII's elder sister Margaret was queen. Margaret was attended by two 'More lasses' called Elen and Margaret, who served as her personal maidservants, much as Catalina served Catherine. King James IV also employed a 'More taubronar', that is to say a drummer, who lived at court with his wife and child. Although the precise nature of his profession is unclear, Peter the More appears repeatedly in royal household accounts and clearly enjoyed a position of honour at the Scottish court. He received a pension, and travelled and lodged at royal expense. In 1508, two 'More friars' had their living expenses paid for by the Scottish treasury, in the same year that a joust was held 'for the black lady', who granted the victor a kiss. In the ports around the British Isles that were centres of international trade, Africans as well as Europeans would be encountered on the various ships pressed against the quayside, although these visitors left fewer traces in documentary records. One ship docked at Southampton in 1491/2 had a musician described simply as 'a blackman' and Maria Moriana, a servant in the household of the Southampton-based merchant Filippo Cini, may also have been of African origin.[4]

According to British mythology, England and Wales had always had an immigrant population. 'Britain' itself, so the hugely influential chronicler Geoffrey of Monmouth had claimed, was named after Brutus – a Trojan who was guided to the country by divine visions, and who founded London ('New Troy') before sending his fellow Trojans to throw all the giants out of Cornwall. Similar foundation myths could be found north of the border – Scotland's dynasty was allegedly founded by an Egyptian princess named Scota. Not to be outdone, the Welsh claimed to be the descendants of Noah's grandson Gomer. Wales was also one of the last outposts of the original Britons, who had been hounded out of their lands by the Saxons during the Dark Ages. Since then, there had been wave after wave of invasions – the Vikings in the ninth century, the Normans in the eleventh, the Angevin Plantagenets in the twelfth – all leaving their mark on the language and place-names of England. The most recent invasion had been that of the Tudor dynasty itself, which arrived with substantial armed support from France and Scotland in August 1485. As well as these military incursions, England had also played host to more peaceable visitors. International marriage repeatedly brought influxes of foreign courtiers, from Bohemia, Savoy, Navarre, France and most recently from Aragon. And, as international trade expanded, English merchants moved to foreign ports, while their European counterparts settled everywhere from London to Bristol, Southampton to Hull and York to Dorchester.

Walking the streets of London, one could expect to encounter foreign goods and accents with regularity: it was a city, one Scottish visitor claimed, 'visited by the ships of all nations'.[5] In the Thameside steelyard, Hanse merchants had carved out a niche of German trade in the very heart of the city. Lombard Street was not only the financial centre of London, but also the centre of an

Italian community that included a branch of the powerful Bardi banking family of Florence. Under Henry VII, two foreign guilds had established themselves near Blackfriars within the city: the Franco-Norman Brotherhood of the Conception of Our Blessed Lady and the Brotherhood of the Holy Trinity of the 'Strangers' of the Low Countries and Spain. Around Gracechurch Street was a cluster of goldsmiths who had journeyed from the Low Countries, France and Germany to ply their trade, and beyond the walls in Farringdon Without Ward lived a collection of French crossbow-makers. In the shade of the lead roof of St Paul's Cathedral could be heard the myriad tongues of men from as far afield as Florence, Lucca, Castile, Pisa, and the Rhine valley – it was a veritable tower of Babel.

As the largest city in England, London was always a magnet for migrants both international and domestic, but there was a foreign presence far beyond the metropolis. The Dutch brothers Frederick and Gerard Freez, now settled in York, were part of a nationwide influx of printers and booksellers from the Continent. Most famously, Wynkyn de Worde (who was either Dutch or Alsatian) had taken over William Caxton's press at the sign of the Red Pale in Westminster. Richard III had actively encouraged the immigrant printing trade, passing an act of parliament that removed any impediment for an 'artificer or merchant stranger of what[ever] nation or country he be' practising the craft of 'writer, limner, binder or printer of such books', 'bringing into this realm, or selling retail or otherwise, any kind of books, written or printed, or dwelling within the said realm for the same purpose'.[6] As a result of this royal approval, there were many foreign printers around the country. In 1509 the mellifluously named Garret Godfrey and Nicholas Speryng could be found binding books in Cambridge, having emigrated from the Low Countries. Ingelbert Haghe of Rouen issued a Hereford *Breviary* in 1505, and also worked as a stationer in London.

The church was another locus for careers that crossed national boundaries. The bishop of Worcester and royal chaplain Silvestro Gigli had been born in Lucca, but like previous generations of his family made his career in England: in 1505 it was he who had brought the papal dispensation that allowed Henry's marriage to Catherine of Aragon. He probably assisted his Lucchese nephew Felix Massarozee to become rector of Tredington in the diocese of Worcester.

The West Country had a large population of 'aliens', with French families working in a wide variety of trades. The eastern coastal areas of Dorset were home to French sailors and servants; while Normans settled in the valleys of the rivers Frome and Piddle were probably dairymen, bringing their expertise to the lush pastures and water meadows of Owermoigne and Winfrith Newburgh. In Shaftesbury a settlement of 'Duchemen' participated in the local wool and cloth trade. Deep into Cornwall, Breton labourers and Frenchmen like John Aparys brought their knowledge to the mines, producing the tin, iron and lead that were the backbone of Cornish industry.

The highest concentration of immigrants could be found in port towns, where low Venetian galleys bristling with oars nestled alongside the great 200-ton carracks of Genoa and Portugal. Bristol had a thriving trade with Ireland, Iceland, Spain and Bordeaux, and acted as a stopping point for, or home to, many merchants of those lands – not to mention a Welsh population who had crossed the Bristol Channel to settle there. Goods from across the Bristol Channel – timber, iron, cloth and wool – were unloaded in the aptly named Welsh Back, while the deliveries from great seafaring ships – stockfish, wine, woad, wax and salt – waited downriver at the large quay on the Kingroad at the mouth of the Avon until the tide was in their favour. Buildings had crept out from the docks, slowly clawing their way up the surrounding hillsides as more and more were drawn to Bristol's international trade.

Southampton, too, was a town adapted to the needs of its merchants. Its three main roads all ran down to the quayside, and the wide thoroughfares, especially the High Street, enabled the transport of goods from the harbour cranes to storehouses and beyond. There were sometimes a thousand Mediterranean 'strangers' in the narrow streets of Southampton, enjoying the ale in the Dolphin or Crown taverns. At the blast of trumpets from the galleys, the Venetian fleet was recalled to ship and any crew lodging in the town departed to begin the perilous journey back across the English Channel.

Prominent among the merchants trading in England was the Marini family of Genoa. There had been Marini in London since the mid-fifteenth century, and by 1509 they had built up considerable influence in the international port of Southampton. The head of the family was Brancino de Marini, who lived with his family of young sons in the West Hall of Southampton, which had been rented by previous generations of Italians far back in the last century. The West Hall was chosen not only for its location in the busiest quarter of town, with entrances into both main thoroughfares and easy access to the Water and West gates, but also because it was a magnificent expression of the wealth and importance of the family. The Marinis made extensive improvements during their tenancy. There was a central hall for Brancino and his household to dine in, with fitted cupboards built into the angles of the walls and long glass windows letting in light from the street. A courtyard was bordered with storehouses, stables and offices, and Brancino could conduct his business in a study away from the hubbub below, surrounded by papers and account books, glancing out the window to oversee the movement of his goods. The large cellars beneath the hall stored the family's merchandise – a common arrangement for households where trade was the bedrock of wealth.

Brancino enjoyed considerable success as a merchant, exporting English cloth and wool from the Cotswolds to the Mediterranean. He was unusual in being one of the few Italians shipping from England to Gascony, carrying cloth to exchange for wine and woad. He was successful enough to own at least one ship: a 190-ton vessel he had bought for thirty pounds in Southampton in 1504. His decision to immediately purchase two pieces of ordnance from the town stores is testament to the dangers of international trade in this era: piracy or attack by Turkish galleys was far from unusual for ships making the run to the Mediterranean, and mariners had to be willing to fight as well as sail. Merchants were not even necessarily safe in port: in 1495 the Venetian consul had been dining on his flagship at dusk when French corsairs crept up Southampton Water and seized him, the ship and all its crew. For the internationally renowned seamen of Venice, this had been a very public humiliation.

Although the Marinis had been in England for generations and used English ships, masters and wool traders in their daily business, they maintained closer connections to their countrymen than they built with the English. In a will left by Brancino's cousin, Niccolò de Marini de Egra, only one Englishman is mentioned, the prominent Sotonian Sampson Thomas. All the other names and bequests belong to Italians. Immigrants to England were always considered 'aliens' unless they sought letters of denization, and Brancino never did so.* When there were disputes with other traders, he

---

* Denization is an obsolete process whereby a foreigner, through 'letters patent' (i.e. by written order of the sovereign), became a denizen, thereby obtaining certain rights of citizenship. It did not offer any retrospective

would take his concerns to his own consular court. There were Venetian, Genoese and Florentine consuls based in London and Southampton, who in many ways acted like guilds for the foreign merchants.

At the docks of Southampton, merchants like Brancino watched hawk-eyed as their goods were hauled by crane from ship to quayside. All the luxuries – as well as the necessities – of daily life were there. Venetian galleys came laden with bales of parchment and reams of writing paper, as well as cargoes of ink-producing oak galls and feather quills to write on them. One galley brought all the paraphernalia of a chapel: singing books for services, rosaries, crucifixes, mass bells, wax candles, incense and church vestments. Ships from Malaga and Valencia brought the finest leatherwork of Cordoba, while from Lucca and Florence came goldsmiths' work and silks woven with golden thread. Venetian and Genoese captains ventured as far as Asia Minor, bringing back bales of cotton wool, sweet wines, spices and Turkish silks. From North Africa, ships returned laden with ostrich plumes, leopard skins, ivory, sugar – and even live monkeys, for wealthy ladies to keep as pets. Queen Catherine's native lands were the source for Mediterranean fruits: oranges, figs, almonds, lemons, pomegranates and raisins.

But despite this constant influx of international goods and workers, the English could be remarkably insular, and the treatment of many foreigners was a far cry from the exotic bonhomie of the Shrove celebrations at Henry VIII's court. More than one foreign visitor noted English arrogance:

---

rights, so could not benefit children born before the date of the grant. Many children with mixed native- and foreign-born parents preferred instead to go through the more time-consuming process of taking out an act of naturalization, by bill in parliament, which gave them the same rights as native-born citizens.

The English are great lovers of themselves, and of everything
belonging to them; they think that there are no other men than
themselves and no other world but England; and whenever they
see a handsome foreigner they say... 'it is a great pity that he
should not be an Englishman'.[7]

During periods of economic unrest, this narrow-mindedness
twisted into mistrust of the 'strangers' in England – and on more
than one occasion in living memory had erupted into violence.
The economic downturn that began in the 1450s led to a string
of attacks on the Italian population of London, which ultimately
caused a number of merchants to withdraw to Southampton and
Winchester. Even Southampton was not immune to xenophobia,
and beginning in 1472, the mayoralty of Thomas Payne led to a rise
in ill-treatment of, and distortion of the law so as to discriminate
against, the Spanish, Gascon and Italian settlers in the port. The
most recent outbreak of serious xenophobic violence had arisen in
1493, when the entire steelyard in London was besieged by mercers'
servants and other youths who first 'began to rifle and to spoil
such chamber and other houses' of the 'Easterlings' in the Steelyard, and then – when forced out – threw themselves at the locked
gates, 'beating and rushing and heaving at the gates to have broken
them up'.[8]

So large a crowd gathered at the gates of the steelyard that the
mayor of London could barely press through it on horseback, and
it was several hours before order was restored. By that time the
steelyard had been 'defensively arrayed with guns, crossbows and
other ordnance for the war' – it was probably a mercy that none
of the youths did manage to break in. The cause of all this trouble?
The youths claimed that the Easterlings had impoverished their
masters by monopolizing the trade with Flanders.

There was a protectionist impulse in English economic thought, which meant that the profits of immigrants working in England were seen as taking directly from the coffers of native workers. A Venetian visitor complained that there was a general 'antipathy to foreigners' as the English 'imagine that they never come into their lands but to make themselves masters of it'. His opinion is echoed on the English side by merchants of the Cely family, who bemoaned the lack of wool available to purchase, 'for the wool of Cotswold is bought by Lombards'. The parliament of Richard III in 1484 recited substantial grievances against immigrants working in England, complaining that they hoarded merchandise until prices were inflated, forcing the English to pay over the odds; that they sent the proceeds of their trade overseas or left the country completely after enriching themselves; that they encouraged other foreigners to stay with them in order to make nefarious secret bargains; that they and their families refused honest hard work 'such as carting and ploughing and other similar work' in favour of making 'cloth and other handicrafts and easy occupations'. They were even, parliament claimed, refusing to allow Englishmen to work *for* them, insisting that they would 'only take into their employment people born in their own countries'. The 'devious and crafty means of the foreigners' were blamed for all manner of economic woes. They had ruined towns, which 'daily fall into great poverty and decay', and increased criminality among the English, since 'the king's said subjects, for lack of occupation, fall into idleness, and be thieves, beggars, vagabonds, and people of vicious living'.[9]

Various acts were passed in the parliament of 1484 in an attempt to deny immigrants the economic benefits they were allegedly abusing, including one that made it illegal for any foreign artisan to take on alien apprentices or workers. It was also forbidden for a 'stranger' to host immigrants of a different nation from his own – which can have done little to prevent ghettoization of those immigrants already in the country. Immigrants to England, even those who had been raised in the country since infancy like the Venetian Sebastian Cabot, were legally considered 'aliens' or 'strangers'. Unless someone was born 'under the king's obedience', he was no true Englishman. Thus, although Brancino Marini had worked for years in Southampton, he was considered an alien, whereas his son Niccolò, who was born in Hampshire in 1509 but grew up in Genoa from the age of five, was legally English. In York, men like John Colyn and Alex Ambler vehemently contested aspersions that they were Scottish strangers, since to be 'noted and defamed' as such would deny them free status to trade in the city as natives.[10]

Enfranchisement was a crucial economic concern for anyone wishing to forge an urban career. Guilds defended their monopoly of trade from any outside competition, and particularly from foreign workers. Casual work undertaken by visitors to the country was actively discouraged. When Italian tailors among the Venetian galley crews docking in Southampton tried to expand their business into the town, local tailors petitioned the mayor in complaint. As a result, it was forbidden for the alien tailors to work unless they paid a fee to, and worked under the supervision of, the local artisans. This stricture can be found in the ordinances of most guilds by 1509. As the ordinances of the Wiresellers of London put it: 'No foreign-held house or shop... [may] work in the said occupation until he be presented by a freeman of the Craft to the Umpire and Wardens, and sworn to obey the rules.'[11]

Gaining the freedom of the city – which required an oath of allegiance from foreigners – was another important step for anyone wishing to progress in the local area. The Dutch printer Frederick Freez was entered into the Register of Freemen of York in 1497, and three years later both he and his wife were admitted as members of the Corpus Christi Guild, a prominent local religious fraternity. His home in Coney Street was leased to him in 1506 as a 'dutchman and alien enfranchised', making it clear that his free status mitigated his being a stranger.[12] In Southampton, where the immigrant population was relatively large, foreign workers who were enfranchised and contributed to the town's finances could even progress into public office. Benedetto Spinola became a burgess of Southampton, as did Antonio Cavallari of Lucca, who was naturalized as English in 1509. Christopher Ambrose – or Cristoforo Ambruogi to give him his Florentine name – arrived in Southampton as a clerk in 1462, received letters of denization a decade later, forged connections with merchants nationally and internationally, and was ultimately made mayor and sheriff. His was an exceptional case, but it demonstrates a positive extreme of the immigrant experience.

At the other end of the spectrum, aliens were discriminated against at every turn: they were not permitted to purchase English property, inherit English lands nor pass their own English lands and property on to their children. In order to gain the same rights as their neighbours, an immigrant needed a letter of denization from the crown, the price of which was an oath of allegiance and a fee to be delivered into the royal coffers. A denizen could then be treated as an English subject, able to acquire land and property, plead in English courts, and pay the same taxes and customs as his neighbours. While the right to taxation may not seem a benefit, it exempted denizens from the extra subsidies that had been imposed on 'aliens' with increasing severity throughout the fifteenth century. Every immigrant over the age of twelve was subject to these payments, and although there had been no demand for a subsidy since 1487 it was only a matter of time before Henry VIII would resurrect this lucrative revenue generator. In 1512, with war overseas brewing, parliament granted a new type of subsidy, with alien residents expected to pay double the sum due from their English neighbours. In 1514 parliament went further, imposing a poll tax on *all* aliens over the age of fifteen who would not otherwise have met the tax threshold. Spanish, Breton and German merchants had managed to gain exemption from the subsidy in Richard III's reign, but the Italians who were the focus of so much of the 1484 parliament's ire were subject to it.

In spite of the benefits, in 1509 and 1510 only eight people took up denization: three were Italian, one Spanish, one Scottish and three from central Europe. This low number was no doubt in part because England was enjoying a period of international peace. During periods of international conflict in Henry VIII's reign, taxation fell more heavily on foreigners, and requests for denization increased. Towards the end of Henry's reign, during the last round of Anglo-French wars, men who had been settled in England since the reign of Henry VII without seeking denization came in vast numbers to register themselves as loyal Englishmen. Had they failed to do so, they faced expulsion or forced labour in the king's galleys. Many of these future denizens were only children in 1509, arriving with their families to a life that would be English as much as foreign. Among their number were the Cabots of Venice, a family of navigators who settled in St Nicholas Street, Bristol. And they were to play their part in expanding the frontiers of the known world.

Thirty years earlier *mappae mundi* – flat, pictoral maps of the world – contained three continents: Europe, Asia and Africa. These three continents reflected the Holy Trinity of Christian understanding, and *mappae mundi* often went further in mirroring Catholic theories, inserting a Garden of Eden or images of Adam and Eve in one corner. Maps could be oriented towards any direction, but frequently had the east (the *'Oriens'*) at the top. While mythical beasts and imaginary islands dotted the maps, they were not wholly inaccurate records of the world's appearance. Europe was often clearly drawn, reflecting the greater cartographical knowledge of its limits, and the north of Africa was recognizably rotund. But the further south and east the cartographer got, the shakier his sketch became. The vast landmass of Asia dwindled away in the far east, its most distant border sometimes left dangling in space, with the enticing promise that it could be reached if only one could get across the intervening Atlantic Ocean. Only two years earlier, a map had been printed that once and for all drew a dividing limit between that Asian continent and the new lands in the Atlantic. It was the work of Martin Waldseemüller, among the earliest cartographers to draw the New Found Lands as a separate landmass from Asia. In honour of the recent explorer of the New Found Lands Amerigo Vespucci, Waldseemüller gave the southern territories a name that would later come to apply to the whole continent: America.

Whether the topography of these continents matched the images on the maps was not really the point, since these charts were not intended to act as navigational guides. No mariner worth his sea-salt would carry a map of the world on his voyage. To keep track of their routes, masters used 'rutters', personal notebooks containing information and advice that had been passed by word of mouth through generations of sailors. These noted distances between ports and capes, information on tidal currents, times of high water at various stages of the moon, soundings (depths), and the meaning of changes in the colour of the water. Sailing was intuitive as much as scientific.

Alongside *mappae mundi*, many humanists, princes and navigators also now possessed globes. The head of the Cabot family,

John, had presented his own globe to Henry VII in 1497, and his son Sebastian was already gaining the skills that would make him a renowned cartographer in the years to come. The shape of these painted orbs reflected an understanding of the earth that had been in existence for millennia – the idea that the world was round was no new theory. From the time of the Ancient Greeks writers had expressed belief in a spherical earth; the Northumbrian chronicler Bede had repeated it in the eighth century; and Roger Bacon and 'Sir John Mandeville' shared it in the thirteenth and fourteenth centuries.* Such globes put a vast ocean between Europe and the eastern tip of Asia – with no American landmass or Pacific Ocean in between – and there was a tantalizing possibility that if a ship could cross that ocean, it would open up a new route to the spices and silks of the East. Reports from the thirteenth-century Venetian traveller Marco Polo of a land called Cipango (Japan) to the east of China, and the discovery of various Atlantic islands that seemed to confirm the possibility of potential refuelling points for ships traversing the ocean, made this fantasy of a western route to Asia seem like a real, workable possibility. The Genoese navigator Christopher Columbus was one of those so convinced. Funded by Catherine of Aragon's parents, Ferdinand and Isabella of Spain, Columbus set forth in 1492 on an expedition to find the western passage. But Columbus made a serious miscalculation: he underestimated the circumference of the globe, vastly underselling the oceanic distances involved in reaching Asia. For this reason, his scheme for a westward route had been rejected in Portugal and initially also turned down in Spain. Ferdinand and Isabella ultimately supported Columbus more in hope than expectation, and only

---

* Mandeville was probably a fictitious character, but this name was given to the alleged narrator of a compilation of travel writing in the fourteenth century.

once they had successfully completed the *Reconquista* by captur-
ing Granada. If Columbus were successful, Spain could challenge
Portuguese maritime dominance. If he was not, he would in all
likelihood never return to trouble them again. The simple fact
is that had it not been for the extraordinary – and unforeseen –
discovery of a vast landmass in his path, Columbus's expedition
would have ended with him and his crew starving to death in the
middle of the ocean. As it was, he returned to his sponsors with
tales of gold-adorned natives and tropical climes ripe for plunder.
Further Spanish voyages of exploration were eagerly launched,
although no Iberian expedition set foot on the North American
continent proper until 1513. Columbus died in 1506, still convinced
that he had discovered Cathay in Asia.*

England did not stand idly by during this scrabble for transatlantic enrichment. Having missed out on, or passed up, a chance
to patronize Christopher Columbus, Henry VII was swift to take
up the cause of another navigator when the opportunity arose.
Fate handed him the Bristol-based navigator John Cabot. Cabot
was known in his native Venice as Zuan Caboto and his surname
was a pun on his trade: *'Cabotare'* is Italian for 'to sail along a coast'.
He believed that Columbus had sailed too far south and asserted
(correctly) that there was a greater landmass to the north, which
he insisted (incorrectly) was a route to Asia. Control of the Asian
market, with its lucrative access to spices and silks, was hotly
contested in the second half of the fifteenth century. When the
Muslim Ottoman Turks surged out of their Anatolian heartland
to seize control of the Eastern Mediterranean ports after the fall
of Constantinople in 1453, they also swallowed up a large portion

---

* Cathay was a word used by medieval travellers – such as Ibn Battuta and
Marco Polo – to refer to the northern part of China.

of the overland caravan route along which these Asian goods travelled. The Venetians were the only Christian traders who were able to get through, but the expense of transporting goods first by land and then in Venetian galleys meant that by the time they reached England, they were prohibitively expensive. The seafaring Portuguese had literally found a way round this problem, by opening up a tortuous but ultimately successful southern sea route around Africa and into the Indian Ocean. Bypassing the Arabs, Ottomans and Venetians, the Portuguese thus gained a rewarding foothold in Asia. If England could find the mythical western route to Asia, past the legendary Isles of Brasil, the Seven Cities and Cipango, then they would gain the upper hand in international trade for the first time. It was with this intention, bankrolled by Bristolian merchants and legitimized by a royal patent, that John Cabot set out up the Bristol Channel in 1496. When poor weather, low supplies and mutinous crew drove him back shortly thereafter, he was undeterred. He had a ship ready to leave the following spring: the fifty-ton caravel the *Matthew*.

When Cabot stepped aboard the *Matthew* in 1497 he would have found a small, three-masted vessel with smoke emerging through the hatches from the cook-box in the hold below. The deck was crowded with cages containing livestock to be eaten on the voyage and butts to catch rainwater. The ballast was made up of sand, shingle and cobbles, so that when Cabot ventured below to check on supplies, he had to crouch to keep his head from striking the oak beams above. There was not much room for a crew of eighteen. In balmy waters, the men could sleep on deck, rolled in blankets, but if the weather turned squally, they had to endure the fetid, close confines below deck. When storms rolled in or wind dropped from the sails, leaving the ship struggling to make headway across the vast open ocean, Cabot might have called on

St Nicholas for help. If things got particularly dire, he and his crew members could promise to go on pilgrimage upon their return: to Rome, to Santiago or to Canterbury. To try to keep the weather onside, it was recommended that they did not gamble, blaspheme, swear or do anything else 'provoking of God's most just wrath'.[13] Some days that would have been easier than others. The only way to properly clean out the ship was to 'rummage' it at the end of a voyage: throw out the ballast to be cleaned by the tide, scrape the filth from the hold, scrub it with vinegar and replace the ballast with clean stones. During the voyage, the ship was left to stink. In the ten weeks it took to journey to and from the New Found Land, unwashed, anxious and barefooted on a deck salty with evaporated sea-water, slick with rain or soiled by vomit and the waste of man and beast, tempers would inevitably fray. Perhaps this is why crews so frequently 'confounded' and rebelled against their masters. Cabot had suffered mutiny in 1496 and his voyage of 1497 ended in him accidentally sailing to Brittany rather than England, because his crew insisted he change his more northerly course. Columbus faced the same trouble, as did Cabot's fellow Bristolian explorers Robert Thorne and Hugh Elyot.

The food on board would not have helped matters much. Barrels of pickled pork, stockfish, 'salt horse' (beef packed in brine) and ship's biscuits named 'hardtack' were all that was on the menu – at least until the livestock on deck were butchered. Beer also made up a substantial proportion of a sailor's diet, which can hardly have lessened the likelihood of mutiny. These slim offerings were cooked in the space below the spar-deck, where a cook-box fire was maintained. Christopher Columbus's son Ferdinand wrote that on his father's fourth and final voyage across the Atlantic, men waited to eat until it was dark so that they would not see the maggots in their biscuit; there were so many it was not worth picking them out, and 'out of sight, out of mind' seems to have been the sailor's motto. Noticeably absent from this diet were fresh fruit and vegetables, and after months or years of this limited fare sailors were prone to scurvy. This disease could be debilitating: the sailor would feel weak, his legs would swell and he would lose strength until he could not stand. Spots would develop on his skin and his mouth would start to stink as his gums rotted away, the flesh bleeding and his teeth falling out. At its most serious, scurvy could kill.

Cabot was relatively fortunate that his journey to the New Found Land took only thirty-five days. At midsummer 1497 he and his men set foot on the coast of North America. They raised banners with the symbols of Henry VII and 'the Holy Father', before cautiously exploring the surrounding area, although they 'did not dare advance inland beyond the shooting distance of a crossbow'.[14] What they found was sufficient to convince them that the land was populated – farm animal manure, the ashes of a fire, a pierced, carved and painted stick – and Cabot posited that dye-producing brazilwood and silk might be native there too. The greatest bounty was in the sea, which Cabot claimed was so swarming with fish that no net was needed – they could just let baskets down into the water and draw them back up, overflowing. Cabot explored along the coast of New Found Land for about a month, before setting sail for home, eager to bring news of his discovery to England. On his return, he was feted by the English. Henry VII invited him for a royal audience, ambassadors wrote admiringly of his expert seafaring abilities and the 'English run after him like mad'.[15]

Cabot's success marked the beginning of a period of intense exploration, largely by Bristolian and Azorean sailors confident in seamanship. Yet despite Cabot's achievement in reaching North America, England gained little from these transatlantic voyages. Without the native supplies of salt needed to preserve such huge quantities of fish, it was impossible for England to capitalize on the bountiful supplies of cod in the waters off New Found Land. Instead, the Portuguese and French, with their richer native salt-mining industries, moved in to seize the initiative – the saltiest seadogs carrying the day. To make matters even more complicated for Henry VII and the mariners seeking his patronage, the Treaty of Tordesillas of 1494 had divided the 'newly discovered world' between Spain and Portugal. The latter were to have Brazil, the Azores and the African coast; while Spain gained control not only of Columbus's discovered islands but also of the northern territories where Cabot later landed. To ensure they could make the most of their gains, the pope also gave permission for Spain and Portugal to enslave the people of these lands. This left England in a difficult position. For Henry VII or his son to encourage further expeditions to North America could be seen as an act of aggression against Spain, endangering the carefully cultivated Anglo-Spanish alliance cemented by the marriages of Henry VIII's brother Arthur and later Henry himself to Catherine of Aragon. While Henry VII continued to sponsor transatlantic expeditions, he did so in the face of dwindling merchant interest and increasing diplomatic vulnerability.

In 1498, John Cabot's second voyage to the new lands ended in a mystery: we know his fleet of five ships sailed from Bristol and that one was forced back to Ireland, but whether they ever reached the New Found Land again or whether they safely returned to England is still hotly debated five hundred years later. Certainly, there is no sign of Cabot in the historical record after 1500. Cabot's son Sebastian may well have taken part in at least one of his father's voyages, and had enough of a reputation by 1508 to win support for his own transatlantic venture. According to his own report, Sebastian took 300 men in two vessels at his own expense, but it is highly unlikely that he could have funded so large an operation without the financial support of either Henry VII, his merchant associates, or both. He encountered little more than icebergs and fog: 'The sea [was] full of large masses of ice which drifted hither and thither, and the ships were in great danger of colliding with them.'[16] Cabot's fleet reached Labrador and explored along the eastern coast of North America but was eventually forced back to England when the crew rebelled.

When Sebastian arrived back in Bristol in 1509 it was to the news of the old king's death and the accession of a young prince with little interest in extending his cod supplies.* The New Found Land of the Cabots was not the gold-dusted, tropical paradise of Christopher Columbus and Amerigo Vespucci. And if Henry VIII was going to send a fleet anywhere, it was to France, to regain the lost glories of his ancestors in the early days of the Hundred Years War.

HENRY'S DESIRE FOR war with France had been evident from the very beginning of his reign. The Venetian ambassador Andrea Badoer had written of the newly crowned monarch that he was 'magnificent, liberal and a great enemy of the French'. Henry had even sworn 'immediately after his coronation to make war on the King of France'.[17] But since that bellicose promise had been made, the king had been thwarted at every turn. Unfortunately for Henry's ambitions, he had inherited a diplomatic situation that was completely unfavourable to the successful conducting of a war with France. Only months before his father's death, the major powers of Europe had created an alliance to combat the

---

* So minimal was the response to Sebastian's voyage, in fact, that we are not entirely certain he went on one.

increasing dominance on the Italian peninsula of the Venetian Republic. The League of Cambrai, as it was known, united the French king Louis XII with the very rulers from whom Henry would have hoped to elicit support from for his war: his father-in-law Ferdinand of Spain, the Holy Roman Emperor Maximilian,* and – worst of all for anyone hoping to wage war on a fellow Christian monarch – Pope Julius II. It was within the papacy's power to declare an Interdict on any state that offended the Roman Church – or indeed just angered the pope – which would forbid priests in the affected land from celebrating divine services. For countries under Interdict, there would be no burial in Christian ground, no marital rites and no mass. Venice had been placed under Interdict by Pope Julius when the League opened hostilities against it, and were Henry to launch a precipitate attack on a papal ally while it was fighting its war, England would almost certainly find itself sharing Venice's fate.

Besides which, England was not the mighty power it had been during the Hundred Years War. Its only foothold in France was the pale around Calais in the north. What Henry needed were powerful allies. Thus, before he could hope to declare war, he first needed to disentangle the great rulers of Europe from the allegiances that bound them to the League and persuade them that turning their swords on France was in their interests. Unfortunately for Henry, many of his fellow rulers stood rather in awe of France, 'the unrelenting disturbers of peace' as Ferdinand called them, with its vast army and pre-eminent position on the European diplomatic stage. The only ally England looked likely to have was Venice, which was far from conveniently located to launch an assault on France.

---

* The Holy Roman Empire under Maximilian was a conglomeration of German territories in central Europe.

Even Spain, usually all too eager to diminish French dominance by encouraging attacks against it, seemed cowed. King Ferdinand, ruling Aragon in his own right and Castile in place of his mad daughter Joanna, counselled patience. Henry's English envoy to Aragon repeated the king's advice: 'his majesty [was] not counselling or advising [Henry] as yet for to move any war unto any outward princes'. Henry must 'appear to be as good a friend of France as his father was... He can afterwards easily find a pretext for quarrelling with [the King of France].'[18] It seemed that all the great powers of early sixteenth-century Europe were in agreement: they were all too busy pursuing their own concerns in Italy to care about an Anglo-French campaign.

The royal council, led by Richard Fox, bishop of Winchester, was no more inclined to wage war than the kings and emperors of Europe. The historian Polydore Vergil reported how 'many came to the conclusion on several grounds that there was no need to take up arms'. Not least among their concerns was the likelihood that lukewarm allies would give up their quarrel with the French as soon as they had achieved their own aims, and then 'the whole burden of the war would fall on this country, which would thus be involved in war while its allies were enjoying peace'. It seemed wisest to wait and see how things fell out once the war in the Italian peninsula was resolved, one way or another. 'Another year something will be done,' Fox told the Venetian ambassador laconically. 'Our king is young; he is exerting himself with the King of Spain... Let this year glide by.'[19]

But Henry was not willing to let time 'glide by'. He wanted glory on the battlefield, and he wanted it now. 'His ambition', said Vergil, 'was not merely to equal but indeed to exceed the glorious deeds of his ancestors.' And this was not mere vanity, for Henry saw it as 'his duty to seek fame by military skill'.[20] In his eagerness to wage war, he was not always careful to mind his behaviour in public, despite Ferdinand's advice. In August 1509, the corpulent abbot of Fécamp came to Westminster as French ambassador, bearing a message from his master King Louis XII. Someone, apparently without Henry's permission, had written to Louis appealing for peace between England and France, and now that Louis had written to confirm that peace, Henry was outraged. In his anger he belittled King Louis, humiliated the French ambassador and showed a worrying lack of unity with his own royal councillors: 'King Henry took offence, and, turning towards his attendants, exclaimed, "Who wrote this letter? I ask peace of the King of France, who dare not look me in the face, still less make war on me!"'[21] When there was a display of arms in the palace tiltyard later that day, the abbot arrived at the viewing gallery to find that, in a further breach with protocol, no seat had been reserved for him. Henry seemed determined to rouse the French ambassador to anger.

But all of this baiting was for naught. By spring, Fox and the other peacemakers on the council had won their argument. Much to Henry's chagrin, on 23 March a treaty of peace was agreed between England and France. 'The King of England did not wish to conclude the treaty with France,' the Spanish ambassador Luis Caroz reported to King Ferdinand, but 'some of his most intimate councillors insisted so much on it that he at last gave way'. The councillors told Henry that 'no other choice had been left them than to conclude the treaty of peace with France, because the king being young and not having a son, it would have been dangerous to engage in a war'. To Henry it must have seemed an unwelcome return to the days of his father, when elder statesmen forced him to put dynastic concern before his own wishes. His father might have been dead almost a year, but his policies were still alive and well.

Safe peace was to be preferred to costly, dangerous war. Henry's glory and fame would have to wait a while longer.

But despite this very public frustration of his schemes, Henry was not deterred, resolving that 'as soon as he had concluded such [necessary] alliances and God had given him a son, he would be more at liberty to do what he wished'.[22] Even as the ink was drying on the Anglo-French treaty, he was already forming plans to break the alliance and make one more to his liking. If his councillors insisted that he must wait until he had a son, then so be it. That time seemed close at hand. For as Henry ungirdled his scimitar and his younger sister Princess Mary scrubbed off her body paint at the end of the Shrove festivities, Catherine's mind was on an even more important occasion. The Shrove feast was to be her last public engagement for some weeks. Catalina and her fellow women of the bedchamber had already begun preparations for the queen's removal from public life and entry into her 'confinement' for the final stages of her pregnancy. It was hoped that soon there would be a flesh-and-blood symbol of international unity – a Tudor heir with Spanish blood in its veins. And when it arrived, nothing would stop Henry from waging his longed-for war.

XI

LADY DAY 1510

Conception

IN THE WARM darkness of the bedchamber, the queen lay waiting. Around her all was muffled. The door and the windows – with their sweeping views of Greenwich Palace grounds – were sealed with arras. The fire was dutifully stoked, with sweet-smelling herbs burning, and the tapestries on the walls showed only serene and pleasant scenes. Her servants' footsteps fell on smothering carpets. Everything that could alarm or invigorate the confined queen had been removed. When Catalina the Moorish servant crept in to change her linens or when Lady Elizabeth Fitzwalter rearranged Queen Catherine's ermine-furred mantel, they did so in silence. Excited whispering had given way to mute anxiety. Weeks had passed since the queen entered her confinement, and still there was no sign of a baby. Just before leaving the world of men and politics Catherine had bled, but her physician and her ladies assured her all was well. Her belly still swelled. Four months had passed since the baby's quickening and all the outward signs suggested she was still with child. Hope overcame caution. The elaborate ritual of lying-in, of cloistering herself among her women, had been carried out. A cradle had been ordered for when the baby was publicly displayed to the royal court. The cradle was enormous: five feet long and three feet wide, with a headboard proudly emblazoned with the royal arms. The same silver font in which King Henry had been baptized eighteen years before had been called forth from Canterbury. A girdle from the shrine of Our Lady of Walsingham lay nearby, ready to be placed on the queen's swollen belly when her labour began. All the ritual symbols, all the necessary steps, were in place. But as the year turned and Lady Day arrived again on 25 March, no baby appeared.

There was still time, the queen's attendants said. Perhaps they had confused the date of conception and the prince would be born in April. Such mistakes in arithmetic were not unknown. Prayer was wise, but there was no reason to despair. More experienced ladies like Lady Elizabeth Fitzwalter, who had attended the last queen during her confinements and was herself a mother twice over, could offer Catherine reassurance and advice. For Catherine's anxieties about the birth, even before its worrying delay, were well founded; while childbirth was natural it was not without its dangers. Perhaps ten in a thousand pregnancies ended in the mother's death, and Lady Fitzwalter knew as well as Catherine that her last royal mistress had died nine days after childbirth.[1] Catherine's own sister Isabella had died after giving birth to a short-lived prince of Portugal a decade ago. Expectant mothers were encouraged to make confession before their labour because of the uncertainty of their survival.

Like most women preparing for childbirth, Catherine had secluded herself in a purely female sanctuary. From the ritual that marked her entrance into her lying-in chambers through to the moment when she re-emerged for her 'churching' a month after birth, Catherine would have only female attendants.* The ceremony

---

* 'Churching' was the ceremony by which a woman was welcomed back into the world outside the birthing chamber, and purified before she took mass.

might be more elaborate for the queen, but this female cloistering was an experience shared by most mothers-to-be, particularly if it was their first pregnancy. Women lower down the social scale, like the child bride Agnes Barbron or the mercer's wife Alice Middleton, were attended by female relatives and friends during their lying-in; women who could provide moral support and invaluable practical experience. The expectant mother would also be attended by midwives. These women of local standing and good character would ideally have slim ringless fingers and herbal expertise, ready to induce the birth if the child proved recalcitrant and even – in extremis – to baptize a dying child. Theirs was a semi-sacral role that inspired awe and respect, but also some suspicion among the otherwise exclusively male echelons of physicians and priests.

During these few weeks of isolation, Henry and other fathers-to-be had to amuse themselves. Labouring heads of households might be expected to take up a little of the domestic slack while their womenfolk were otherwise engaged. For Henry, lacking the necessity of such duties, there were other distractions. Chief among them was Lady Anne Hastings. High-cheekboned and dark-eyed, Anne was a Stafford by birth, the younger sibling of Lady Fitzwalter and the duke of Buckingham. Last December, the king had given her a gift of money to celebrate her second marriage, to the courtier Lord George Hastings. As a twice-married widow without the encumbrance of children, Anne had legitimate sexual experience without being matronly. With his wife removed from his attentions, Henry was free to pursue his interest in Anne, and he did so with impunity.

Henry had no permitted outlet otherwise for his sexual desires. The church forbade sex between husband and wife during her confinement and for the month or so until her 'churching', when she returned to the world of men. Royal and noble women usually employed wetnurses, so Henry would at least be spared the further restriction on marital sex while his wife was breastfeeding. These rules were just the tip of the iceberg when it came to religious proscription of sexual activity. Sex was also forbidden on Wednesdays, Fridays and Sundays; throughout Lent, Advent and Pentecost; before major holy days; when a woman was menstruating; three days before Communion; during daylight hours; naked; or in any position other than missionary. And it was not merely time, place and position that were circumscribed; any sexual act going against the 'natural order' – which is to say marital sex for the purpose of procreation – was forbidden. Sexual wrongdoing existed on a continuum, so that everything from the lesser sins of wet dreams and masturbation through the condemned practices of oral sex or transgressive sexual positions, right through to the 'abominable vices' of incest, bestiality and homosexual acts, were legally classed as 'sodomy'.* Marriage was the only moral outlet for sexual activity and even then the participants needed to ensure they were not enjoying it too much – St Jerome had written that in the eyes of God, taking too much pleasure in one's spouse was tantamount to adultery.

Manuals for priests – known as penitentials – had existed for centuries, advising how best to cater to the confessional needs of their parishioners, and specifically how much penance was required for different sins. Sexual sins took up a considerable amount of space in these manuals, sometimes in rather startling detail. The eleventh-century *Corrector and Physician of Burchard of Worms* had a sliding scale of penance, with laypeople receiving less punishment than the religious for sexual transgressions. If a cleric

---

* Sodomy was an official and broad legal category of sexual 'perversions' considered unnatural by the Catholic Church.

committed adultery and begat a child, he was to do seven years' penance, fasting on bread and water for at least three days every week. If he committed adultery but did not beget a child 'and the act does not come to the notice of men', only three years' penance was imposed, which rather suggests that the loss of face was considered worse than the crime itself. Incidentally, three years was the same period of penance given for a layman who fornicated either with himself, with a beast of burden, any quadruped, or 'anyone [who] intentionally cuts off any of his own members', although one might imagine that such a sin was punishment enough.[2]

The Shropshire prior John Mirk, who wrote two penitentials in the early fifteenth century, suggested that a confessor must be careful not to ask too many questions about his parishioner's sex life – had they fornicated in a specific way, for instance? – for fear of giving them ideas. Beyond sexual acts, sexual positions were also of concern to the authors of pentitentials. Couples were expected to have sex in the approved manner – the husband on top, the woman supine underneath – so as not to subvert the expected roles of the sexes. This was having sex 'like a man', and to do otherwise could be considered an attempt at contraception, which was forbidden by the church. In one absurd fourteenth-century tale from Boccaccio's *Decameron*, a gullible rustic believed himself to be pregnant because his wife insisted on being on top during sex.[3]

The danger that the church was trying to avert was that sex was enjoyed so much in its own right that people indulged in it for reasons other than procreation. The church did not have moral qualms about its daughters and sons having sex within marriage to produce children – God himself had told Adam and Eve to 'go forth and multiply'. But since the expulsion from Paradise, all humans had been tainted by Adam and Eve's sin and could no longer have sex without potentially arousing feelings of lust.

The thirteenth-century theologian Peter Lombard compared pre-expulsion sexual interaction as being like the movement of the hand to the mouth to feed oneself, and lamented the fact that sex now brought on 'itching of the flesh', which could lead to damnation.[4] Lust encouraged masturbation in the young, fornication among the unwed and adultery in the married. If not sated, it could even lead to homosexual acts or bestiality. Curiously, one of the few sexual transgressions that the church winked at was prostitution. This was still considered to be an evil, but it was often claimed that without the availability of prostitutes and the sexual outlet they offered, male lust might be sated on 'respectable' women, causing violence, rape and the breakdown of social order. The Church Father St Augustine of Hippo had argued that if a man was going to have sex for non-procreative reasons, it was better that he did so with a woman who was already corrupted, rather than infecting his wife with his immorality.

Religious notions of sexuality, written largely by celibate men, were inevitably going to be divorced from reality, but those people who hoped to gain some clarity on sexual matters from the medical world would only be disappointed. Contemporary theories about sex were frequently contradictory, and many must have felt that they were damned if they did and damned if they didn't. The highly influential medical writings of ancient Greeks like Hippocrates and Galen held that both sexes produced 'seed', which was the means by which new life was created. Like all constituent parts of the body, seed needed to be kept in balance – both too much and too little could cause illness. Exactly how people maintained this balance was where the trouble started. The ancient Greek philosopher Aristotle had warned that sex could drain the mind of strength, robbing both men and women of reason. In similar vein, John Fisher, bishop of Rochester and confessor to Henry's grandmother Margaret Beaufort, claimed that 'filthy lust of the flesh' robbed men of their potency: 'Physicians say that a man taketh more hurt by the effusion of a little seed than by shedding of ten times so much blood.'[5] However, if a man did *not* vent his seed, he might be driven to more and more depraved acts of sexual transgression, including incest, bestiality and rape. On the Continent, cities like Florence and Dijon licensed brothels for the specific purpose of enticing men away from homosexuality or the rape of 'respectable' women.

According to Galenic theory, serious illness awaited women who did not vent their seed through sexual intercourse or menstruation: they might fall victim to convulsions, fainting spells, breathing difficulty or even madness. All of these infirmities were caused by the poisonous reaction of festering seed within a woman's womb, which caused the uterus either to emit noxious fumes or even, according to some physicians, actually move around the body (the phenomenon of the so-called wandering womb). In either case, the uterus damaged internal organs and suffocated the woman. To drive away the fumes, or return the womb to its proper place in the abdomen, fumigation and bathing were generally prescribed. The theory was that sweet smells attracted the womb and unpleasant odours drove it away, so perfumes or sweetly scented oils might be applied to a woman's genitals to draw the uterus south, or foul-smelling items like feather or hair burned under her nose to prevent it moving any further north. Pessaries or herbal baths might also be used, with similar intentions. Some physicians, of course, rejected both the idea that the womb moved inside the body and that fumigating it was an effective treatment. Perhaps surprisingly, one recommended treatment for 'uterine suffocation' was sex. The 'moistening properties' of male semen would counteract the woman's noxious seed and bring her back to health. It was partly according to this logic that women were believed to be more sexually voracious than men, because their wombs were constantly desirous of the neutralizing effects of male seed. Indeed, in cases where women went too long without sex, it could have serious implications for their health, as the enormously popular corpus of medical texts known as the *Trotula* spelled out:*

> [When] women are not able to use men... the semen abounds in them a lot, which Nature wishes to draw out by means of the male. From this superabundant and corrupt semen, a certain cold fumiosity is released and it ascends to the organs.

If a woman was not able to have sex – for instance, if she was a nun – the *Trotula* prescribed medical pessaries, massage and exercise as potential alternatives.[6]

All this theory had one crucial outcome: it privileged male sexual desire. A build-up of seed in women was harmful only to themselves, but in men it threatened the entire social order. Women might be vilified as the more lascivious sex, never satisfied and constantly desiring male semen, but in practice it was men whose desires dictated sexual activity. Women's sexuality was condemned; men's was legitimized, morally and medically.

There was one potentially positive aspect to this 'two seed' theory: if both men and women emitted seed, then both were equally responsible for procreation, and female sexual pleasure must be as necessary a part of sex as male.† Unfortunately, there

---

* The *Troluta* texts are attributed to a female physician of eleventh- or twelfth-century Salerno, in northern Italy. They were widely translated into the vernacular in the fifteenth century.

† Aristotle, incidentally, disagreed with the notion that women produced seed, viewing them only as 'matter for the semen to work upon'.

was considerable confusion about what the female orgasm involved, with physicians who followed Galen and Hippocrates assuming that it was simply the release of seed. According to this logic, virtually any vaginal emission would do – it could be caused by genuine arousal or it might just as easily be menstrual blood or vaginal discharge. Hippocrates argued that female orgasm took place in the womb and was the result of rising heat caused by sexual friction, being stopped abruptly by male ejaculation: '[a] man's sperm arriving in the womb extinguishes both the heat and the pleasure of the woman'.[7] However, there was clearly not total ignorance of how female sexual pleasure worked, even within the medical profession. As far back as the eleventh century, the writings of the Syrian polymath Avicenna had gone into vivid detail when describing the signs of approaching female orgasm. He argued that men should look out for such signals so they could ensure conception. Avicenna's works were translated into Latin by the late twelfth century and editions of his *Canon Medicinae* proliferated in the fifteenth and early sixteenth centuries, so they would have been available to medical professionals and other interested parties at this time.

Notions of male orgasm were founded in similar Hippo-Galenic theories: the male erection was believed to be caused by blood combining with *pneuma*, the air and life spirit that sustained the vital organs and enabled movement. This 'elevating windiness' in the penis built until it was eventually expelled, which caused pleasure to the man. Problems with male potency could therefore be treated by eating 'windy' foods like peas and beans, whereas issues with female fertility were usually caused by an over-dry or slippery womb, and therefore required pessaries or fumigants. Although in cases of infertility blame was generally laid at the wife's door, certain medical treatises recognized that both parties could be the cause. The *Trotula* said that 'conception is impeded as much by the fault of the man as by the fault of the woman'. In order to work out where the issue lay, the work suggested taking two pots of wheat bran, one containing the urine of the man and one of the woman. When the pots were checked after nine or ten days, whoever's urine had developed a smell, with bran sunk to the bottom, was the party who required treatment.[8]

Procreation was so important to concepts of sex that a spouse's inability or unwillingness to pay their 'marital debt' of sex was cause for divorce. Even St Paul – hardly renowned for notions of sexual equality – placed the onus for this debt on both parties in a marriage:

Let the husband render to his wife what is her due, and likewise the wife to her husband. A wife has no authority over her body but her husband; likewise, the husband has no authority over his body but his wife. You must not refuse each other except perhaps by consent, for a time.[9]

Where a woman found her husband impotent, she could sue for divorce. Church courts appointed 'women of good opinion, worthy of faith, and expert in the works of marriage' to investigate the claim, with both husband and wife undergoing inspection. In extremis, a husband's impotence might be put to the test before witnesses, by a woman 'expert in the works of marriage', who was probably – given what was involved – a prostitute. In a fifteenth-century case in York, a man called John had his potency tested by a woman who 'exposed her naked breasts and, with her hands warmed at the said fire, she held and rubbed the penis and testicles of the said John. And she embraced and frequently kissed the same John', all to no avail. According to her expert testimony, 'the whole time aforesaid the said penis was scarcely three inches long... remaining without any increase or decrease'. John was reprimanded for tricking his wife into a marriage with no hope of children.[10] The prospect of impotence was a real concern to some men. In 1515, Robert Harding was hauled before the Court of Aldermen in London for bedding the prostitute Katherine Worsley. Robert claimed Katherine had blackmailed him into it, threatening that unless he could prove his virility to her she would tell the women of the parish that he was impotent. As Robert was courting a wealthy local widow at the time, such a report could have serious implications for his future economic security.

Attitudes towards the marital debt could have more disturbing consequences. Legitimate reasons for seeking, as St Paul put it, 'to refuse each other... by consent' were not always accepted, and while legal writers condemned the rape of a fiancée, they did not generally forbid rape of a wife. The surgeon William Hobbys angrily reproached his wife when she refused him access to her bed, even though she only did so on learning that Hobbys had been visiting prostitutes for years. The fifteenth-century mystic Margery Kempe asked her husband to end their marital relations because she feared that they 'had displeased God by their inordinate love and the great delectation they each had in using the other'. Margery's husband insisted that they continue to sleep together and 'he used her as he had done before, he would not spare' even though she only 'obeyed with great weeping and sorrowing' and now found sex to be 'very painful and horrible'. It took years for Margery to convince her husband to release her from her marital debt and live chastely together.[11]

The image conjured up by the church's strictures and medical writing is of circumspect sex undertaken by married couples, in the missionary position, beneath layers of nightgowns and bed-sheets. But the reality revealed by court records is quite different.

Where couples are accused of illicit sex they do so in back alleys or kitchens, on shop floors, against haystacks, under market stalls and even – least romantically of all – 'in a pit' beside St George's Field in London. One French couple 'had sex together in [her] home, in the vineyards outside their village, and even near the communal fountain', not to mention a literal roll in the hay. Illicit sex, unsurprisingly, was often associated with the young. For many of the youths sent to noble households or teenaged apprentices and servants working in cities, this would have been the first time they lived away from home, and perhaps the first time they were thrown into close quarters with members of the opposite sex. There was a great deal of temptation and not always much supervision. In the absence of their own private space, servants had sex in their master's bed while he was out of the house or resorted to locations of the sort mentioned above. For the nobly or gently born, children as young as seven might find themselves being brought up in something akin to a dormitory, surrounded by other children and adolescents, with almost no privacy. The example of one Tudor teenager called Catherine is probably representative of a number of youthful indiscretions of the era.[12]

Catherine was brought up in her grandmother's household with a large group of other young men and women. The sexes were supposed to be divided, and Catherine slept in the 'maidens' chamber' where the girls were two to a bed. However, Catherine was not much for rules, so she stole her grandmother's keys and invited the young men of the household in to join the 'maidens' in midnight feasting – and also in their beds. Catherine had already been involved with the household music tutor, but after exchanging gifts with a slightly older youth called Francis she began a sexual relationship with him. Francis later claimed that he 'knew her carnally many times both in his doublet and [hose between] the sheets and in naked bed, alleging three women [as witnesses]'.[13] Clearly what happened in the maidens' chamber did not always stay in the maidens' chamber, because Catherine's grandmother found out what was going on and responded in a manner characteristic of much Tudor guardianship: she beat Catherine, and for good measure also hit her usual bedfellow, Joan. The rest of the family treated the young people's dalliances as amusing, to be lightly admonished, which suggests that, at least for the upper classes, Catherine and her friends were not doing anything particularly unusual.*

However, youthful dalliances were not always winked at, and lower down the social scale, extramarital sex was seen as an issue of social order, which local people felt they had a duty to prevent. The relationship between Thomas Wulley and Margaret Isot seems to have concerned half their local community in London. Most immediately, it impacted on Thomas's parents, who clearly felt Margaret was not the woman for their son. When Mrs Wulley discovered her son in Margaret's bed, she hid his shoes so he would be forced to walk home wearing Margaret's footwear – an attempt to shame him into good behaviour that proved unsuccessful. Thomas's father took more official action, calling on the local constable to arrest the pair in the hopes that a night in the sheriff's prison would cool their ardour. The constable was all too happy to oblige, as for three months he had been receiving reports from concerned neighbours about Thomas and Margaret's liaisons. In fact, so keen

---

* The teenager in question was Catherine Howard, who went on to marry Henry VIII in 1540. She was raised in the home of her grandmother, the dowager duchess of Norfolk, in the 1530s. Thanks to investigations into her sexual history once she was queen of England, we know more about what she got up to in her youth than almost any other contemporary teenager. Her sexual intrigues would, eventually, be her undoing.

was the constable to take action that he enlisted the support of four dinner guests who happened to be in his house at the time to assist in catching the pair red-handed (did the quartet come along purely for their own amusement, or was this another attempt to shame the fornicating duo?). The constable, Thomas's father and the four tag-alongs found Margaret and Thomas in the basement of a neighbour's house at ten o'clock at night, struggling back into their clothes. Evidently they had been interrupted, as Thomas still had his gown around his head and his hose and shoes under his arm. The pair were brought back to the constable's house where, in front of yet more dinner guests, Thomas surprised everyone by announcing that he and Margaret were married. The constable was understandably sceptical, so the couple repeated their vows. Since they were now no longer fornicating but legitimately paying their marital debt, the couple were free to go.

While Thomas Wulley had been unable to escape his family's interference in his sex life, one might have imagined that the king of England could do as he pleased. In fact, as Henry was to learn, even a monarch had to answer to the collective moral judgement of his community. His attentions towards Lady Anne Hastings during the queen's confinement had not gone unnoticed. A noblewoman's honour, even more so than a man's, was a matter of concern to her entire family. So when Anne's sister, the queen's attendant Lady Elizabeth Fitzwalter, realized where the king's eyes had wandered, she called for an intervention. Not with Anne herself, but rather the family members most likely to be affected by her actions: Anne's husband Lord George Hastings, Elizabeth's husband Lord Fitzwalter and Elizabeth and Anne's brother, the duke of Buckingham. Despite his wife being the focus of the king's attentions, Lord Hastings was not the first to respond to the rumours. Perhaps he saw some personal benefit arising from royal interest in his wife, or he may just have been more cool-headed than the choleric Buckingham, who marched straight to his sister's chambers to give her a piece of his mind. By spectacular ill-fortune, his arrival at Anne's private apartments coincided with a visit from the king's closest servant and childhood friend William Compton. Was Compton simply acting as go-between for his royal master? The Spanish ambassador Luis Caroz thought this the most likely reason for Compton's involvement, but others at court claimed it was Compton himself who was paying suit to the enticing Lady Hastings. Whatever the truth, Compton's presence in Anne's private chambers baited the already angered duke, who launched into a ferocious tirade and 'severely reproached [Compton] in many and very hard words'.[14]

Compton was not going to put up with such treatment, and immediately reported the duke's behaviour to the king. Henry followed the duke's lead and flew into a rage. What right did Buckingham have to interfere in his affairs? Henry 'reprimanded the duke [so] angrily' that Buckingham immediately stormed from the court. For all Compton was groom of the stool, he was still the son of a nobody from Warwickshire and it must have rankled with the proud Buckingham to be allowed no latitude in his behaviour towards him, particularly as this was a question of his own family honour. What happened next would have done little to cool the duke's ire, and it certainly did not silence the rumours about Henry's interest in Lady Hastings. The king was so incensed by what he saw as needless meddling on Lady Fitzwalter's part that he ordered both her and her husband to be turned out of the palace. Perhaps Henry was so angry because the object of his affection had been stolen from him. Lord Hastings, finally taking action, had removed Anne from court and 'placed her in a convent sixty miles from here, that no one may see her'.

The Spanish ambassador reported all this with some amusement and attached no blame to the king for his behaviour – indeed, he was more concerned with how the queen reacted to news of her husband's liaison:

Almost all the court knew that the queen had been vexed with the king, and the king with her, and thus this storm went on between them... I thought that the queen should have acted [differently]... For in this I think I understand my part, being a married man, and having often treated with married people in similar matters.

Caroz suggests that extramarital affairs should not be of lasting concern, an attitude that finds some support from the future behaviour of Lord and Lady Hastings as well as William Compton. Indeed, Buckingham's occupation of the moral high ground in this case is rather ironic, given that he himself had an affair with the mistress of his children's nursery, Margaret Geddynge, and produced three illegitimate children he unashamedly proclaimed as his own. Like Queen Catherine, the duchess of Buckingham showed her displeasure when she learned of Buckingham's affair with Mistress Geddynge, forcing Buckingham to remove her from his household, 'for', as he explained to Lady Fitzwalter, 'we think the demeanour of my lady is such that Margaret Geddynge will be loth to be about her'.[15]

Even once removed from exile, Lady Anne Hastings was not completely forgotten by the king. In 1513, she was given the remarkably generous royal gift of a silver gilt cup, thirty ounces in weight. This seems to have been the last special sign of notice from Henry, but Compton maintained a lifelong connection with Lady Hastings, even after marrying the wealthy widow Werburga

Brereton in 1512. When he wrote his will in 1523, he left property and prayers to Anne as well as his wife, establishing chantries for 'daily service to pray for the souls of the king, the queen, my lady Anne Hastings, for the souls of my wife, my ancestors and all Christian souls'.[16] He also gave Anne a life interest in some of his estates and the right to will them as she chose at her own death. Yet according to an oath he took in 1527, Compton claimed not to have committed adultery with Anne – at least during his own marriage. If that was true it must have been a remarkable platonic friendship for Compton to single Anne out for so much attention in his will. Such a large endowment on a woman outside of a kinship group was very unusual, although not unique. In 1509 Sir Thomas Brandon, uncle of the king's jousting companion Charles Brandon, left real estate and prayers to the widowed Lady Jane Guildford in his will. Lady Jane and Sir Thomas were not related, yet Jane's servants cared for Brandon throughout his last illness and in her own will almost thirty years later she requested prayers for his soul, suggesting a close relationship akin to Anne and Compton's.

Despite the enduring connection between Compton and Anne, both enjoyed apparently contented lives with their spouses. Anne and Lord Hastings had eight children and in 1525 he wrote a letter brimming with affection for his wife: 'Mine own good Anne, with all my whole heart, I recommend me unto you as he that is most glad to hear that you be merry and in good health.'[17] Both Compton and Lord Hastings made their wives the executors of their wills, a position of trust that not all husbands afforded their widows, and Compton even requested burial with Werburga in his family church.

Evidently Catherine could not turn the other cheek so early in her marriage. She was far from alone in feeling betrayed by a spouse's infidelity. Philip Cruce of Smithfield was said to have died 'of sadness' after catching his wife in adultery.[18] It is suggestive of the low opinion taken of the unfaithful that communities tended to ostracize those suspected of marital infidelity. When Anastasia Reygate of London accused Thomas Hay of committing adultery, his wife and his local community actively avoided his company. Even colleagues could turn on you, as the royal surgeon and physician William Hobbys learned when his wife sued him for divorce in 1476. Despite being married for twenty years, Hobbys was accused of visiting prostitutes everywhere from Calais to Southwark. His colleagues in the medical profession flocked to condemn him, taking the stand as witnesses to insist that they had upbraided him for his sexual impropriety.

Adulterous partners were condemned by society, but what happened to the children that resulted from adultery? In some cases, parents seem to have made efforts to ensure a child's birth was not associated with them. Those wealthy enough probably followed the example of Henry VII's physician, Lewis of Caerleon, when he impregnated his servant Margaret: he twice sent her off to the country to give birth and then welcomed her back into his home afterwards to take up where they left off. However, some illegitimate children were brought within the family fold and apparently accepted by their relations. When Henry, Lord Grey, and Sir Ralph Bigod made their wills, they asked their wives to continue to raise their illegitimate sons – since both their spouses were also their executors, they had presumably discussed their request during life. The morally upright Margaret Paston left ten marks to her illegitimate grandchild in her will. Even those who had broken religious vows to produce offspring could feel themselves duty-bound to assist their children. Henry VIII's recently appointed royal almoner Thomas Wolsey had two illegitimate children by 'Mistress Lark'

of Suffolk: he ensured his son Thomas received a thorough education and an ecclesiastical position in his teens, while his daughter
Dorothy became a nun at Shaftesbury Abbey. Noble and gentle
households must have housed a number of illegitimate offspring
alongside the cousins, neighbours and patronized youths of allied
families. When he made his will in 1512, Henry VIII's jousting companion Edward Howard asked that of his 'two bastards' the king
should have 'the choice of them' to raise as he saw fit. 'The other I
bequeath to my special trusty friend Charles Brandon, praying him
to be good master unto him.'[19]

So much for the privileged and wealthy. For those further down
the social scale, an unwanted pregnancy could end in a mother
giving up her baby. Some single mothers in London might repair to
the hospital at St Bartholomew's, where illegitimate children could
be secretly taken in, allowing the mother to go on to live another
life. At Salisbury, Holy Trinity hospital had been founded to care
for orphans, widows and 'lying-in women' who had no other
support. A number of Holy Trinity's patients would have been
single women and illegitimate children. Unfortunately, such maternity and foundling hospitals were still rare in England, and many
women must have been driven to take more desperate measures.
Medical texts often contain references to the causes of miscarriage,
or advice on how to provoke menstruation – information which
could just as easily have been turned to the purpose of ridding
women of unwanted pregnancies. Excessive eating, bathing and
movement were well known and relatively uncomplicated ways to
bring on a miscarriage. Herbal mixtures – potentially lethal brews
of poisonous savin,* tansy, willow leaves, ivy, pennyroyal and white

---

* Savin was a form of poison derived from the young shoots of leaves of
the juniper plant.

poplar bark – might be poured into the bath, or introduced into pessaries, or even drunk. Such toxic concoctions were not without their accidental victims. When the chaplain of Alne in Yorkshire attempted to rid his servant of their unborn child, he accidentally killed the mother as well.

To avoid such unfortunate consequences, many couples tried to prevent conception in the first place. Like abortion, contraception was condemned by the church, although an exception could be made in those rare cases where a woman's life would be endangered by birth. One medical text warned that 'such things should not be known to young fools but only to save good and wise women from peril'. For poorer families, contraception was an economic necessity and demographic studies suggest that many limited the sizes of their own families. The obvious contraceptive method, which was the focus of much penitential hand-wringing, was *coitus interruptus*. Breastfeeding acted as a natural contraceptive, and was a method that even the church could not disapprove of. Less effective were the wearing of amulets or the use of douches to 'cool' the womb. One such mixture called for egg whites, opium poppy, goose fat, honey and 'the milk of a woman'. The *Trotula* recommends that a woman who wishes to prevent pregnancy should carry around the testicles of a castrated weasel in her bosom. One imagines that would at least successfully cool a lover's ardour. Remarkably, the future Pope John XXI had written a popular treatise including advice on birth control: he recommended a plaster of hemlock for the testicles before sex.[20]

Clearly, for all the church's rhetoric forbidding non-procreative sex, a lot of it was going on. Since homosexual activities were definitively not for reproduction, they were condemned strongly. According to one early medieval penitential, male homosexual acts were the moral equivalent of bestiality and demanded ten years of penance. Lesbianism, on the other hand, carried a considerably more lenient penance of three years.[21] Presumably because they generally lived among their own sex – or perhaps just because of a general assumption of sexual transgression in the church – homosexuality was particularly associated with the religious, but it was believed that any man or woman could succumb to it. To Tudors homosexuality, which fell under the umbrella of 'sodomy', was a question of morality rather than personal identity. It is difficult to discern the inner lives of gay men and women in this period for, since homosexual acts were proscribed, they were carried out in secret to avoid discovery and punishment. As a result, few examples survive. The French teenagers Laurence and Jehanne were unfortunate that their illicit lesbian liaison was discovered. Both were married when the affair began, in the local fields where they worked. Jehanne was the pursuer – at least according to Laurence's later testimony – and promised that 'if you will be my sweetheart, I will do you much good'. Theirs was an unequivocally sexual relationship, with Jehanne having sex with Laurence 'as a man does [with] a woman'. When Laurence tried to break off the affair after further encounters, Jehanne responded violently and Laurence ended up imprisoned for her actions. Their fate is not recorded.[22]

Sometimes it is questionable whether the people involved in a same-sex relationship saw it as homosexual. In the late fifteenth century a German woman called Katherina Hetzeldorfer had a number of female sexual partners, but she cross-dressed convincingly as a man and sexually 'behaved exactly like a man with women'. A more fluid approach to sexuality was demonstrated by the late fourteenth-century English prostitute John Rykener, also known as Eleanor. Rykener was a man, but he occasionally disguised himself as a woman and was happy to have sex as either, with partners of any sex: in one town, 'as a man, [he] had sex with a certain Joan... and also there two foreign Franciscans had sex with him as a woman'. Sometimes his clients were 'unsuspecting' and appear to have genuinely believed they were sleeping with a woman. He claimed he 'accommodated priests more readily than other people because they wished to give [him] more than others'.[23]

Rykener was paid for his services in money – anywhere between one and two shillings – and also in goods. He was not above blackmailing and stealing from his clients if necessary, poaching two gowns from a rector in Essex. Prostitution was a thriving trade, particularly in urban areas where large numbers of passing traders or merchants offered regular business. In some towns, prostitution was even officially sanctioned: Southampton had an official 'Bawd of the Stews'.* Sandwich city council regulated 'a house... for common women', where 'serving maids' were charged sixteen pence a week for room and board. Another area infamous for prostitution was Southwark on the south bank of the Thames. To assuage the complaints of local citizens, prostitutes were expected to leave the stewhouses of Southwark for most of the day and could not board there. Instead, they had to rent rooms for fourteen pence a week to ply their trade. What made Southwark unusual was its landlord: the bishop of Winchester. He personally owned two of the dozen brothels in Southwark and received revenues from all the others as arbiter of local justice.†

Indeed, prostitution was a thriving trade that lined the pockets of many local officials. In Hull, the town walls and foreland were

---

* 'Stews' were originally bathhouses, where prostitutes were renowned for plying their trade, but it had come to be the name for any area in which prostitution was rife.

† Hence the mid-sixteenth-century term 'Winchester goose' for a venereal disease caught in these episcopally owned bordellos.

rented out for the use of prostitutes, and Winchelsea was one among many towns that used fines for prostitution as a money-spinner, making provision for regular quarterly payments of fines for women who were out after curfew or carried on prostitution within the town walls. As a result, the same names appear repeatedly over the years, being fined for the same offences. Southampton fined any men who slept with prostitutes outside of the appointed stews and also occasionally raided the brothels to fine the foreigners they discovered there. In general civic officials were not driven by a desire to wipe out prostitution completely, but simply to ensure that it operated in a way that benefited them and did not cause too much public nuisance.

From the late fifteenth century, the 'stews' and brothels in Southampton's East Street and West Quay were home to woman in distinctive striped hoods plying their trade. 'Ray hoods' were demanded by many towns to ensure that prostitutes constantly displayed their sexual availability, preventing any 'respectable' women from accidentally being associated with the trade and thereby becoming victims of sexual harassment. Evidently not all prostitutes were happy to wear the hoods however, as in Great Yarmouth there are several cases of women caught out without them. To get around this, Hull town provided the hoods themselves.

Some made a lifelong career of brothelkeeping and prostitution, like Margaret Curtys of Oxford, who was eventually put on the pillory for her 'great notorious and long-continued whoredom'. Although the law sometimes demanded that brothels be kept only by men, a third to half of all documented brothelkeepers were women. Alice Dymmok of Great Yarmouth carried on her trade for at least a decade, and appears repeatedly in criminal records for crimes connected to prostitution, including illegally selling ale (taverns were notorious for acting as meeting places for prostitutes and their clients), keeping a 'suspicious house', assault and adultery. She was even banished as a suspected leper in 1500. Leprosy was one of a number of diseases that was associated with sex during this period, even though the disease is not in fact a sexually transmitted one, nor is it highly contagious. 'Lepers' could also be suffering from a range of different skin-damaging complaints. Any women found to have 'burning sickness' was banished from the stews of Southwark to prevent her passing it on to her clients. In a period when syphilis was spreading wildly throughout Europe, proximity to a venereal disease was a significant cause for alarm among neighbours and customers.[24]

Some women put on their ray hoods for brief periods to raise a little extra cash then left them behind, but there were also inevitably a number who had been entrapped into prostitution and found themselves incapable of escape. These were women like Ellen Butler, who came to London seeking work as a servant but was tricked by Thomas Bowde ('bawd' being another term for a pimp or brothel-owner) into following him to his house on the 'stews' side of the river. There, he attempted to force Ellen to work for him by claiming that she was now in his debt and he kept her a prisoner for as long as she refused to do so. Joan Rawlyns from Hertfordshire was similarly entrapped after moving to London, but her story had a happier outcome. She met a man called John Barton on the highway from Willesden and he promised to help her find 'good and honest service in this city'. Instead, he got her lost and abandoned her in a waterman's house in Southwark while he found a bawd to sell her to. Joan was able to escape only because she appealed to the waterman's wife, praying on bended knee that the woman help her escape, 'for Our Lady's sake'. Rawlyns took Barton to court and successfully had him imprisoned, publicly humiliated, put in the pillory and then banished – but she was an exceptionally fortunate woman to escape his snares. The records teem with references to abducted and vulnerable young women – some of them girls not yet in their teens – pimped out by master, mistress, strangers like Barton and Bowde or even their own parents. The servant Isabella Putnam, 'a pure virgin', was enticed to the house of Margaret and Richard Peryn where she was 'shut and sealed... against her will and crying out, in a room' before being sold to a merchant who raped her and passed her on to his friends. In Sandown, Kent, the ex-prostitute Joan Chapman acted as bawd for her own fifteen-year-old daughter, passing her around 'the Easterlings and Flemings in the Downs'.[25]

THAT JOAN CHAPMAN even had a daughter was contrary to contemporary medical opinion, which held that prostitutes rarely had children because their wombs were too slippery for seed to take root there. But whether legitimate, nobly born offspring or illegitimate child of a prostitute, every member of the community was expected to go through certain rituals, the first and perhaps most celebrated being their baptism. Catherine and Henry had already made arrangements for their child's christening. Red cloth would cover the steps to the magnificent silver font, dressed in finest Holland linen and a vast canopy was prepared to hang over the cradle of estate in the nursery where the baby would be displayed. But childhood was fragile, and while a child's baptism was an occasion for celebration and hope, it could also be an anxious time. Infant mortality is difficult to establish, but some estimates suggest that in the early sixteenth century a fifth of all newborns died as infants, and thirty per cent of children died before the age of ten.[26] Even in the royal family, where the most extensive medical attention was available, infant death was far from unknown. The king's mother had gone through eight childbirths, the last killing her – and only three royal children still lived. The king's sister, Queen Margaret of Scotland, had six children from her first marriage, of whom only one would live to see his third birthday. Catherine's father Ferdinand of Aragon had lost three children to stillbirth. For all that, children were still cared for and parents felt their loss keenly. The chronicler Edward Hall described Queen Catherine's grief at the death of a child later in life as extreme, but not unusual: she made 'much lamentation' like a 'natural woman'. The stillbirth of the only child of Thomas and Agnes Parkinson of Bedale filled them with such grief that they parted, to live celibate lives. Thomas became a hermit. One Tudor mother kept the baptismal cloths that had been wrapped around her babies when they went to the font for decades after their deaths – only two out of her eight children reached adulthood.[27]

Catherine had already lost one infant – the miscarried daughter of January. Now, as April gave way to May and still no child appeared, she finally realized what those around her had long suspected. There was no baby. Her belly stopped swelling, and sagged back to its original size. She bled again. By May, she had to face the truth. This confinement would yield no prince of Wales. For any woman it would be distressing, but for Queen Catherine it was also a mortifying political blunder. The primary function of a queen was to provide an heir, and on her first attempt she had failed to do so. The king's councillors muttered darkly about her fertility before her first wedding anniversary had even arrived. Was she capable of carrying a child to full term? Catherine screwed up her courage to break the news to Henry, whose disappointment must have been combined with anxiety about the future of the Tudor dynasty. The Venetian ambassador reported that 'the queen had had a miscarriage, to the great sorrow of every one', but in fact anger seemed to be the emotion predominantly on display at court. The Spanish ambassador Caroz wrote incensed to Ferdinand of Aragon, questioning how a royal physician could persist in the delusion that the queen was pregnant even after a miscarriage and menstruation. The English councillors railed against Catherine's ladies for misleading her.[28]

Did Catherine blame herself? Caroz suggested that the queen's excessive fasting and history of irregular menstruation lay at the root of her failure to conceive. The queen was certainly anxious enough about events to try to suppress the reality of her complicated obstetric history. She forbade her Spanish ambassadors and servants from writing to her father – although they did – and when she wrote to him to break the news herself, she deliberately conflated her miscarriage in January with her phantom pregnancy and confinement. She told him that she had given birth to a stillborn daughter 'some days before', claiming that this was why she '[had] not written sooner, or permitted any other person to send the news of her confinement'. Rather pathetically, she pleaded with 'him not to be angry with her, for it has been the will of God'. This was at the end of May, and Catherine was still hiding herself away from prying eyes. Her faithful confessor Fray Diego told Ferdinand that Catherine was 'very healthy, and the most beautiful creature in the world, with the greatest gaiety and contentment that ever was', but the reality could not have been more different. Caroz confessed that the English 'wish she should go out and be no longer withdrawn; it is, however, not yet known when she will go out'. It seems Catherine was in a deep depression.[29] Whatever his private misgivings, Henry publicly made no show of disappointment in his wife. Catherine wrote to her father that she 'thanks God and him that he has given her such a husband as the King of England'. Fray Diego was singing from the same song sheet: 'The king my lord adores her, and her highness him.'

But this sorry chapter of Henry and Catherine's marriage had a happy conclusion. Either Henry had not kept to the strictures of church law and abjured his wife's company during confinement, or he and Catherine had been sleeping together right up to the moment she took to her chambers, because when Catherine finally returned to public view, she was in the early stages of a real pregnancy. After her mortifying experience Catherine chose to deny it 'to all the world and to the king' but Fray Diego was told, and in short measure the royal physicians and the entire court were also sure of it. This time the child – a longed-for prince of Wales – would be carried to full term.[30]

XII

1510 AND BEYOND

Fortune's wheel

Suddenly thus Fortune can both smile and frown
Suddenly set up and suddenly cast down.[1]

FORTUNE'S WHEEL WAS a familiar image in 1509. It appeared in literature and Books of Hours: a crowned king sat atop a glorified spinning-wheel. To one side of him a figure climbed up the wheel to reach him, and on the other side a man slipped off to his doom. As far as someone rose in the world, it was seen as inevitable that they would eventually fall. This was a lesson that Empson and Dudley learned to their cost. As the new year rolled around once more, they both still languished in the Tower of London. It was months since they had been condemned to die as traitors. While Empson appears to have been rather more resigned to his fate, using his time in prison to put his affairs in order for his surviving family, Edmund Dudley had done everything in his power to convince King Henry that he was innocent of wrongdoing, and that he could be useful to the new regime. He had tried to meet with his old colleague on the royal council, Richard Fox, to offer a personal appeal, and when Fox refused he had drawn up a long list of those persons who had been wronged by the financial extractions of Henry VII, 'for the help and relief of [the late king's] soul'. Dudley addressed this list to Fox and his influential ally in the royal council, Sir Thomas Lovell, using it as an opportunity to protest his innocence: 'I never offended in treason or thing like to it to my knowledge,' he wrote, 'as my sinful soul be saved.' During the course of his imprisonment he had also written *The Tree of Commonwealth*, giving advice for good governance. Perhaps he hoped it would impress the young monarch. In *The Tree of Commonwealth*'s closing lines he again lamented his unfortunate position in the Tower, claiming to be 'in worldly vexation and troubled with the sorrowful and bitter remembrance of death'. When his words garnered no response, he even contemplated an escape attempt. All to no avail.[2]

Did the king delay Empson and Dudley's execution because he had had a change of heart? It was one thing to denounce and imprison royal ministers, but quite another to have them executed simply for serving their old master too diligently. Or was Henry VIII simply too distracted by his own entertainments to make the necessary last arrangements for execution? As his own councillors whispered to the Spanish ambassador Luis Caroz, 'the king... is young, and does not care to occupy himself with anything but the pleasures of his age. All other affairs he neglects.' And there were many pleasures to savour as spring gave way to summer. On 22 May a great green tree bearing a painted white shield was set up in Greenwich Park and two knights declared themselves ready to fight all challengers 'at the feat called the barriers'. Every Thursday and Monday from then until 20 June, twelve hours of the day would be given over to the tournament, 'to eschew idleness, the ground of all vice, and give honorable and healthy exercise'. According to Caroz, this was just the beginning of the court's entertainments:

The King of England amuses himself almost every day of the week with running the ring, and with jousts and tournaments on foot, in which one single person fights with an appointed adversary... The most interested in the combats is the king himself, who never omits being present at them.[3]

Caroz agreed with the circle of statesmen around the king that Henry did 'not like to occupy himself much with business'. When he attempted to bend the king's ear, he was told 'to arrange the details with [Henry's] councillors'. It seemed that 'all business affairs [were] in the hands of the Bishop of Durham and the Bishop of Winchester.' Thomas Ruthall, royal secretary and bishop of Durham, and Richard Fox, bishop of Winchester, were now pre-eminent on the royal council. So comfortably were they ensconced atop Fortune's wheel that the Venetian ambassador, Andrea Badoer, described Fox as *'alter rex'* – another king.[4] As Henry himself recognized, Fox was a shrewd operator. 'Here in England they think he is a fox,' the king told Caroz, 'and such is his name.'[5]

However, Fox was not without challengers. In recent months a rival had developed in the form of Thomas Howard, earl of Surrey. Dark-eyed and slim-featured, Surrey was the hero of military campaigns against Scotland and had acted with Fox as an executor of Henry VII's will. His family had never fully recovered the pre-eminent position they had occupied under Richard III, and which they had so spectacularly lost when the Tudors took the throne in 1485. For the offence of fighting for Richard rather than Henry VII at the Battle of Bosworth – a cause in which his father John was killed – Thomas Howard had been attainted as a traitor and imprisoned. Attainder 'tainted' the entire bloodline of those it was imposed upon, stripping Howard of all claims to family land and title and preventing him from transferring such claims to future generations. For three years, Howard was a prisoner of the Tower and it had taken over a decade of careful fostering of Henry VII's trust before he regained anything approaching his previous authority. By fighting for Henry against various pretenders and over the border, Howard had proven his worth and loyalty, and slowly but steadily, his family's inheritance was restored: first the earldom of Surrey, then increasingly large portions of their East Anglian estate. The duchy of Norfolk was still denied him, but Howard had hopes that in the fullness of time that too would be regained.

By the time of Henry VII's death, Fox and the revived earl of Surrey had both become trusted chief ministers, with positions on the royal council and in the Order of the Garter. Perhaps it was inevitable that they would compete for supremacy. The royally appointed historian Polydore Vergil believed that 'these men... had long nursed secret quarrels between themselves, which their rivalry made bigger and bigger every day'.[6] With the accession of a young prince eager for feats of arms, Surrey had seen an opportunity to increase his own family's influence. As a bishop, Fox was able to command armies in the king's name – indeed, he had done so when Henry VII invaded France in 1492 – but he was not permitted to engage in the chivalric endeavours of the tiltyard. In the tournament to celebrate Henry VIII's coronation, Surrey seized the opportunity to promote his family in the king's estimation. The team of six challengers who appeared before the king in green velvet embroidered with golden roses and pomegranates as 'enterprisers of the jousts' were virtually all from the Surrey clan: his heir Thomas, his younger sons Edward (who had worn the late king's armour at his funeral) and Edmund, and his son-in-law Thomas Knyvett. Even the gold-armoured Charles Brandon was closely connected to the family, thanks to his brotherly relationship with

Edward Howard, forged in the sweat and skill of the joust. In the early months of 1510, Surrey received the greatest signs of royal favour yet: he was awarded the position of earl marshal for life, and his son Thomas was made a Knight of the Garter. Two generations of the same family serving in the Order of the Garter was common enough for royalty, but not for the nobility. This association of the Howards with all that was best in chivalry went even further in the role of earl marshal, a hereditary right that had been lost in 1485. Now regranted it for the duration of his life, the earl marshalship entitled Surrey to oversee the College of Arms, which refereed tournaments and granted coats of arms to noble families. It also meant that he could act as the king's deputy and lead royal armies to war. As a visible sign of his importance, the earl marshal would bear a golden baton, instead of the usual white staff of office.

To counteract the increasing dominance of the Howard family, Fox had promoted a lowborn chaplain approaching middle age, but in whom he clearly saw the sparks of greatness: Thomas Wolsey. Wolsey, the portly son of a Suffolk butcher, had a knack for securing patronage from the great and the good. While completing his studies at Oxford University he had tutored the younger children of the marquess of Dorset at Bradgate Park in Leicestershire.* The marquess helped Wolsey to a living in Somerset, and when he passed away in 1501 Wolsey was able to make an even more influential connection, becoming chaplain to the then archbishop of Canterbury, Henry Deane. Chaplains were expected to undertake religious services in the private chapels of their benefactors and as such would be frequently in their company. It was therefore relatively easy for a man of Wolsey's keen intelligence – he had

---

* This marquess was the father – and, confusingly for future generations, the exact namesake – of Thomas Grey, marquess of Dorset, who had been imprisoned by Henry VII and was pardoned by Henry VIII in 1509.

become a Bachelor of the Arts at fifteen, which was 'a rare thing, seldom seen' – to build relationships swiftly with his influential patrons. On Deane's death Wolsey moved into the household of the deputy lieutenant of Calais, a trusted servant of the Tudor king called Sir Richard Nanfan. Wolsey seems to have taken up much of the strain of Nanfan's administration and 'through his instant labour and especial favour, [he] was promoted to the king's service and made his chaplain'.[7]

Once in the orbit of Henry VII, Wolsey made it his business to know whose star was in the ascendant, and where real power lay. As his biographer and gentleman usher George Cavendish later put it, Wolsey 'gave his attendance on those whom he thought to bear most rule in the council and to be most in favour with the king, which at the time were Dr Fox, bishop of Winchester... and also Sir Thomas Lovell'. Wolsey made a point of courting Fox and Lovell, who, having 'perceived this chaplain to have a very fine wit, and what wisdom was packed in his head', promoted his services to the king. The chaplain successfully undertook diplomatic missions to Scotland and the Holy Roman Empire, for which he was rewarded with the deanery of Lincoln Cathedral.

Once Henry VIII succeeded and the royal council gained greater influence, Wolsey rose even further owing to Fox's desire to keep the scales of power tipped in his favour. As early as August 1509 there were mutterings that Fox was not able to use 'his own craft and policy... to rule the king's grace and put out of favour the Earl of Surrey'.[8] Perceiving the increasing Howard dominance of Henry VIII's tiltyard and household, Fox 'took care' that Wolsey should be appointed royal almoner in November 1509, a position that gave him a seat on the royal council and closer access to the king. Now Fox had another ally to add to the ranks of Lovell and Ruthall, promoting their own authority with King Henry. By summer 1510, Wolsey, Fox and the royal council sat in judgement of the affairs of the highest nobleman in the land, considering the duke of Buckingham's claim to be hereditary constable of England. It was quite some ascent, for a butcher's boy to hold power over a duke's desires.

However, in recent months neither Surrey nor Fox had done much to further their causes, for both were hindering the king in his most fervently expressed desire: making war on France. In March, Henry had very reluctantly been forced to conclude an Anglo-French treaty of peace, as 'his most intimate councillors insisted so much on it'. The English commissioners of the treaty were listed as 'Richard [Fox], bishop of Winchester; Thomas [Ruthall], bishop of Durham; and Thomas [Howard], earl of Surrey'.[9] While peace with France was the wisest course of action as long as the country's future stability rested on one eighteen-year-old's continuing good health, Henry was consumed by his desire to win fame and glory on the battlefield. The council had intimated that when the king had an heir, the matter could be reconsidered, but with Catherine's recent procreative confusions, that day still seemed a long way off. Even in late May, she still had not told Henry that she believed herself to be pregnant again. Perhaps Surrey, Fox and Ruthall underestimated Henry's determination, or overestimated their own sway over the teenaged king. For Henry was not willing to let time 'glide by' as they wished, waiting for an heir while the prospect of a glorious war grew ever more distant.[10] He was resolved to make it happen. Even while he enjoyed the month of jousts that supposedly distracted him from anything but pleasure, Henry was encouraging Caroz to promote plans for an alternative alliance between England and Spain. If Henry and Caroz succeeded, they would have a treaty that would to all intents and purposes negate that made with France. Meanwhile, Henry kept up a barrage of ambassadorial missives, sending envoys to the courts of Emperor Maximilian and the pope, as well as staying in close contact with Ferdinand through Caroz. His intention was that the Anglo-Spanish alliance would be the first step towards a greater union against France, in which the papacy, the emperor, the doge of Venice and Prince Charles of Castile – the grandson of both Ferdinand and Maximilian, and currently betrothed to Henry's sister Mary – would all participate. For good measure, Ferdinand recommended that Henry also approach Maximilian's daughter Margaret of Austria, who ruled as regent for Charles in the Low Countries. To make matters even better, by May 1510 King Louis of France was playing right into Henry's hands. Ferdinand wrote in a panic to his regent in Naples that:

> The King of France is marching to Italy by way of Lyons, Grenoble, and Milan, with so powerful an army that there is no doubt he intends to conquer the whole of Venice, Siena, and in fact as much of the rest of Italy as he can, to depose the present Pope, and to set up another of his own making.[11]

Others besides Henry had become concerned about French military dominance. While Ferdinand still insisted that any Anglo-Spanish alliance remain secret and that, outwardly at least, they should maintain 'amity' with France, he now sanctioned Caroz to make an official agreement with Henry as quickly as possible. On 24 May, the treaty was concluded, including a clause that if either party was attacked by the king of France, the other would personally go to war in response. Henry now had an alliance that would not only support a possible future invasion of France, but required him to lead the English army himself.

Thus, by the summer of 1510, Henry VIII's long-desired scheme to wage war against France was finally on track. Revelling in his own success, he set off on progress through Surrey, Hampshire and the West Country to enjoy further martial sports. But even there, his subjects were determined to make their king remember his day job. As Henry travelled, he was repeatedly confronted by bands of commoners presenting him with 'grievous bills and complaints against Dudley and Empson'.[12] It had now been a year since the pair were condemned, and still they ate, drank and enjoyed the relative comfort of imprisonment in the Tower of London. The king's commissions and general pardons were all well and good, but the people wanted blood for what Empson and Dudley (and, although none of them said it out loud, Henry VII) had done. In the face of such vehement protest, the king finally sent orders to the earl of Oxford, constable of the Tower, to put the pair to death.

On 17 August 1510, Empson and Dudley were escorted out of the shadows of the middle gateway of the Tower of London to meet their fate. In one regard at least, the king was merciful. They were to escape the full traitor's death of hanging, drawing and quartering. Not for them the shameful, painful haul behind a horse to Tyburn. Their sentence was commuted to a public beheading. They walked to their execution on Tower Hill through crowds eager to see the despised royal councillors finally get what they deserved. They mounted the scaffold steps, a priest at their side, the executioner's block and axe already standing waiting. Then, as the *Great Chronicle of London* succinctly puts it, 'their heads were stricken off'. Since posterity does not record a botched job, we can only assume that their ends were mercifully swift. Empson was buried at Whitefriars in Fleet Street and Dudley at Blackfriars on Ludgate Hill. They were far from the first ministers to meet their ends as a result of public ire at their master's policies – and they would certainly not be the last.[13]

Sir Richard Empson's confiscated Thameside house, Le Parsonage, was transferred at royal command into the keeping of Thomas Wolsey. In later years this would seem a prophetic gift, for Wolsey would become a closer adviser, and a more powerful minister, than Empson or Dudley had ever been. Despite his beatific smile, Wolsey was the shrewdest of political animals. Under Henry VII, he had gained the patronage of Fox and Lovell. Now that Henry VIII had succeeded, rather than relying on his allies in the council, Wolsey sidestepped them all and moved straight for the king himself. For Wolsey saw what some of the royal council still could not: that for all his inexperience, Henry was determined to rule himself, not to be ruled by his elders. In other words, as the king had proven in his international endeavours, what Henry wanted, Henry would get – and Wolsey would do everything in his power to ease that process. When war with France finally broke out in 1512, Wolsey would be the man who organized logistics on the king's behalf. His astute mind was well suited to the task. The war itself would be a costly disaster, but Wolsey's endeavours would raise him immeasurably in the king's esteem. As George Cavendish noted, 'all [Wolsey's] endeavour was only to satisfy the king's mind, knowing right well that it was the… right course to bring him to high promotion'.[14] By making his royal master's life easier, Wolsey slowly but surely made himself indispensable to King Henry. In a matter of years, Wolsey would outfox even Fox himself, usurping the title of *alter rex* from his old patron.

Much would change in the course of the next four decades of Henry VIII's rule. The England of 1547, when Henry died, would have been almost unrecognizable to the English of 1509. Fortune's wheel would elevate many and grind still more beneath it. Some rose higher than any would have thought possible – within four years, the lowly Knight of the Spears Charles Brandon was not only created duke of Suffolk but also became the king's brother-in-law, having made a staggeringly bold illicit marriage to Henry's younger sister Mary.

The mediator between Mary, Brandon and the enraged king in 1515 was none other than Wolsey, yet again proving himself useful to the powerful and wealthy. His obscure origins might never be forgotten, but Wolsey would far outreach any of his contemporaries at court: lord chancellor, chief minister, archbishop of York, *alter rex*. All these positions were his, and yet all fell away before he died, dishonoured and condemned by his royal master, en route to the Tower of London in 1530.

But of course, as one man fell, another rose. The London lawyer Thomas More, brother-in-law of John Rastell, would be the man to replace Wolsey. By then he had married a wealthy mercer's widow by the name of Alice Middleton, who was never slow to give her opinion. More wore the chain of lord chancellor for long enough to witness the enormous changes of fortune that would have an impact far beyond the small world of Henry VIII's court. He would also be one of the many destroyed by them.

The loyal Catherine, who had waited so long and worked so hard to become queen of England, would end her days in a humiliating exile that grotesquely mirrored her years as widowed princess of Wales. Five more times she would suggest the hope of an heir for the throne, and five times she would disappoint: miscarriages, stillbirths, a short-lived Prince Henry, a daughter who stubbornly survived but was not male and so was not a secure enough peg on which to hang the dynasty's hopes. Little wonder that when Catherine died in 1536, borne to the lowest point of Fortune's wheel, legally separated from Henry and forcibly parted from her daughter Mary, her heart was said to have turned black with grief.

Five queens took their seat on Catherine's vacated throne in

Henry's increasingly desperate drive to produce a son: rising up the wheel and falling down, rising up, falling down. Before Henry's reign no queen of England had ever been executed. By the time he died in 1547, two had fallen to the executioner's blade.

Henry's fear for a safe succession took its toll on the highest nobility in the land. When he left to wage his French war in person in 1513, Henry first tied up a loose end in the form of the 'white rose' Edmund de la Pole, by having him beheaded on Tower Hill. Apparently the king had feared that those of his subjects 'eager for a revolution' might 'snatch Edmund forcibly from the Tower, give him his liberty' and declare him king in Henry's absence. The duke of Buckingham ultimately met the same fate in 1521, condemned for treason for saying 'he would make it his business to seize the crown if it should come about that Henry died without children'. Even Henry's cousin, Margaret Pole, by then in her sixties, would meet her end in the Tower of London, butchered by an incompetent executioner for the crime of having royal blood and offspring of suspect loyalty.[15]

But the impact of Henry's inability to beget a male heir would be felt far beyond the royal court. Henry's quest for a divorce from Catherine, in order to remarry and produce a legitimate heir elsewhere, would see England sundered from the rest of Europe and – most cataclysmically – from the Catholic Church. The entire ritual rhythm of the year would be shattered as a result, along with many of the visual signs of the church's power. Plate, relics and figures of saints would be ripped from parish churches, the religious dragged to execution still wearing their habits and robes, boy bishops outlawed, holy days cut back, the awesome shrine of St Thomas Becket at Canterbury dismantled. Ringing church bells for souls in purgatory became a suspect sign of idolatry, pilgrimage was questioned, monasteries torn down and their riches scattered.

Religious routes to education, to medical care, to alms were all ripped away.

The wheel kept on turning. Harvests failed, famine stalked the land, rebellion flared in the north, war with France twice sent soldiers streaming across the English Channel for no obvious reward, taxation increased, the coins in English pockets were barely made of silver any more. And in the end, the wheel still bearing men to their doom, Henry himself would die, bloated, paranoid, feared more than he was loved – and failing where his father had succeeded. His child's succession would be less assured than his own. In 1547 the treasury was empty and his heir, Edward, a big-eyed, pudgy-cheeked child resembling his Yorkist ancestors, was only nine years old.

BUT WE CAN turn back Fortune's wheel. Restore it to its position in early June 1510, when the anniversary of Catherine and Henry's joint coronation approaches.

The queen is pregnant, the king still only eighteen years old and gaining confidence in his own ability. The royal council has already started to lose its firm grip on him. When war with France arrives they will argue fiercely that he should stay at home, but Henry is determined to lead his troops in person. Increasingly, the bouts between king and council will be weighted in Henry's favour.

Across England, Henry's subjects are enjoying the early signs of summer. Thomasine Percyvale rides her horse, resplendent in its blue velvet saddle and harness, through the streets of London, where youths squeeze their way through the crowds to bring kindling and wood to the city bonfire and aldermen anxiously busy themselves, preparing their livery for the night-time procession. Perhaps Thomasine passes John Rastell toiling at his printing press off Fleet Street. Through a warped window she may even glimpse

Alice Middleton, in black mourning clothes that are just a touch too fine for her station, her finger following the letters of a Book of Hours as her daughters recite the words they read there.

Beyond the city walls, lepers beg for alms on the roads heading west, towards the rented Bristol apartments of the Cabot family, awaiting word of Sebastian's return from the New Found Land. They hope for news of untold riches, but will receive only reports of icebergs and codfish.

Far to the north in York, Thomas Drawswerd inspects the pageants for the city's Corpus Christi productions. He is considering running for election as a member of parliament – perhaps even as mayor – against the bellicose William Nelson. Meanwhile, the printer Frederick Freez and his wife Joanna prepare for their guild's celebratory procession from Holy Trinity Priory. Frederick will be among the guild members bearing torches as the procession sets off at dawn to the pealing of bells, his feet falling on streets strewn with rushes and flowers.

In Lincolnshire, the labourer Stephen Green welcomes his son William home from grammar school. William has high ambitions, to go to Cambridge and become a priest, but for now he will have to be content with helping his father at the long-saw in the local yard. Not far away John Barnes, the porter of Lincoln Cathedral, checks that the cathedral clock is running to time and that the various mechanical props are ready for their next dramatic production. Carefully stored for future use are gloves for the Virgin Mary, a star for the shepherds to follow and a dove to be released at Pentecost.

In the tiltyard at Greenwich, Henry VIII rides before his loving wife Catherine in gleaming armour, surrounded by comrades and councillors. Among their number are the Tudor-made men, Charles Brandon and Thomas Wolsey; veteran Lancastrian

loyalists Richard Fox and Sir Thomas Lovell; and once-excluded
Yorkists like the earl of Surrey and the marquess of Dorset. Henry
VIII is living up to his reputation as the 'rose both white and red',
the living embodiment of his father's Tudor rhetoric. England is
at peace with itself. On Fortune's wheel, the Tudor rose is in the
ascendant.

KEY CHARACTERS

The Royal Family

HENRY VII (1457–1509)

First king of the 'Tudor' dynasty, descended from the Lancastrian line on his mother Margaret BEAUFORT's side. He spent fourteen of the first twenty-eight years of his life in hiding from the Yorkist kings in Brittany and France. Controlling and inclined to avarice in his waning years, he left an enormous stockpile of wealth in the royal treasury for his son to inherit.

HENRY VIII (1491–1547)

Eldest surviving son of HENRY VII and Elizabeth of York. Energetic, keen to prove himself and more than a little vain, he was a 'renaissance man'. Alongside his enthusiasm for warfare and the joust he was also learned in music, religion and languages. He famously went on to have six wives and establish an English church divorced from the church in Rome.

CATHERINE OF ARAGON (1485–1536)

Princess of Spain (her parents were the co-rulers Isabella of Castile and Ferdinand of Aragon) and widow of HENRY VII's first-born son, Prince Arthur, who died in 1502. Cultivated, pious and intelligent but occasionally prone to melodrama, Catherine spent the years between 1502 and 1509 in England, uncertain of her eventual fate. Her marriage to HENRY VIII ended in annulment and their separation triggered England's eventual split from the Catholic Church.

MARGARET BEAUFORT (1443–1509)

Matriarch of the Tudor dynasty and mother of HENRY VII. A real survivor of the Wars of the Roses. Very pious, prudent and, like her son, inclined to micromanagement of her interests. A patron of printers and founder of two Cambridge colleges, she published her own translations of religious works.

QUEEN MARGARET OF SCOTLAND (1489–1541)

Eldest surviving child of HENRY VII. Married in 1503 to King James IV of Scotland. It was through her bloodline that the Scottish throne was eventually united with the English in 1603.

PRINCESS MARY (1496–1533)

Youngest surviving child of HENRY VII. Betrothed in 1509 to Prince Charles of Ghent, heir to half of Europe. Due to changes in international diplomacy she went on to marry instead King Louis of France in 1514 and then illicitly remarried Charles BRANDON in 1515.

The Court

CHARLES BRANDON (c.1484–1545)

Only surviving son of Sir William Brandon, killed at the Battle of Bosworth holding the standard for HENRY VII. Entered court service and became one of the King's Spears, jousting in royal tournaments. Remained one of HENRY VIII's closest friends until his death, despite illicitly marrying his sister PRINCESS MARY in 1515.

EDWARD STAFFORD, DUKE OF BUCKINGHAM (1478–1521)

One of the foremost noblemen in the country and cousin to HENRY VIII. Brought up in Margaret BEAUFORT's household and a fixture at the royal court throughout his life, the proud duke was prone to excess and elaborate expense in his dress. Feeling himself the rightful counsellor of kings, his high opinions got him arrested in 1521 and he was executed for treason.

WILLIAM COMPTON (c.1482–1528)

HENRY VIII's childhood attendant and lifelong friend. After Henry's accession he was given the trusted position of groom of the stool and became embroiled in the king's love life, forming a long-lasting relationship with the duke of BUCKINGHAM's sister Lady Anne Hastings. He died of the sweating sickness.

THOMAS GREY, MARQUESS OF DORSET (1477–1530)

Yorkist cousin of HENRY VIII and when 1509 dawned imprisoned in Calais Castle for suspected involvement in a Yorkist plot. A celebrated jouster in royal tournaments, he was restored to favour under the new king and remained a loyal presence at the Tudor court.

EDMUND DUDLEY (c.1462–1510)

One-time lawyer and Speaker of the House of Commons, by 1509 Dudley and his colleague richard EMPSON had become HENRY VII's leading councillors. He was particularly associated with the harsh financial controls imposed by the king on his subjects and after Henry's death was swiftly arrested. He was executed in 1510.

SIR RICHARD EMPSON (c.1450–1510)

Having trained as a lawyer, Empson was on the king's council by 1494 and thereafter became, with Edmund DUDLEY, one of the most influential royal councillors and 'the king's hatchet man'. He was executed with Dudley on Tower Hill in 1510.

RICHARD FOX, BISHOP OF WINCHESTER (1447/8–1528)

Associated with HENRY VII while he was still a traitor in exile, Fox acted as his secretary and on Henry's accession was made keeper of the privy seal. He was one of Henry's leading ministers, heading his council and becoming embroiled in his unpopular financial controls. In 1509 he was a natural adviser for HENRY VIII and continued to be highly influential in the early years of his reign, his name often linked to Thomas LOVELL and Thomas RUTHALL.

THOMAS LOVELL (c.1449–1524)

A long-term and loyal supporter of HENRY VII, he had been part of his rebel army before he was king. He was rewarded with the position of treasurer of the royal chamber and later of the king's household. Part of the 'inner ring' of power under Henry VII, he worked closely with other royal councillors such as Richard FOX and led armies in support of the king. As deputy lieutenant of the Tower of London he was frequently involved in the movement of royal prisoners.

HENRY ALGERNON PERCY, EARL OF NORTHUMBERLAND (1478–1527)

Denied the regional power his ancestors had held in the north, Northumberland was regularly involved in local power struggles with rival lords and occasionally with the crown. One of the richest peers in the country, he kept a magnificent household that rivalled that of his brother-in-law the duke of BUCKINGHAM.

DAME MARGARET POLE (1473–1541)

Cousin of Queen Elizabeth of York. Her father George, duke of Clarence, was executed in the Tower of London when she was a child and her brother Edward, earl of Warwick, suffered the same fate in 1499. By 1509, she was a widow with several children but her rightful title as countess of Salisbury was withheld. A member of Catherine of Aragon's household in 1509. Like her father and brother, she was eventually executed for treason inside the Tower of London.

THOMAS RUTHALL, BISHOP OF DURHAM (d.1523)

Royal secretary and privy councillor, Ruthall was an ally of Richard FOX and Sir Thomas LOVELL on the council.

EDMUND DE LA POLE, EARL OF SUFFOLK (c.1472–1513)

A Yorkist relative of HENRY VIII imprisoned in the Tower of London from 1506 for plotting invasion and asserting his own right to the throne. His brother Richard remained an active threat to the Tudors, and perhaps for this reason Edmund was executed in 1513.

THOMAS HOWARD, EARL OF SURREY (1443–1524)

After fighting in support of Richard III at the Battle of Bosworth, Howard lost his title and lands, and was imprisoned in the Tower of London. By 1509 he had been restored to HENRY VII's favour and proved a loyal servant of the dynasty, but an even more zealous promoter of his own family's interests. His sons were prominent in tournaments during HENRY VIII's early years as king.

The Country

THOMAS DRAWSWERD (c.1476–1528)

From a family of image-makers and carvers, Thomas Drawswerd was an alderman of York in 1509. Later he became mayor of York and a member of parliament.

FREDERICK FREEZ (?–?)

Dutch printer living in York with his brother and fellow printer Gerard Freez. Enfranchised, married and with his wife a member of the local Corpus Christi Guild.

ALICE MIDDLETON (c.1474–c.1551)

In 1509, wife of the London mercer John Middleton and mother to two daughters. After Middleton's death she remarried a family friend,

Thomas MORE, and thanks to his later fame we know that she was considered proud, confident and sometimes unnervingly straight-talking. She survived More's execution in 1535 and appears in the grand portrait of Thomas More's family painted by Hans Holbein, looking uncharacteristically docile.

JOHN MIDDLETON (d.1509)

Husband of Alice MIDDLETON, based in London. A wealthy mercer (cloth merchant) and Merchant of the Staple of Calais, dealing with import and export.

THOMAS MORE (1478–1535)

London lawyer and humanist scholar. In 1509 he had just become a freeman of the Mercers' Guild. Later entering royal service, he rose to the position of lord chancellor but was eventually executed by HENRY VIII for opposing his break from the Roman Catholic Church. His brother-in-law was the Coventry lawyer and printer John RASTELL.

CATALINA OF MOTRIL (?–?)

Moorish servant ('once the slave') of CATHERINE OF ARAGON. Probably taken into the Spanish royal household after the violent conquest of her native Granada, Catalina accompanied her mistress to England and served in her bedchamber for years. She later married a crossbow-maker called Oviedo, had children and returned to Granada. A search was made for her when HENRY VIII aunched divorce proceedings against Catherine, but if she was found her testimony does not survive.

THOMASINE PERCYVALE (d.1512)

Tailor in London. Born in Week St Mary, Cornwall, she moved to London as a servant and married three tailors of the city. In 1509 she was a widow continuing the business with her own apprentices, including Ralph Walker, and had founded a school in her home town.

JOHN RASTELL (*c.*1475–1536)

A native of Coventry and member of its Corpus Christi Guild. After legal training in London he served as the city coroner. In 1509 he has moved his family (he was married to Thomas MORE's sister) to London to establish a legal practice and set up as a printer. Later in life he converted to Protestantism and died in poverty in the Tower of London.

YORKISTS, LANCASTRIANS AND TUDORS

A Royal Family Tree

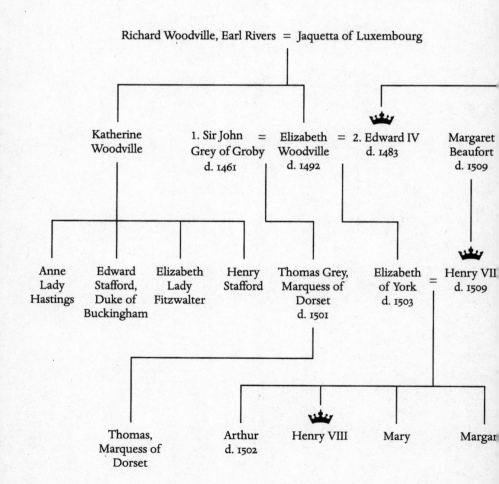

Richard Woodville, Earl Rivers = Jaquetta of Luxembourg

Katherine Woodville

1. Sir John Grey of Groby d. 1461 = Elizabeth Woodville d. 1492 = 2. Edward IV d. 1483

Margaret Beaufort d. 1509

Anne Lady Hastings

Edward Stafford, Duke of Buckingham

Elizabeth Lady Fitzwalter

Henry Stafford

Thomas Grey, Marquess of Dorset d. 1501

Elizabeth of York d. 1503 = Henry VII d. 1509

Thomas, Marquess of Dorset

Arthur d. 1502

Henry VIII

Mary

Margar

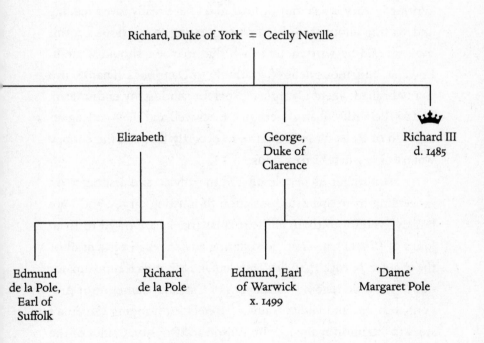

ACKNOWLEDGEMENTS

Writing history is a labour of love, and I have really loved reading and writing about 1509. For first suggesting that a book on this topic should be written, and then that maybe I should write it, I owe an enormous debt of gratitude to Dan Jones. Thanks also to my brilliant agent Georgina Capel for sharing my enthusiasm, and to Richard Milbank, Georgina Blackwell and their colleagues at Head of Zeus for steering me so expertly through the choppy waters of my first history book.

A vast number of people offered me advice and assistance on everything from Spanish translation to jousting targes, and I am hugely grateful to them all. Particular thanks are owed to Evan Jones of Bristol University for offering advice on an early draft of the chapter 'Shrove'; to Giles Tremlett and Miranda Kaufmann, for our conversations about the identity of Catalina, Catherine of Aragon's servant, and Nadia Nadif of *Untold* for bringing Catalina's story to attention again; to John Wilson and Royston Griffey of the Matthew Trust in Bristol; to Annie Gray and Richard Fitch, who lent their ineffable culinary wisdom to my chapter on Christmas; Dicky de Winter, who helped me make sense of Catholic mysteries; Briony Paxman for her assistance at the National Archives; Ray Nicklin and Derek Brown for their advice on printing founts; Gloria Sanders and Sarah Elkan for help with Spanish translation;

Hilary Wood with the Latin; Mark Griffin for sharing his knowledge of scoring in the joust; Megan Gooch for advice about Tudor coinage; Stephanie Selmayr and Laura Sheldon for their advice on masque costumes; Sally Pointer for sharing her thoughts on lampblack; Amy Rhodes and Alex Rowe, who have cheerfully chauffeured my pedestrian self to churches and forests across the country; and many extremely helpful Twitterstorians. Thanks also to the staff of the British Library, the London Library and National Archives, who were their customary helpful selves.

Pete Holdway deserves particular mention for not only lending me his translation skills in the question of the King of the Bean but also for reading my first draft. Other readers who cast their eyes over my manuscript and offered invaluable guidance include Anne Carroll, Claire Chate, Emma Hatton, Georgina Hildick-Smith, Charles Neville and Anne, Keith and Luke Johnson.

As always, I owe a debt of gratitude to my friends and colleagues at Past Pleasures Ltd, for their flexibility, enthusiasm and support while I was burying myself in papers at the British Library.

Most of all, I owe thanks to my family, especially my ever-generous Mum and Dad for providing me with the best writing retreat in the country, and putting up with me dragging them to historical sites all over Europe for the past twenty-plus years. The final word of thanks has to go to Joe, who has been proofreader, comma-corrector and chief cheerleader throughout. Without you I might never have written more than the date.

ENDNOTES

ABBREVIATIONS

Anglica Historia: Denys Hay (ed.), *The Anglica Historia of Polydore Vergil*: AD *1485–1537* (Camden Series, Volume 74, 1950)

Cal, SP, Spain: *Calendar of State Papers, Spain* (online edition)

Cal, SP, Ven: *Calendar of State Papers Relating To English Affairs in the Archives of Venice* (online edition)

Great Chronicle: A. H. Thomas and I. D. Thornley (eds), *The Great Chronicle of London* (Alan Sutton, 1983)

Hall's Chronicle: Edward Hall, *Hall's Chronicle: Containing the History of England, during the Reign of Henry IV and the Succeeding Monarchs, to the End of the Reign of Henry VIII in which are Particularly Described the Manners and Customs of those Periods* (London, 1809)

Household Ordinances: *A collection of ordinances and regulations for the government of the royal household, made in divers reigns: from King Edward III to King William and Queen Mary* (Society of Antiquaries of London, 1790)

NS: New Series

LP: *Letters and Papers, Foreign and Domestic, Henry VIII* (online edition)

Parliament Rolls: *Parliament Rolls of Medieval England* (online edition)

Sneyd: Charlotte Augusta Sneyd (trans.), *A relation, or rather a true account, of the island of England: with sundry particulars of the customs of these people, and of the royal revenues under King Henry the Seventh, about the year 1500* (Camden Society 37, 1847)

INTRODUCTION

1 John Skelton, 'Lawd and Praise made for our Sovereign Lord the King', in Philip Henderson (ed.), *The Complete Poems of John Skelton, Laureate* (J. M. Dent & Sons Ltd, 1948), p. 131.

I. LADY DAY 1509: TIME TO PAY YOUR DEBTS

1 Henry Littlehales (ed.), *The Medieval Records of a London City Church* (Early English Text Society, original series, No. 128; 1905), pp. xl, 275; LP, I, preface; Eamon Duffy, *Marking the Hours: English People and their Prayers, 1240–1570* (Yale University Press, 2006), p. 4; Deborah Youngs, 'Servants and Labourers on a Late Medieval Demesne: The Case of Newton, Cheshire, 1498–1520', The Agricultural History Review, Vol. 47, No. 2 (1999), pp. 145–60, 152–4.

2 *The Petition of Edmund Dudley*, written in 1509–10, provides a list of all those whom he could specifically remember using 'hardly' during his term of office. It runs to over eighty entries. C. J. Harrison, 'The Petition of Edmund Dudley', *English Historical Review*, Vol. 87, No. 342 (January 1972).

3 In May 1509 *The Great Chronicle of London* records four London citizens being condemned to the pillory as 'chieftains of all the questmongers' working in the city for Dudley and Empson. They included a bowyer, fuller, carpenter and fishmonger. *Great Chronicle*, p. 339.

4 Angelo Raine (ed.), *York Civic Records*, Vol. I (Yorkshire Archaeological Society Record Series, Vol. XCVIII, 1938), pp. 53, 127, 138.

5 *Anglica Historia*, p. 129.

6 Cal, SP, Spain, I, no. 360.

II. EASTER: TO EVERYTHING A TIME AND PLACE

1 Sneyd, pp. 23, 40.

2 C. F. C. Beeson, *English Church Clocks 1280–1850: History and Classification* (Antiquarian Horological Society, 1971), p. 23.

3 Christopher Dyer, *Making a Living in the Middle Ages: The People of Britain, 850–1520* (Penguin Books, 2003), p. 318.

4 D. M. Brodie (ed.), *The Tree of Commonwealth: A Treatise Written by Edmund Dudley* (Cambridge University Press, 1948), pp. 45–6.

5   *Oxford English Dictionary* (online edition), 'Body Politic'. Maria
    Hayward, *Rich Apparel: Clothing and the Law in Henry VIII's England*
    (Ashgate, 2009), p. 43.
6   Sneyd, p. 22.
7   Sneyd, p. 25. Desiderius Erasmus (Eleanor Merchant, trans.),
    A Handbook on Good Manners for Children (Preface, 2008), pp. 10–11,
    14, 65.
8   Edith Rickert and L. J. Naylor (trans.), *The Babees' Book: Medieval
    Manners for the Young* (In Parentheses Publications, Middle English
    Series, 2000), p. 22.
9   W. D. Robson-Scott, *German Travellers in England: 1400–1800* (Basil
    Blackwell, 1953), p. 9.
10 Robson-Scott, *German Travellers in England*, p. 8.
11 Sir Thomas Elyot, *The Book Named the Governor*, (S. E. Lehmberg,
    ed.) (J. M. Dent & Sons Ltd, 1962), p. 163; Maria Hayward, *Dress at the
    Court of King Henry VIII* (Maney, 2007), p. 42; Sneyd, p. 22; the Venetian
    ambassador in 1513, CSP, Venice, II, no. 219.
    In June 1529 the papal legate Cardinal Campeggio complained
    that 'we are still wearing our winter clothing, and use fires as if it
    were January. Never did I witness more inconstant weather.' LP, IV,
    no. 5636.
12 Hayward, *Rich Apparel*, p. 5.
13 John Guy, *A Daughter's Love: Thomas and Margaret More* (Fourth Estate,
    2008), p. 42.
14 John Chandler, *John Leland's Itinerary: Travels in Tudor England* (Alan
    Sutton, 1993), p. 514; C. H. Williams (ed.), *English Historical Documents,
    Volume V: 1485–1558* (Eyre & Spottiswoode, 1967), p. 189.
15 Hayward, *Rich Apparel*, p. 98.
16 In May 1538 John Husee advised his mistress Lady Lisle that her 'old
    damask gown… will never be good tawny, [but] it will take a good
    black' dye. Tawny was a light brown or orange colour, popular
    in Tudor England. Muriel St Clare Byrne (ed.), *The Lisle Letters:
    An Abridgement* (Secker & Warburg, 1983), p. 245.
17 St Clare Byrne, *The Lisle Letters*, p. 98.
18 A. G. Dickens (ed.), *Clifford Letters of the Sixteenth Century* (Surtees
    Society, Vol. CLXXII, 1962), p. 21.
19 Hayward, *Rich Apparel*, p. 134.

20 Erasmus, *A Handbook on Good Manners for Children*,
pp. 9, 33.

III. ST GEORGE'S DAY: AN EDUCATION

1 LP, I, no. 11.
2 Sylvia L. Thrupp, *The Merchant Class of Medieval London [1300–1500]*
(University of Chicago Press, 1948), pp. 155–8; Jo Ann Hoeppner
Moran, *The Growth of English Schooling 1340–1548: Learning, Literacy
and Laicization in Pre-Reformation York Diocese* (Princeton University
Press, 1985), pp. 20, 150; Julia Boffey, 'Women Authors and Women's
Literacy in Fourteenth- and Fifteenth-Century England', in Carol
M. Meale (ed.), *Women and Literature in Britain, 1150–1500* (Cambridge
University Press, 1993), p. 165; Adam Fox, *Oral and Literate Culture in
England, 1500–1700* (Oxford Studies in Social History, Oxford University
Press, 2002), pp. 13–19; M. T. Clanchy, 'Learning to Read in the Middle
Ages and the Role of Mothers' in Greg Brooks and A. K. Pugh (eds),
Studies in the History of Reading (Centre for the Teaching of Reading,
University of Reading School of Education, 1984), p. 33.
3 Sneyd, pp. 24–5.
4 Joan Kirby (ed.), *The Plumpton Letters and Papers* (Camden Society,
Fifth Series, 8; 1996), pp. 182–3.
5 Such provision for education was relatively unusual: only seven out of
390 Bedfordshire wills made between 1480 and 1519 make reference to
schools or learning. Maria Hayward, *Rich Apparel: Clothing and the Law
in Henry VIII's England* (Ashgate, 2009), p. 6; Carol M. Meale, '"…all
the bokes that I haue of latyn, englisch, and frensch": laywomen and
their books in late medieval England', in Carol Meale (ed.), *Women
and Literature in Britain, 1150–1500* (Cambridge University Press, 1993),
p. 131.
6 M. P. Davies, 'Dame Thomasine Percyvale "the maid of Week"
(d. 1512)', in C. M. Barron and A. F. Sutton (eds), *Medieval London
Widows, 1300–1500* (Bloomsbury, 1994), pp. 192–7.
7 William Caxton (M. Y. Offord, ed.), *The Book of the Knight of the Tower*
(Early English Text Society, Supplementary Series No. 2, 1971) p. 122.
8 PROB 11/17/239.

9   Arthur F. Leach, *Educational Charters and Documents, 598–1909* (Cambridge University Press, 1911), pp. 425, 431.

10 In 1502 Dame Jane Chamberleyn left money for the 'exhibition of pure [poor] childer apt to learn at schools'. Moran, *The Growth of English Schooling*, p. 164.

11 Wages varied, but 'common labourers' in Henry VIII's household were paid four pence a day, and the same was paid to a man 'for carrying of rubbish out of the churchyard' of St Mary at Hill, London, in 1512–13. Moran, *The Growth of English Schooling*, p. 49; Henry Littlehales (ed.), *The Medieval Records of a London City Church* (Early English Text Society, original series, No. 128; 1905), p. 281.

12 Nicholas Orme, *Medieval Schools: From Roman Britain to Renaissance England* (Yale University Press, 2006), p. 239.

13 Joan Simon, *Education and Society in Tudor England* (Cambridge University Press, 1979), pp. 28, 31–2.

14 Moran, *The Growth of English Schooling*, p. 176.

15 Orme, *Medieval Schools*, p. 279. For the following see Orme, pp. 278–87.

16 Dorothy Gardiner, *English Girlhood at School: A Study of Women's Education through Twelve Centuries* (Oxford University Press, 1929), pp. 134, 138; H. Arthur Doubleday and William Page (eds), *A History of the County of Hampshire*: Volume 2 (London, 1903), British History Online.

17 Cal, SP, Spain, I, No. 398.

18 David Starkey, *Henry: Virtuous Prince* (Harper Press, 2008), p. 355.

19 In a 1512 lawsuit at York 300 printed missals, primers, and other works in Latin and English were estimated to be worth approximately ten pounds. In 1520s Oxford twenty-four 'ABC's in paper sold for ten pence. Moran, *The Growth of English Schooling*, p. 35.

20 E. Gordon Duff, *The English Provincial Printers, Stationers and Bookbinders to 1557* (Cambridge University Press, 1912), pp. 124–5.

21 Angelo Raine (ed.), *York Civic Records*, Vol. I (Yorkshire Archaeological Society Record Series, Vol. XCVIII, 1938), p. 20.

22 Wynkyn de Worde is named in Gerard's will of 1510 as being owed forty shillings. Robert Davies, *A Memoir of the York Press, with Notices of Authors, Printers and Stationers, in the Sixteenth, Seventeenth and Eighteenth Centuries* (Nichols and Sons, 1868), p. 9.

23 Shannon McSheffrey, *Gender and Heresy, Women and Men in Lollard Communities, 1420–1530* (University of Pennsylvania Press, 1995), p. 200.
24 Rob Lutton, 'Connections between Lollards, Townsfolk and Gentry in Tenterden in the Late Fifteenth and Early Sixteenth Centuries', in Margaret Aston and Colin Richmond (eds), *Lollardy and the Gentry in the Later Middle Ages* (Sutton Publishing, 1997), pp. 200–2.
25 Shannon McSheffrey and Norman Tanner (ed. and trans.), *Lollards of Coventry, 1486–1522* (Cambridge University Press, 2003), pp. 41, 218; Susan Brigden, *London and the Reformation* (Clarendon Press, 1989), p. 89.
26 Brigden, *London and the Reformation*, p. 201.
27 McSheffrey and Tanner, *Lollards of Coventry*, p. 153; McSheffrey, *Gender and Heresy*, p. 99.
28 LP, I, no. 933.
29 W. H. St J. Hope (ed.), 'The last testament and inventory of John de Veer, thirteenth earl of Oxford', *Archaeologia*, Vol. 66 (1915), pp. 276–7.

IV. MAY: 'YOUTH MUST HAVE SOME DALLIANCE'

1 Starkey, *Virtuous Prince*, p. 278.
2 LP, I, no. 84; Starkey, *Virtuous Prince*, p. 280; Thomas Penn, *Winter King: The Dawn of Tudor England* (Allen Lane, 2011), p. 357.
3 Sir Thomas Elyot, *The Book Named the Governor* (S. E. Lehmberg, ed.), (J. M. Dent & Sons Ltd, 1962), pp. 91–2.
4 19 Henry VII c. 14, c. 24, *Parliament Rolls*.
5 Among these distractions: Cornish hurling, quoits, maypole-dancing, bell-ringing and 'Christmas games'. Steven Gunn, 'Archery Practice in Early Tudor England', *Past and Present*, No. 209 (November 2010), p. 65.
6 Giles Tremlett, *Catherine of Aragon: Henry's Spanish Queen. A Biography* (Faber & Faber, 2010), p. 153.
7 Starkey, *Virtuous Prince*, pp. 266–8; Penn, *Winter King*, pp. 349–50.
8 Out of a sample of fifty-three marriages made by aristocratic brides between 1450 and 1550, forty-one were aged sixteen or under, and twenty-nine were between the ages of thirteen and sixteen. Barbara J. Harris, *English Aristocratic Women, 1450–1550: Marriage and Family, Property and Careers* (Oxford University Press, 2002), p. 56.

9   R. Stewart-Brown, *Lancashire and Cheshire Cases in the Court of Star Chamber*, Part I (The Record Society, 1916), pp. 28, 31.

10   Sylvia Thrupp, *Merchant Class of Medieval London* [1300–1500] (University of Chicago Press, 1948), p. 193.

11   Harris, *Aristocratic Women*, p. 46.

12   All quotations about the Brews/Paston marriage are from Norman Davis, *The Paston Letters: A Selection in Modern Spelling* (1477) (Oxford University Press, 1983), pp. 233–41.

13   Harris, *Aristocratic Women*, p. 55.

14   Patricia Thomson, *Sir Thomas Wyatt and his Background* (Stanford University Press, 1964), pp. 11–12.

15   Barbara J. Harris, 'Power, Profit and Passion: Mary Tudor, Charles Brandon and the Arranged Marriage in Early Tudor England', *Feminist Studies*, Vol. 15, No. 1: Women, Family and Work (Spring 1989), p. 62.

16   Shannon McSheffrey, *Marriage, Sex, and Civic Culture in Late Medieval London* (University of Pennsylvania Press, 2006), pp. 25, 70.

17   *Paston Letters*, pp. 181–3.

18   For the following see P. J. P. Goldberg, *Women, Work and Life Cycle in a Medieval Economy: Women in York and Yorkshire c.1300–1520* (Clarendon Press, 1992), p. 247.

19   Details survive of the words exchanged at Henry VIII's last wedding, to Katherine Parr, in 1543. Her vow was this:

     'I, Katharine, take thee Henry to my wedded husband, to have and to hold from this day forward, for better for worse, for richer for poorer, in sickness and in health, to be bonayr and buxome in bed and at board, till death us depart, and thereto I plight unto thee my troth.'

     Henry said the same, but without a promise to be 'bonayr and buxome'. LP, XVIII (i), no. 873.

20   *Paston Letters*, pp. 60, 178.

21   Patricia Thomson, 'Courtly Love' in *Sir Thomas Wyatt and his Background* (Stanford University Press, 1964), p. 10.

22   (Knyvett: 1515; Oxford, 1520) Harris, *English Aristocratic Women*, p. 78; (Frechwell, 1512) David G. Edwards, *Derbyshire Wills Proved in the Prerogative Court of Canterbury, 1393–1574* (Derbyshire Record Society, Volume XXVI, 1998), p. 42.

23 Harris, *Aristocratic Women*, p. 79.

24 LP, XII (ii), no. 976.

25 McSheffrey, *Marriage, Sex, and Civic Culture*, pp. 139–41, 153.

26 Margaret Kebell's story is reported in detail in Eric Ives, "'Agaynst Taking Awaye of Women": the Inception and Operation of the Abduction Act of 1487' in E. E. Ives, J. R. Knecht, J. J. Scarisbrick, *Wealth and Power in Tudor England: Essays Presented to S. T. Bindoff* (Athlone Press, 1978).

27 Cal, SP, Spain, II, No. 17.

V. MIDSUMMER: 'ALL ENGLAND IS IN ECSTASIES'

1 Elizabeth Worship first appears in the accounts as royal silkwoman in 1510–11, but was probably the same Elizabeth Langton who had worked for Queen Elizabeth of York in 1502–6. Maria Hayward, *Dress at the Court of King Henry VIII* (Maney, 2007), p. 327.

2 *Hall's Chronicle*, p. 507.

3 Angelo Raine (ed.), *York Civic Records*, Volume I (Yorkshire Archaeological Society Record Series, Vol. XCVIII, 1938), p. 5; Stanley J. Kahrl, *Records of Plays and Players in Lincolnshire, 1300–1585* (Collections, Volume VIII; the Malone Society, 1974), p. 43.

4 The Noah play in Hull was performed annually on Plough Monday in January, and was more of a procession than a pageant, as it lacked a dramatic cycle of events. E. K. Chambers, *The Mediaeval Stage*, Volume II (Oxford University Press, 1925), pp. 119–20, 139.

5 *Hall's Chronicle*, p. 511.

6 Sydney Anglo, *Spectacle, Pageantry and Early Tudor Policy* (Clarendon Press, 1969), p. 100; Gordon Kipling (ed.), *The Receyt of the Ladie Kateryne* (Early English Text Society, No. 296, 1990), p. 54.

7 *Great Chronicle*, p. 343.

8 Arthur F. Leach, 'Some English plays and players, 1220–1548', in W. P. Ker, A. S. Napier and W. W. Skeat (eds), *An English Miscellany: Presented to Dr Furnivall in Honour of his Seventy-Fifth Birthday* (Clarendon Press, 1901), p. 217.

9 Joshua Toulmin Smith and Lucy Toulmin Smith (eds), *English Gilds. The original ordinances of more than one hundred early English Gilds: together with the olde usages of the cite of Wynchestre; the ordinances of*

Worcester... From original MSS. of the fourteenth and fifteenth centuries (Early English Text Society, original series, No. 40, 1860; repr. Oxford University Press, 1963), pp. 50, 193, 169–70.

10 C1/252/13; C1/304/33; C1/369/3.

11 Ruth Mazo Karras, *Common Women: Prostitution and Sexuality in Medieval England* (Oxford University Press, 1996), p. 60; Percy D. Mundy, *Abstracts of Star Chamber Proceedings relating to the County of Sussex: Henry VII to Philip and Mary* (Sussex Record Society, Volume XVI, 1913), p. 5.

12 John Skelton, 'Lawd and Praise made for our Sovereign Lord the King', in Henderson (ed.), *The Complete Poems of John Skelton*, p. 131.

13 *The Complete Works of St. Thomas More, Volume 3, Part II: Latin Poems* (Clarence H. Miller, Leicester Bradner, Charles A. Lynch and Revilo P. Oliver, eds) (Yale University Press, 1984), pp. 100–5.

14 LP, I, No. 51.

15 *Complete Works of St. Thomas More, Volume 3, Part II*, pp. 114–15.

16 Starkey, *Virtuous Prince*, p. 296.

17 'Encerrado como a dama.' Gutierre Gomez de Fuensalida, *Correspondencia de Gutierre Gomez de Fuensalida, embajador en Alemania, Flandes é Inglaterra* (Madrid, 1907), p. 449.

VI. LAMMAS: GOOD AND BAD LORDSHIP

1 D. M. Brodie, 'Edmund Dudley: Minister of Henry VII: (The Alexander Prize Essay)', *Transactions of the Royal Historical Society, Fourth Series*, Vol. 15 (1932), pp. 150–1.

2 The Black Book of Edward IV instructed the Clerk of the Market to make these preparations. Quoted in Simon Thurley, *The Royal Palaces of Tudor England: Architecture and Court Life, 1460–1547* (Yale University Press, 1993), p. 72.

3 Eamonn Duffy, 'Religious Belief' in Rosemary Horrox and W. Mark Ormrod (eds), *A Social History of England 1200–1500* (Cambridge University Press, 2006), p. 319.

4 Sneyd, pp. 30–1.

5 W. D. Robson-Scott, *German Travellers in England: 1400–1800* (Basil Blackwell, 1953), p. 7. For unicorn horns see Sneyd, p. 29.

6 LP, III, No. 950.

7 W. G. Hoskins, 'The Leicestershire Farmer in the Sixteenth Century', in *Essays in Leicestershire History* (Liverpool University Press, 1950), p. 131; Christopher Dyer, *Making a Living in the Middle Ages: The People of Britain, 850–1520* (Penguin, 2003), p. 354. See also S. A. Peyton, 'The Village Population in the Tudor Lay Subsidy Rolls', *The English Historical Review*, Vol. 30, No. 118 (April 1915), p. 247.

8 Barbara Jean Harris, *Edward Stafford, Third Duke of Buckingham, 1478–1521* (Stanford University Press, 1986), pp. 113–14.

9 Newton inherited his estate in 1498. Deborah Youngs, 'Servants and Labourers on a Late Medieval Demesne: The Case of Newton, Cheshire, 1498–1520', *The Agricultural History Review*, Vol. 47, No. 2 (1999), p. 147.

10 George Owen of Henllys, *The Description of Pembrokeshire* (Dilwyn Miles, ed.) (Gomer Press, 1994), p. 73.

11 (Willesthorpe, 1514; Doddershall, 1495) C. G. Bayne (ed.), *Select Cases in the Council of Henry VII* (Selden Society, Vol. 75, 1958), pp. cxli–cxlii; Dyer, *Making a Living*, p. 344.

12 G. Bradford (ed.), *Proceedings in the Court of Star Chamber in the Reigns of Henry VII and Henry VIII* (Somerset Record Society, Volume 27, 1911), p. 80.

13 Sir John Seymour was made a knight of the body to Henry VIII on 1 August 1509 and in his new role is likely to have accompanied the king on progress. Lady Barnardiston's case was brought in 1508; the bishop of Salisbury's in 1514. LP, I, No. 3409; Bayne, *Select Cases in the Council of Henry VII* (Selden Society, Volume 75, 1958), p. cxxvii.

14 Bradford, *Proceedings in the Court of Star Chamber*, pp. 72–81.

15 The case rolled on for twenty years. Under subsequent chancellors, Mulsho and the inhabitants of Thingden (Finedon) repeatedly had their previous decisions overturned. For details of the dispute see I. S. Leadam, *Select Cases before the King's Council in the Star Chamber, commonly called The Court of Star Chamber, Vol. II: 1509–1544* (Selden Society, 1911; repr. Professional Books Ltd, 1986), pp. lix–lxxv.

VII. ALL SAINTS AND ALL SOULS:
'WE ARE BUT DUST, AND DIE WE MUST'

1 John Skelton, 'Upon a Deadman's Head', in Henderson (ed.),
   The Complete Poems of John Skelton (J. M. Dent & Sons Ltd, 1948), p. 19.

2 Ten years later, John's brother Thomas repeated these words almost
   verbatim in his own will. Peter Heath, 'Urban Piety in the Later
   Middle Ages: The Evidence of Hull Wills', in Barrie Dobson (ed.),
   The Church, Politics and Patronage in the Fifteenth Century (Alan Sutton,
   1984), p. 213. The will of John de Vere, earl of Oxford, written in
   April 1509, began: 'I, John de Vere... knowing and considering well
   the uncertainty and unstableness of this wretched life; and that there
   is nothing so certain to any creature in this world living as is the
   departure from the same; And nonetheless nothing so uncertain as
   the time and hour thereof.' Similarly, Margaret Beaufort wrote her
   will in 1508, having 'called to our remembrance the unstableness of
   this transitory world, and that every creature living is mortal, and
   the time and place of death to every creature [is] uncertain'. W. H.
   St J. Hope (ed.), 'The last testament and inventory of John de Veer,
   thirteenth earl of Oxford', *Archaeologia*, 66 (1915), pp. 276–7; N. H.
   Nicholas (ed.), *Testamenta Vetusta*, [Volume II] (London, 1826), p. 517.

3 *Hall's Chronicle*, p. 512.

4 Forestier, quoted in Bishop of Arusiens, *A litil boke the whiche traytied
   and reherced many gode thinges necessaries for the... Pestilence... made by
   the... Bisshop of Arusiens... [London], [1485?]* (Manchester University
   Press, 1910).

5 'Hippocrates' may in fact have been multiple authors, whose
   works were compiled into one text in the third century BC. Galen
   (b. *c.* AD 129) was the Greek physician to Roman emperor Marcus
   Aurelius. Carole Rawcliffe, *Medicine and Society in Later Medieval
   England* (Sutton, 1995), p. 31.

6 Rawcliffe, *Medicine and Society*, pp. 82–3.

7 *Litil Boke*, folio 3.

8 *Litil Boke*, folio 4.

9 Andrew Boorde, *The Fyrst Boke of the Introduction of Knowledge:
   A Compendious Regyment or A Dyetary of Helth Made in Mountpyllier,
   Barnes in the Defence of the Berde* (F. J. Furnivall, ed.) (Elibron Classics,
   2005), pp. 88, 228, 244. The following is based on unpublished research

I did for *Past Pleasures Ltd* and *Historic Royal Palaces*, which became a lecture paper delivered at Queen Mary University London in 2012.

10 For more on the distinction between artificial and natural fools see Suzannah Lipscomb, 'All the King's Fools', *History Today*, Vol. 61, No. 8 (August 2011) and John Southworth, *Fools and Jesters at the English Court* (Sutton, 1998).

11 *Litil Boke*, folio 3.

12 Carole Rawcliffe, 'The Hospitals of Later Medieval London', *Medical History*, Vol. 28, No. 1 (1984), p. 10.

13 PROB/11/16.

14 This was the case for John Pendilton in 1558. He asked to be placed 'as nigh to the end of my wife's pew where she sitteth as conveniently may be' in St Nicholas, Rochester. John Brode made his will in 1512. Nicholas Rogers, 'Hic Iacet... The Location of Monuments in Late Medieval Parish Churches', in Clive Burgess and Eamon Duffy (eds), *The Parish in Late Medieval England: Proceedings of the 2002 Harlaxton Symposium* (Shaun Tyas, 2006), p. 267.

15 PROB/11/16.

16 Rogers, 'Hic Iacet... The Location of Monuments in Late Medieval Parish Churches', p. 267.

17 *A History of the County of Warwick: Vol. 2*, ed. William Page (London, 1908), from 'Victoria County History', *British History Online*.

18 Carole Rawcliffe, 'The Hospitals of Later Medieval London', *Medical History*, Vol. 28, No. 1 (1984), p. 2.

19 Joshua Toulmin Smith and Lucy Toulmin Smith (eds.), *English Gilds. The original ordinances of more than one hundred early English Gilds: together with the olde usages of the cite of Wynchestre; the ordinances of Worcester... From original MSS. of the fourteenth and fifteenth centuries* (Early English Text Society, Original Series, No. 40, 1860; repr. Oxford University Press, 1963), p. 194.

20 For life expectancy: Caroline M. Barron, *London in the Later Middle Ages: Government and People, 1200–1500* (Oxford University Press, 2004), p. 295; Ian Mortimer, *The Time Traveller's Guide to Medieval England: A Handbook for Visitors to the Fourteenth Century* (Vintage, 2009), p. 35; Roger Wrigley and E. A. Schofield, *Population History* (Edward Arnold, 1981), p. 528; Christopher Dyer, *Standards of Living in the*

Later Middle Ages: Social Change in England, c.1200–1520 (Cambridge University Press, 1989), p. 182.

21 Rawcliffe, 'The Hospitals of Later Medieval London', p. 4.

22 *A History of the County of Warwick.*

23 Rawcliffe, 'The Hospitals of Later Medieval London', p. 11.

24 Cal, SP, Spain, II, no. 23.

VIII. CHRISTMAS: FEAST AND FAST

1 James Stokes (ed.), *Records of Early English Drama: Lincolnshire* (British Library, 2009) Vol. II, p. 673.

2 Richard Leighton Greene, *The Early English Carols* (Clarendon Press, 1977), pp. 2–5.

3 W. D. Robson-Scott, *German Travellers in England 1460–1800* (Basil Blackwell, 1953), pp. 9–10.

4 Giles Tremlett, *Catherine of Aragon: Henry's Spanish Queen. A Biography* (Faber & Faber, 2010), p. 115.

5 *Cambridge University Library*, possibly written by James Ryman, c.1492. Reprinted in Richard Leighton Greene, *The Early English Carols* (Clarendon Press, 1977), pp. 1–2.

6 LP, XVI, No. 380, f. 111.

7 *Household Ordinances*, p. 120.

8 All numbers from J. Gage (ed.), 'Extracts from the household book of Edward Stafford... 1507–8' *Archaeologia*, Vol. XXV (1834), pp. 321–9.

9 Greene, *The Early English Carols*, p. 80.

10 (1517) Cal, SP, Ven, II, No. 918.

11 Ian Lancashire, 'Orders for Twelfth Day and Night c.1515 in the Second Northumberland House Book', *English Literary Renaissance*, Vol. 10 (1980), p. 14.

12 This guide to dining etiquette is based on Desiderius Erasmus, *A Handbook on Good Manners for Children*, trans. Eleanor Merchant (Preface, 2008), pp. 41–59.

13 Lancashire, 'Orders for Twelfth Day and Night', p. 14.

14 John Elliott Jr, Alan H. Helson, Alexandra F. Johnston and Diana Wyatt (eds), *Records of Early English Drama: Oxford*, Vol. I (British Library and Toronto University Press, 2004), Vol. I, p. 37.

15 Olga Horner, 'Christmas at the Inns of Court' in Meg Twycross (ed.), *Festive Drama: Papers from the Sixth Triennial Colloquium of the International Society for the Study of Medieval Theatre, Lancaster, 13–19 July 1989* (D. S. Brewer, 1996), p. 49.

16 For the following see *Hall's Chronicle*, p. 513.

17 Cal, SP, Spain, II, No. 45.

IX. PLOUGH DAY: FEAR GOD, HONOUR THE KING

1 Angelo Raine (ed.), *York Civic Records*, Vol. III (Yorkshire Archaeological Society Record Series, Vol. CVI, 1942), pp. 30–1.

2 Boston's Noah ship was carried during the feasts of Pentecost and Corpus Christi. James Stokes (ed.), *Records of Early English Drama: Lincolnshire* (British Library, 2009), Volume II, pp. 620–8.

3 C. H. Williams (ed.), *English Historical Documents, Volume V: 1485–1558* (Eyre & Spottiswoode, 1967), pp. 588–9.

4 S. J. Gunn, *Early Tudor Government, 1485–1558* (Macmillan, 1995), pp. 72–86.

5 William Brown (ed.), *Yorkshire Star Chamber Proceedings* (Yorkshire Archaeological Society Record Series, Vol. XLI, 1908), p. 9. (1499).

6 R. Stewart-Brown, *Lancashire and Cheshire Cases in the Court of Star Chamber, Part I* (The Record Society, 1916), p. 26.

7 C1/300/44.

8 C1/300/4.

9 *The Great Chronicle of London* records pirates being drowned in the Thames in 1496 and 1504. John Stafford was executed in 1484, while in 1505 a London coiner was hanged, drawn and quartered at Tyburn. *Great Chronicle*, pp. 260, 328; Angelo Raine, *York Civic Records, Vol. I*, pp. 107–9.

10 LP, I, No. 559.

11 John Bellamy, *The Tudor Law of Treason: An Introduction* (Routledge & Kegan Paul, 1979), p. 92; C. H. Williams, 'The Rebellion of Humphrey Stafford', *English Historical Review*, Vol. 43, No. 170 (1928).

12 *Great Chronicle*, p. 328.

13 *Great Chronicle*, pp. 258, 262.

14 (1479) Karen Jones, *Gender and Petty Crime in Late Medieval England: The Local Courts in Kent, 1460–1560* (Boydell Press, 2006), pp. 123–4.

15 Jones, *Gender and Petty Crime*, pp. 123–6.

16 (1526) Jones, *Gender and Petty Crime*, p. 202.

17 Ruth Mazo Karras, *Common Women: Prostitution and Sexuality in Medieval England* (Oxford University Press, 1996), pp. 77–8.

18 Goyte did her penance in 1488; Brewster abjured his heresy in 1506. Shannon McSheffrey and Norman Tanner (eds & trans.), *Lollards of Coventry, 1486–1522* (Cambridge University Press, 2003), p. 7; Norman Tanner, 'Penances imposed on Kentish Lollards by Archbishop Warham, 1511–12', in Margaret Aston and Colin Richmond (eds.), *Lollardy and the Gentry in the Later Middle Ages* (Sutton Publishing, 1997) p. 234.

19 The same penance was given to John Scrivener's children when he was executed in 1522. Shannon McSheffrey, *Gender and Heresy, Women and Men in Lollard Communities, 1420–1530* (University of Pennsylvania Press, 1995), p. 97.

20 Tanner, 'Penances imposed on Kentish Lollards', pp. 235–42.

21 *Great Chronicle*, p. 257.

22 John Baker, *The Oxford History of the Laws of England Volume VI: 1483–1558* (Oxford University Press, 2003), p. 512.

23 *Great Chronicle*, p. 365.

X. SHROVE: CONTRITION AND SUSPICION

1 *Hall's Chronicle*, pp. 513–14.

2 'Faser la cama de su altera y de servier en las cosas secretras de su camara', PRO 31 / 11 / 12. An English translation is given at Cal, SP, Spain, IV (i), No. 574. Catalina of Motril has frequently been conflated with a higher-status Spanish lady of Catherine's bedchamber called Catalina de Cardones or Cardenas, whose name appears second in a list of Catherine's household officers in England. Given Catalina's circumstances – she was described as Catherine's slave, married a Moorish bowmaker and returned to relative obscurity in Granada in the 1520s – it is highly unlikely that she would have been the second-highest-ranking lady in Catherine's bedchamber. I am grateful for conversations with Miranda Kaufmann and Giles Tremlett, and especially for research I undertook for Nadia Nadif and Untold, for helping me untangle the two Catalinas.

3   Gordon Kipling (ed.), *Receyt of the Ladie Kateryne* (Early English Text Society, No. 296, 1990), p. 33.

4   Peter Fryer, *Staying Power: The History of Black People in Britain* (Pluto Press, 1984), p. 1; Miranda Kaufmann, 'Africans in Britain, 1500–1640', unpublished PhD thesis (Oxford, 2011), pp. 263–4; Onyeka, *Blackamoore: Africans in Tudor England: Their Presence, Status and Origins* (Narrative Eye and the Circle with a Dot, 2013), pp. 182–3; Alwyn A. Ruddock, *Italian Merchants and Shipping in Southampton 1270–1600* (Southampton University College, 1951), p. 127.

5   John Major, *A History of Greater Britain as well England as Scotland compiled from the Ancient Authorities* (Archibald Constable, ed.) (Scottish History Society, 1892), p. 21.

6   'Richard III: January 1484', *Parliament Rolls*.

7   Sneyd, p. 21.

8   *Great Chronicle*, p. 248.

9   Sneyd, p. 24; Ruddock, *Italian Merchants and Shipping in Southampton*, p. 141; 'Richard III: January 1484', *Parliament Rolls*.

10 Angelo Raine (ed.), *York Civic Records*, Vol. I (Yorkshire Archaeological Society Record Series, Vol. XCVIII, 1938), pp. 17, 113–14.

11 'Folios 321–33, flyleaf: Feb 1495–6', *Calendar of letter-books of the city of London: L: Edward IV–Henry VII* (British History Online).

12 A. G. Dickens, *Lollards and Protestants in the Diocese of York: 1509–1558* (Hambledon Press, 1982), p. 44; Angelo Raine (ed.), *York Civic Records*, Vol. I (Yorkshire Archaeological Society Record Series, Vol. XCVIII, 1938), p. 20.

13 Samuel Eliot Morison, *The European Discovery of America: The Northern Voyages, AD 1500–1600* (Oxford University Press, 1971), p. 142.

14 James A. Williamson, *The Cabot Voyages and Bristol Discovery Under Henry VII* (Cambridge University Press, 1962), pp. 212–14.

15 Williamson, *The Cabot Voyages*, p. 207.

16 Peter Firstbrook, *The Voyage of the Matthew: John Cabot and the Discovery of North America* (BBC Books, 1997), p. 158.

17 LP, I, No. 5 (ii).

18 LP, I, No. 162; Cal, SP, Spain, II, No. 27.

19 *Anglica Historia*, p. 161; Cal, SP, Ven, II, No. 63.

20 *Anglica Historia*, p. 161.

21 Cal, SP, Ven, II, No. 11; LP, I, No. 156.
22 Cal, SP, Spain, II, Nos. 27, 44.

XI. LADY DAY 1510: CONCEPTION

1   Getting accurate figures for maternal mortality in this period is very
    difficult, but the 'best estimate' is that in the later sixteenth century
    just under ten in a thousand women died in childbirth. Maternal
    mortality was higher in London, and in the same period the records
    of the parish of St Botolph without Aldgate show that just over
    twenty-three out of a thousand baptisms ended in the mother's
    death. Mortality also varied over time, being somewhat lower in the
    sixteenth century than the seventeenth, and with age and parity. First
    births were the most dangerous and women over thirty-five were at
    greater risk than their younger counterparts. For more on this, see
    Roger Schofield, 'Did the Mothers Really Die? Three Centuries of
    Maternal Mortality' in Lloyd Bonfield, Richard M. Smith and Keith
    Wrightson (eds), *The World We Have Gained: Histories of Population and
    Social Structure, Essays presented to Peter Laslett on his Seventieth Birthday*
    (Basil Blackwell, 1986).
2   John T. McNeill and Helena M. Gamer (eds), *Medieval Handbooks of
    Penance: A Translation of the Principal Libri Poenitentiales and Selections
    from Related Documents* (Columbia University Press, 1938), pp. 302–3,
    307.
3   Patricia Simons, *The Sex of Men in Pre-modern Europe: A Cultural
    History* (Cambridge University Press, 2011), p. 198.
4   Henrietta Leyser, *Medieval Women: A Social History of Women in
    England, 450–1500* (Ted Smart, 1995), p. 94.
5   James A. Brundage, *Law, Sex and Christian Society in Medieval Europe*
    (University of Chicago Press, 1988), pp. 490–1.
6   Monica H. Green, *The Trotula: An English Translation of the Medieval
    Compendium of Women's Medicine* (University of Pennsylvania Press,
    2002), pp. 71–2, 91.
7   Simons, *The Sex of Men in Pre-modern Europe*, p. 195.
8   Green, *The Trotula*, pp. 76–7, 85.
9   Leyser, *Medieval Women*, p. 95.

10 Ruth Mazo Karras, *Common Women: Prostitution and Sexuality in Medieval England* (OUP, 1996), p. 97.

11 Margery Kempe, *The Book of Margery Kempe* (Barry Windeatt ed.) (Longman, 2000), p. 63.

12 Judith M. Bennett, '"Lesbian-Like" and the Social History of Lesbianisms', *Journal of the History of Sexuality*, Vol. 9, nos. 1–2 (2000), pp. 18–19; Carol Kazmierczak Manzione, 'Sex in Tudor London: Abusing their Bodies with Each Other' in Jacqueline Murray and Konrad Eisenbichler (eds), *Desire and Discipline: Sex and Sexuality in the Premodern West* (University of Toronto Press, 1996), pp. 92–7.

13 LP, XVI, No. 1334.

14 This was all reported by Luis Caroz in May 1510. Cal, SP, Spain: Supplement To Volumes I–II, No. 8.

15 Barbara Jean Harris, *Edward Stafford, Third Duke of Buckingham, 1478–1521* (Stanford University Press, 1986), p. 46.

16 Compton wrote his will in 1523, but did not die until 1528. PROB 11/23/8.

17 Barbara J. Harris, *English Aristocratic Women, 1450–1550: Marriage and Family, Property and Careers* (Oxford University Press, 2002), p. 83.

18 Shannon McSheffrey, *Marriage, Sex, and Civic Culture in Late Medieval London* (University of Pennsylvania Press, 2006), p. 174.

19 N. H. Nicolas (ed.), *Testamenta Vetusta*, Vol. II (Nichols & Son, 1826), p. 534.

20 Lesyer, *Medieval Women*, p. 104; Green, *The Trotula*, p. 78.

21 McNeill and Gamer (eds), *Medieval Handbooks of Penance*, p. 185.

22 Bennett, 'Social History of Lesbianisms', p. 18.

23 Simons, *The Sex of Men in Pre-modern Europe*, p. 36; David Lorenzo Boyd and Ruth Mazo Karras, '"Ut cum muliere": A Male Transvestite Prostitute in Fourteenth-Century London' in Louise Fradenburg and Carl Freccero (eds), *Premodern Sexualities* (Routledge, 1996), pp. 111–12.

24 Mazo Karras, *Common Women*, pp. 19, 68.

25 Mazo Karras, *Common Women*, pp. 49, 57–63.

26 Amy Licence, *In Bed with the Tudors: The Sex Lives of a Dynasty from Elizabeth of York to Elizabeth I* (Amberley, 2013), pp. 94, 97; Roger Schofield and E. A. Wrigley, 'Infant and Child Mortality in the Late Tudor and Early Stuart Period' in Charles Webster (ed.), *Health,*

Medicine and Mortality in the Sixteenth Century (Cambridge University Press, 1979), p. 84.

27 This was Henry VIII's niece Margaret Douglas, whose chambers were searched in 1565, twenty years after the birth and death of her first child. Rosalind K. Marshall, 'Douglas, Lady Margaret, countess of Lennox (1515–1578)', *Oxford Dictionary of National Biography* (Online Edition).

28 Cal, SP, Ven, II, No. 73.

29 Cal, SP, Spain, II, No. 43; Cal, SP, Spain, Supplement to I–II, Nos. 7–8.

30 Cal, SP, Spain, Supplement to I–II, No. 7.

XII. 1510 AND BEYOND: FORTUNE'S WHEEL

1 John Skelton, *Magnificence* (1516), in Henderson (ed.), *The Complete Poems of John Skelton* (J. M. Dent & Sons Ltd, 1948), p. 243.

2 *Petition of Edmund Dudley*, p. 86; D. M. Brodie (ed.), *The Tree of Commonwealth: A Treatise Written by Edmund Dudley* (Cambridge University Press, 1948), p. 104.

3 LP, I, 467; Cal, SP, Spain, II, Nos. 44, 45.

4 Cal, SP, Spain, II, No. 44; Cal, SP, Ven, II, No. 63.

5 Cal, SP, Spain, No. 44.

6 David Starkey, *Henry: Virtuous Prince* (Harper Press, 2008), pp. 362–3.

7 Quotes are from George Cavendish, *The Life and Death of Thomas Wolsey the Great Cardinal of England* (Alcuin Press, 1930), pp. 7–10.

8 P. S. Allen and H. M. Allen (eds), *The Letters of Richard Fox: 1486–1527* (Clarendon Press, 1929), p. 44.

9 Cal, SP, Spain, II, No. 36.

10 Cal, SP, Ven, II, No. 63.

11 Cal, SP, Spain, II, No. 47.

12 *Great Chronicle*, p. 366.

13 *Great Chronicle*, p. 366.

14 Cavendish, *The Life and Death of Thomas Wolsey*, p. 15.

15 *Anglica Historia*, pp. 203, 279

SELECT BIBLIOGRAPHY

Online Sources

Abstracts of Inquisitions Post Mortem for the City of London (via british-history.ac.uk)

A Survey of London, by John Stow (via british-history.ac.uk)

Calendar of letter-books of the city of London: L: Edward IV–Henry VII (via british-history.ac.uk)

Calendar of State Papers Relating to English Affairs in the Archives of Venice (via british-history.ac.uk)

Calendar of State Papers, Spain (via british-history.ac.uk)

England's Immigrants (englandsimmigrants.com)

Letters and Papers, Foreign and Domestic, Henry VIII (via british-history.ac.uk)

Parliament Rolls of Medieval England (via british-history.ac.uk)

Oxford English Dictionary (oed.com)

The Oxford Dictionary of National Biography (oxforddnb.com)

Victoria County History (via british-history.ac.uk)

Unprinted Primary Sources

C1: Pleadings in Chancery (National Archives)

PRO 31: Domestic Records of the Public Record Office (National Archives)

PROB 11: Prerogative Court of Canterbury, Wills (National Archives)

Printed Primary Sources

A collection of ordinances and regulations for the government of the royal household, made in divers reigns: from King Edward III to King William and Queen Mary (Society of Antiquaries of London, 1790)

A litil boke the whiche traytied and reherced many gode thinges necessaries for the… Pestilence… made by the… Bisshop of Arusiens (Manchester University Press, 1910)

Allen, P. S. and H. M. Allen (eds), *The Letters of Richard Fox: 1486–1527* (Clarendon Press, 1929)

Anderson, J. J., *Records of Early English Drama: Newcastle Upon Tyne* (Manchester University Press, 1982)

Arbeau, Thoinot, *Orchesography*, trans. Mary Stewart Evans (Dover Publications, New York, 1967)

Ashmole, Elias, *The Institution, Laws and Ceremonies of the Most Noble Order of the Garter; and a Brief Account of all Other Military Orders of Knighthood in England, Scotland, France, Spain, Germany, Italy, Swedeland, Denmark and c. with the Ensigns of the Several Orders* (Thomas Dring, 1693)

Astle, T. (ed.), *The Will of King Henry VII* (T. Payne and B. White, 1775)

Bayne, C. G. (ed.), *Select Cases in the Council of Henry VII* (Selden Society, Volume 75, 1958)

Boorde, Andrew, *The Fyrst Boke of the Introduction of Knowledge: A Compendious Regyment or A Dyetary of Helth Made in Mountpyllier, Barnes in the Defence of the Berde*, ed. F. J. Furnivall (Elibron Classics, 2005)

Bradford, G. (ed.), *Proceedings in the Court of Star Chamber in the Reigns of Henry VII and Henry VIII* (Somerset Record Society, Volume 27, 1911)

Brodie, D. M. (ed.), *The Tree of Commonwealth: A Treatise Written by Edmund Dudley* (Cambridge University Press, 1948)

Brown, William (ed.), *Yorkshire Star Chamber Proceedings* (Yorkshire Archaeological Society Record Series, Vol. XLI, 1908)

Byrne, Muriel St Clare (ed.), *The Lisle Letters: An Abridgement* (Secker and Warburg, 1983)

Campbell, William (ed.), *Materials for a History of the Reign of Henry VIII from Original Documents Preserved in the Public Record Office, Volume II* (London, 1877)

Castle, Eileen, and Hulton, Mary (eds), *Ten Tudor Families: Coventrian Wills and Inventories* (Coventry Branch of the Historical Association, 1987)

Cavendish, George, *The Life and Death of Thomas Wolsey the Great Cardinal of England* (Alcuin Press, 1930)

Caxton, William, *The Book of the Knight of the Tower*, ed. M. Y. Offord (Early English Text Society, Supplementary Series No. 2, 1971)

Chandler, John, *John Leland's Itinerary: Travels in Tudor England* (Alan Sutton, 1993)

Edwards, David G. (ed.), *Derbyshire Wills Proved in the Prerogative Court of Canterbury, 1393–1574* (Derbyshire Record Society, Volume XXVI, 1998)

Elliott Jr, John, Alan H. Helson, Alexandra F. Johnston and Diana Wyatt (eds), *Records of Early English Drama: Oxford* (British Library and Toronto University Press, 2004), 2 volumes

Ellis, Henry, *Original Letters Illustrative of English History, Volume I* (Harding, Triphook and Lepard, 1824)

Elyot, Sir Thomas, *The Book Named the Governor*, ed. S. E. Lehmberg (J. M. Dent & Sons Ltd, 1962)

Erasmus, Desiderius, *A Handbook on Good Manners for Children*, trans. Eleanor Merchant (Preface, 2008)

Gage, J. (ed.), 'Extracts from the household book of Edward Stafford, duke of Buckingham, 1507–8', *Archaeologia*, Vol. XXV (1834)

Gomez de Fuensalida, Gutierre, *Correspondencia de Gutierre Gomez de Fuensalida, embajador en Alemania, Flandes é Inglaterra* (Madrid, 1907)

Grace, Mary, *Records of the Gild of St George in Norwich, 1389–1547: A Transcript with an Introduction* (Norfolk Record Society, 1937)

Green, Monica H., *The Trotula: An English Translation of the Medieval Compendium of Women's Medicine* (University of Pennsylvania Press, 2002)

Greene, Richard Leighton, *The Early English Carols* (Clarendon Press, 1977)

Hall, Edward, *Hall's Chronicle: Containing the History of England, during the Reign of Henry IV and the Succeeding Monarchs, to the End of the Reign of Henry VIII in which are Particularly Described the Manners and Customs of those Periods* (London, 1809)

Harrison, C. J., 'The Petition of Edmund Dudley', *English Historical Review*, Vol. 87, No. 342 (January 1972)

Hay, Denys, *The Anglica Historia of Polydore Vergil, AD 1485–1537* (Camden Series, Vol. LXXIV; Offices of the Royal Historical Society of Great Britain, 1950)

Hollis, D. (ed.), *Calendar of the Bristol Apprentice Book, 1532–1565, Part I: 1532–1542* (Bristol Record Society, 1949)

Hopper, Clarence (ed.), *London Chronicle during the Reigns of Henry VII and Henry VIII* (Camden Society, Vol. IV, 1859)

Kahrl, Stanley J., *Records of Plays and Players in Lincolnshire, 1300–1585* (Collections, Volume VIII; The Malone Society, 1974)

Kempe, Margery, *The Book of Margery Kempe*, ed. Barry Windeatt (Longman, 2000)

Kipling, Gordon (ed.), *The Receyt of the Ladie Kateryne* (Early English Text Society, No. 296, 1990)

Kirby, Joan (ed.), *The Plumpton Letters and Papers* (Camden Society, Fifth Series, 8; 1996)

Lancashire, Ian, 'Orders for Twelfth Day and Night c.1515 in the Second Northumberland House Book', *English Literary Renaissance*, Vol. 10 (1980)

Leadam, I. S., *Select Cases before the King's Council in the Star Chamber, commonly called The Court of Star Chamber, Volume II: 1509–1544* (Selden Society, 1911; repr. Professional Books Ltd, 1986)

Leadam, I. S. (ed.), *Select Cases in the Court of Requests, AD 1497–1569* (Selden Society, Vol. XII, 1898)

Leland, John, *Joannis Lelandi antiquarii De rebus Britannicis Collectanea cum Thomae Hearnii Praefatione Notis et Indice ad Editionem primam: Editio Alterta, Volume IV* (Gregg International, 1970)

List of Early Chancery Proceedings, Volume IV (PRO, Lists and Indexes, No. XXIX)

Littlehales, Henry (ed.), *The Medieval Records of a London City Church* (Early English Text Society, original series, No. 128; 1905)

McNeill, John T., and Helena M. Gamer (eds), *Medieval Handbooks of Penance: A Translation of the Principal Libri Poenitentiales and Selections from Related Documents* (Columbia University Press, 1938)

Major, John, *A History of Greater Britain as well England as Scotland compiled from the Ancient Authorities*, ed. Archibald Constable (Scottish History Society, 1892)

Mayor, John E. B. (ed.), *The English Works of John Fisher, Bishop of Rochester, Part I* (Early English Text Society, Vol. XXVII, 1876; repr. 1935)

More, Thomas, *The Complete Works of St. Thomas More, Volume 3, Part II: Latin Poems*, eds. Clarence H. Miller, Leicester Bradner, Charles A. Lynch and Revilo P. Oliver (Yale University Press, 1984)

Mundy, Percy D., *Abstracts of Star Chamber Proceedings relating to the County of Sussex: Henry VII to Philip and Mary* (Sussex Record Society, Vol. XVI, 1913)

Nelson, Alan H., and John R. Elliott, Jr (eds), *Records of Early English Drama: Inns of Court* (D. S. Brewer, 2010)

Nichols, John Gough (ed.), *The Chronicle of Calais in the Reigns of Henry VII and Henry VIII to the year 1540* (Camden Society, 1846)

Nicolas, N. H. (ed.), *Testamenta Vetusta*, Volume II (Nichols & Son, 1826)

Owen of Henllys, George, *The Description of Pembrokeshire*, ed. Dilwyn Miles (Gomer Press, 1994)

Page, William (ed.), *Letters of Denization and Acts of Naturalization for Aliens in England, 1509–1603* (Publications of the Huguenot Society of London, Vol. VIII, 1893)

Percy, Thomas, *The Regulations and Establishment of the Household of Henry Algernon Percy, the Fifth Earl of Northumberland, at his Castles of Wresill and Lekinfield in Yorkshire. Begun anno domini M.DXII* (London, 1827)

Pilkington, Mark C. (ed.), *Records of Early English Drama: Bristol* (University of Toronto Press, 1997)

Ralph, Elizabeth, and Nora M. Hardwick (eds), *Calendar of the Bristol Apprentice Book, 1532–1565, Part II: 1542–1555* (Bristol Record Society, 1980)

Raine, Angelo (ed.), *York Civic Records*, Volume I (Yorkshire Archaeological Society Record Series, Vol. XCVIII, 1938)

Raine, Angelo (ed.), *York Civic Records*, Volume III (Yorkshire Archaeological Society Record Series, Vol. CVI, 1942)

Raine, James (ed.), *Testamenta Eboracensia, Volume V* (Surtees Society, Vol. LXXIX, 1884)

Sellers, Maud, *York Mercers and Merchant Adventurers, 1356–1917* (Surtees Society, Vol. CXXIX, 1918)

Skelton, John, *The Complete Poems of John Skelton, Laureate* ed. Philip Henderson (J.M. Dent & Sons Ltd., 1948)

Sneyd, Charlotte Augusta (trans.), *A relation, or rather a true account, of the island of England : with sundry particulars of the customs of these people, and of the royal revenues under King Henry the Seventh, about the year 1500* (Camden Society, Vol. 37, 1847)

Stewart-Brown, R., *Lancashire and Cheshire Cases in the Court of Star Chamber, Part I* (The Record Society, 1916)

Stokes, James (ed.), *Records of Early English Drama: Lincolnshire*, Volume II (British Library, 2009)

Stow, John, *A Summary of the Chronicle of England, diligently collected, abridged and continued unto this present yeare of Christ 1604*, ed. Barrett L. Beer (Edwin Mellen Press, 2007)

Thomas, A. H.,tt and I. D. Thornley (eds), *The Great Chronicle of London* (Alan Sutton, 1983)

Warner, George (ed.), *The Libelle of Englyshe Polycye: A Poem on the Sue of Sea-Power, 1436* (Clarendon Press, 1926)

Williams, C. H. (ed.), *English Historical Documents, Volume V: 1485–1558* (Eyre and Spottiswoode, 1967)

Wriothesley, Charles, *A Chronicle of England during the Reigns of the Tudors, from AD 1485 to 1559, Volume I*, ed. William Douglas Hamilton (Camden Society, New Series XI, 1875)

Secondary Sources

I. LADY DAY 1509

Brodie, D. M., 'Edmund Dudley: Minister of Henry VII: (The Alexander Prize Essay)', *Transactions of the Royal Historical Society*, Fourth Series, Vol. 15, (1932)

Duffy, Eamon, *Marking the Hours: English People and their Prayers, 1240–1570* (Yale University Press, 2006)

Gunn, S. J., 'The Courtiers of Henry VII', *English Historical Review*, Vol. 108, No. 426 (January 1993)

Penn, Thomas, *Winter King: The Dawn of Tudor England* (Allen Lane, 2011)

Rappaport, Steve, *Worlds within Worlds: Structures of Life in Sixteenth Century London* (Cambridge University Press, 1989)

Rose, Susan, *Calais: An English Town in France, 1347–1558* (Boydell Press, 2008)

Ross, James, '"Contrary to the ryght and to the order of the lawe": New Evidence of Edmund Dudley's Activities on Behalf of Henry VII in 1504', *English Historical Review*, Vol. 127, No. 524 (February 2012)

Thomas, W. S. K., *Tudor Wales: 1485–1603* (Gomer Press, 1983)

II. EASTER

Baldwin, Frances Elizabeth, *Sumptuary Legislation and Personal Regulation in England* (John Hopkins Press, 1926)

Beeson, C. F. C., *English Church Clocks 1280–1850: History and Classification* (Antiquarian Horological Society, 1971)

Duffy, Eamon, *Marking The Hours: English People and their Prayers, 1240–1570* (Yale University Press, 2006)

Dyer, Christopher, *Making a Living in the Middle Ages: The People of Britain, 850–1520* (Penguin Books, 2003)

Elton, G. R., 'Henry VII: Rapacity and Remorse', *Historical Journal*, Vol. 1, No. 1 (1958)

Hanawalt, Barbara A., *Growing up in Medieval London: The Experience of Childhood in History* (Oxford University Press, 1993)

Hayward, Maria, *Rich Apparel: Clothing and the Law in Henry VIII's England* (Ashgate, 2009)

Hayward, Maria, *Dress at the Court of King Henry VIII* (Maney, 2007)

Robson-Scott, W. D., *German Travellers in England: 1400–1800* (Basil Blackwell, 1953)

Tittler, Robert, and Norman Jones (eds), *A Companion to Tudor Britain* (Blackwell Publishing, 2004)

III. ST GEORGE'S DAY

Aston, Margaret, and Colin Richmond (eds), *Lollardy and the Gentry in the Later Middle Ages* (Sutton Publishing, 1997)

Brigden, Susan, *London and the Reformation* (Clarendon Press, 1989)

Clanchy, M. T., 'Learning to Read in the Middle Ages and the Role of Mothers', in Greg Brooks and A. K. Pugh (eds), *Studies in the History of Reading* (Centre for the Teaching of Reading, University of Reading School of Education, 1984)

Dale, Marian K., 'The London Silkwomen of the Fifteenth Century', *Economic History Review*, Vol. 4, No. 3 (October 1933)

Davies, M. P., 'Dame Thomasine Percyvale "the maid of Week" (d. 1512)', in C. M. Barron and A. F. Sutton (eds) *Medieval London Widows, 1300–1500* (Bloomsbury, 1994)

Dickens, A. G., *Lollards and Protestants in the Diocese of York: 1509–1558* (Hambledon Press, 1982)

Duff, E. Gordon, *The English Provincial Printers, Stationers and Bookbinders to 1557* (Cambridge University Press, 1912)

Fox, Adam, *Oral and Literate Culture in England, 1500–1700* (Oxford Studies in Social History, Oxford University Press, 2002)

Gardiner, Dorothy, *English Girlhood at School: A Study of Women's Education through Twelve Centuries* (Oxford University Press, 1929)

Geritz, Albert J., and Amos Lee Laine, *John Rastell* (Twayen Publishers, 1983)

Gunn, S. J., 'The Accession of Henry VIII', *Historical Research*, Vol. 64, No. 155 (1991)

McSheffrey, Shannon, *Gender and Heresy, Women and Men in Lollard Communities, 1420–1530* (University of Pennsylvania Press, 1995)

McSheffrey, Shannon, and Norman Tanner (eds and trans.), *Lollards of Coventry, 1486–1522* (Cambridge University Press, 2003)

Meale, Carol M. (ed.), *Women and Literature in Britain, 1150–1500* (Cambridge University Press, 1993)

Moran, Jo Ann Hoeppner, *The Growth of English Schooling 1340–1548: Learning, Literacy and Laicization in Pre-Reformation York Diocese* (Princeton University Press, 1985)

Rex, Richard, *The Lollards* (Palgrave, 2002)

Starkey, David, *Henry: Virtuous Prince* (Harper Press, 2008)

Starkey, David, 'Intimacy and Innovation: The Rise of the Privy Chamber, 1485–1547', in David Starkey, D. A. L. Morgan, John Murphy, Pam Wright, Neil Cuddy and Kevin Sharpe, *The English Court: From the Wars of the Roses to the Civil War* (Longman, 1987)

Storey, R. L., *The Reign of Henry VII* (Blandford Press, 1968)

Thrupp, Sylvia L., *The Merchant Class of Medieval London [1300–1500]* (University of Chicago Press, 1948)

IV. MAY DAY

Goldberg, P. J. P., *Women, Work and Life Cycle in a Medieval Economy: Women in York and Yorkshire c.1300–1520* (Clarendon Press, 1992)

Gunn, Steven, 'Archery Practice in Early Tudor England', *Past and Present*, No. 209 (November 2010)

Harris, Barbara J., 'Power, Profit and Passion: Mary Tudor, Charles Brandon and the Arranged Marriage in Early Tudor England', *Feminist Studies*, Vol. 15, No. 1: Women, Family and Work (Spring 1989)

Harris, Barbara J., *English Aristocratic Women, 1450–1550: Marriage and Family, Property and Careers* (Oxford University Press, 2002)

Ives, Eric, '"Agaynst Taking Awaye of Women": the Inception and Operation of the Abduction Act of 1487', in E. E. Ives, R. J. Knecht,

J. J. Scarisbrick, *Wealth and Power in Tudor England: Essays Presented to S. T. Bindoff* (Athlone Press, 1978)

Loades, David, *The Tudor Court* (Headstart History, 1992)

McSheffrey, Shannon, *Marriage, Sex, and Civic Culture in Late Medieval London* (University of Pennsylvania Press, 2006)

Tremlett, Giles, *Catherine of Aragon: Henry's Spanish Queen. A Biography* (Faber & Faber, 2010)

V. MIDSUMMER

Anglo, Sydney, 'The Court Festivals of Henry VII: A Study Based Upon the Account Books of John Heron, Treasurer of the Chamber', *Bulletin of John Rylands Library*, Vol. 43, No. 1 (September 1960)

Anglo, Sydney, *Spectacle, Pageantry and Early Tudor Policy* (Clarendon Press, 1969)

Anglo, Sydney (ed.), *Chivalry in the Renaissance* (Boydell Press, 1990)

Chambers, E. K., *The Mediaeval Stage, Volume II* (Oxford University Press, 1925)

Davidson, Clifford, *Festivals and Plays in Late Medieval Britain* (Ashgate, 2007)

Leach, Arthur F., 'Some English plays and players, 1220–1548', in W. P. Ker, A. S. Napier and W. W. Skeat (eds), *An English Miscellany: Presented to Dr Furnivall in Honour of his Seventy-Fifth Birthday* (Clarendon Press, 1901)

Toulmin Smith, Joshua, and Lucy Toulmin Smith (eds), *English Gilds. The original ordinances of more than one hundred early English Gilds: together with the olde usages of the cite of Wynchestre; the ordinances of Worcester ... From original MSS. of the fourteenth and fifteenth centuries* (Early English Text Society, original series, No. 40, 1860; repr. Oxford University Press, 1963)

Young, Alan, *Tudor and Jacobean Tournaments* (George Philip, 1987)

VI. LAMMAS

Darby, H. C. (ed.), *An Historical Geography of England Before 1800: Fourteen Studies* (Cambridge University Press, 1936)

Harris, Barbara Jean, *Edward Stafford, Third Duke of Buckingham, 1478–1521* (Stanford University Press, 1986)

Hoskins, W. G., 'The Leicestershire Farmer in the Sixteenth Century', in *Essays in Leicestershire History* (Liverpool University Press, 1950)

Horrox, Rosemary, and W. Mark Ormrod (eds), *A Social History of England 1200–1500* (Cambridge University Press, 2006)

Oestman, Cord, *Lordship and Community: The Lestrange Family and the Village of Hunstanton, Norfolk in the First Half of the Sixteenth Century* (Boydell Press, 1994)

Phythian-Adams, Charles, *Desolation of a City: Coventry and the Urban Crisis of the Late Middle Ages* (Cambridge University Press, 1979)

Thurley, Simon, *The Royal Palaces of Tudor England: Architecture and Court Life, 1460–1547* (Yale University Press, 1993)

Youngs, Deborah, 'Servants and Labourers on a Late Medieval Demesne: The Case of Newton, Cheshire, 1498–1520', *The Agricultural History Review*, Vol. 47, No. 2 (1999)

VII. ALL SAINTS AND ALL SOULS

Barron, Caroline M., *London in the Later Middle Ages: Government and People, 1200–1500* (Oxford University Press, 2004)

Dyer, Christopher, *Standards of Living in the Later Middle Ages: Social Change in England, c.1200–1520* (Cambridge University Press, 1989)

Heath, Peter, 'Urban Piety in the Later Middle Ages: The Evidence of Hull Wills', in Barrie Dobson (ed.), *The Church, Politics and Patronage in the Fifteenth Century* (Alan Sutton, 1984)

Mortimer, Ian, *The Time Traveller's Guide to Medieval England: A Handbook for Visitors to the Fourteenth Century* (Vintage, 2009)

Rawcliffe, Carole, 'The Hospitals of Later Medieval London', *Medical History*, Vol. 28, No. 1 (1984)

Rawcliffe, Carole, *Medicine and Society in Later Medieval England* (Sutton, 1995)

Rogers, Nicholas, 'Hic Iacet... The Location of Monuments in Late Medieval Parish Churches', in Clive Burgess and Eamon Duffy (eds), *The Parish in Late Medieval England: Proceedings of the 2002 Harlaxton Symposium* (Shaun Tyas, 2006)

Wrigley, Roger, and E. A. Schofield, *Population History* (Edward Arnold, 1981)

VIII. CHRISTMAS

Dyer, Christopher, 'English Diet in the Later Middle Ages' in T. H. Ashton *et al.*, *Social Relations and Ideas: Essays in Honour of R. H. Hilton* (Cambridge University Press, 1983)

Hayward, Maria, 'Gift Giving at the Court of Henry VIII: the 1539 New Year's Gift Roll in Context', *The Antiquaries Journal*, Vol. 85, No. 1 (September 2005)

Horner, Olga, 'Christmas at the Inns of Court', in Meg Twycross (ed.), *Festive Drama: Papers from the Sixth Triennial Colloquium of the International Society for the Study of Medieval Theatre, Lancaster, 13–19 July 1989* (D. S. Brewer, 1996)

Hutton, Ronald, *The Rise and Fall of Merrie England 1400–1700* (Oxford University Press, 1994)

Hutton, Ronald, *The Stations of the Sun: A History of the Ritual Year in Britain* (Oxford University Press, 1996)

O'Keeffe, Eleanor, 'Christmas 1535 at the Court of Henry VIII' (unpublished research pack for Historic Royal Palaces and Past Pleasures Ltd, 2008)

Sim, Alison, *Food and Feast in Tudor England* (Sutton, 1997)

Streitberger, W. R., *Court Revels, 1485–1559* (University of Toronto Press, 1994)

IX. PLOUGH DAY

Baker, J. H., *The Legal Profession and the Common Law: Historical Essays* (Hambledon Press, 1986)

Baker, John, *The Oxford History of the Laws of England Volume VI: 1483–1558* (Oxford University Press, 2003)

Bellamy, John, *The Tudor Law of Treason: An Introduction* (Routledge & Kegan Paul, 1979)

Gunn, S. J., *Early Tudor Government, 1485–1558* (Macmillan, 1995)

Guy, John, *Tudor England* (Oxford University Press, 1988)

Jones, Karen, *Gender and Petty Crime in Late Medieval England: The Local Courts in Kent, 1460–1560* (Boydell Press, 2006)

Kermode, Jenny, and Garthine Walker, *Women, Crime and the Courts in Early Modern England* (University College London Press, 1994)

Powell, Edward, 'Jury Trial at Gaol Delivery in the Late Middle Ages: The Midland Circuit, 1400–1429' in J. S. Cockburn and Thomas A. Green (eds), *Twelve Good Men and True: the Criminal Trial Jury in England, 1200–1800* (Princeton University Press, 1988)

Sharpe, J. A., *Judicial Punishment in England* (Faber & Faber, 1990)

Thornley, Isobel, 'The Destruction of Sanctuary' in R. W. Seton Watson (ed.), *Tudor Studies* (Longman, 1924)

Winter, Christine, 'Prisons and Punishments in Late Medieval London' (unpublished PhD thesis, Royal Holloway, University of London, 2012)

X. SHROVE

Butler, Cheryl Bernadette, 'Southampton Book of Fines, 1488–1540' (unpublished PhD thesis, Southampton University, 2003)

Coffin, Cyril, 'Aliens in Dorset, 1525', TheDorsetPage.com (online, 2000)

Firstbrook, Peter, *The Voyage of the Matthew: John Cabot and the Discovery of North America* (BBC Books, 1997)

Fryer, Peter, *Staying Power: The History of Black People in Britain* (Pluto Press, 1984)

Habib, Imtiaz, *Black Lives in the English Archives, 1500–1677* (Ashgate, 2008)

Harvey, P. D. A., *Maps in Tudor England* (Public Record Office, 1993)

Jones, Evan, 'The Matthew of Bristol and the Financiers of John Cabot's 1497 Voyage to North America', *English Historical Review*, Vol. 121, No. 492 (June 2006)

Kaufmann, Miranda, 'Africans in Britain, 1500–1640' (unpublished PhD thesis, University of Oxford, 2011)

Lester, Toby, *The Fourth Part of the World: The Race to the Ends of the Earth, and the Epic Story of the Map That Gave America its Name* (Profile Books, 2009)

Morison, Samuel Eliot, *The European Discovery of America: The Northern Voyages, AD 1500–1600* (Oxford University Press, 1971)

Onyeka, *Blackamoore: Africans in Tudor England: Their Presence, Status and Origins* (Narrative Eye and the Circle with a Dot, 2013)

Page, William (ed.), *Letters of Denization and Acts of Naturalization for Aliens in England, 1509–1603* (Publications of the Huguenot Society of London, Vol. VIII, 1893)

Ruddock, Alwyn A., *Italian Merchants and Shipping in Southampton 1270–1600* (Southampton University College, 1951)

Williamson, James A., *The Cabot Voyages and Bristol Discovery Under Henry VII* (Cambridge University Press, 1962)

XI. LADY DAY 1510

Bennett, Judith M., '"Lesbian-Like" and the Social History of Lesbianisms', *Journal of the History of Sexuality*, Vol. 9, Nos. 1–2 (2000)

Boyd, David Lorenzo, and Ruth Mazo Karras, '"Ut cum muliere": A Male Transvestite Prostitute in Fourteenth Century London', in Louise Fradenburg and Carl Freccero (eds), *Premodern Sexualities* (Routledge, 1996)

Bray, Alan, *Homosexuality in Renaissance England* (Columbia University Press, 1995)

Bray, Alan, *The Friend* (University of Chicago Press, 2003)

Brundage, James A., *Law, Sex and Christian Society in Medieval Europe* (University of Chicago Press, 1988)

Bullough, Vern L. and James A. Brundage, *Handbook of Medieval Sexuality* (Garland, 2000)

Cressy, David, *Birth Marriage & Death: Ritual, Religion and the Life-Cycle in Tudor and Stuart England* (Oxford University Press, 1999)

Goodich, Michael, *The Unmentionable Vice: Homosexuality in the Later Medieval Period* (American Bibliographical Center, Clio Press, 1979)

Karras, Ruth Mazo, *Common Women: Prostitution and Sexuality in Medieval England* (Oxford University Press, 1996)

Leyser, Henrietta, *Medieval Women: A Social History of Women in England, 450–1500* (Ted Smart, 1995)

Licence, Amy, *In Bed with the Tudors: The Sex Lives of a Dynasty from Elizabeth of York to Elizabeth I* (Amberley, 2013)

Manzione, Carol Kazmierczak, 'Sex in Tudor London: Abusing their Bodies with Each Other', in Jacqueline Murray and Konrad Eisenbichler (eds), *Desire and Discipline: Sex and Sexuality in the Premodern West* (University of Toronto Press, 1996)

Schofield, Roger, and E.A. Wrigley, 'Infant and Child Mortality in the Late Tudor and Early Stuart Period', in Charles Webster (ed.), *Health, Medicine and Mortality in the Sixteenth Century* (Cambridge University Press, 1979)

Simons, Patricia, *The Sex of Men in Pre-modern Europe: A Cultural History* (Cambridge University Press, 2011)

Toulan, Sarah, and Kate Fisher (eds), *The Routledge History of Sex and the Body: 1500 to the Present* (Routledge, 2013)

XII. 1510 AND BEYOND

Cameron, T. W., 'The early life of Thomas Wolsey', *English Historical Review*, Vol. 3, No. 11 (1888)

Gwyn, Peter, *The King's Cardinal: The Rise and Fall of Thomas Wolsey* (Barrrie & Jenkins, 1990)

Scarisbrick, J. J., *Henry VIII* (Methuen, 1988)

LIST OF ILLUSTRATIONS

Henry VII, 1505
(© *National Portrait Gallery*)

Henry VIII, *c.* 1513
(*The Berger Collection, Denver, Colorado / Fine Art Images / HIP / Topfoto*)

Henry VII on his deathbed drawn by Sir Thomas Wriothesley
(*British Library Board / Topfoto*)

Richard Fox by Hans Corvus, *c.* 1530
(© *Corpus Christi College, Oxford, UK / Bridgeman Images*)

Henry VII with Richard Empson and Edmund Dudley
(*Belvoir Castle, Leicestershire / Topfoto*)

Sir Thomas Lovell after Pietro Torrigiano, *c.* 1518
(© *National Portrait Gallery*)

Edward Stafford, Duke of Buckingham, 1520
(*Magdalene College, Cambridge / Wikimedia Commons*)

Engraving of the coronation of Henry VIII and Catherine of
Aragon from *A joyfull medytacyon to all englonde* by Stephen Hawes,
1509
(*Cambridge University Library*)

Catherine of Aragon by Michael Sittow, *c.* 1500–5
(*World History Archive / Topfoto*)

Margaret Beaufort by Roland Lockey, *c.* 1598
(*By permission of the Master and Fellows of St John's College, Cambridge*)

Henry VIII in parliament, The Wriothesley Garter Book, *c.* 1530
(*Wikimedia Commons*)

Procession of the knights of the garter attending mass, Black Book
of the Garter, *c.* 1534
(*Royal Collection Trust / © Her Majesty Queen Elizabeth II 2015*)

Henry VIII jousting before Catherine of Aragon, College of Arms
MS The Westminster Tournament Roll, 'le Roy desarmey', 1511
(*Reproduced by permission of the Kings, Heralds and Pursuivants of
Arms*)

Wool dyers at work, British Library Royal MS 15.E
(*British Library Board*)

A merchant returns home through the snow, *The Breviary of Queen
Isabella of Castile*, British Library Add MS 1885
(*British Library Board / Topfoto*)

Men and women performing harvest duties, *Les Très Riches Heures du
Duc de Berry*
(*Wikimedia Commons*)

A spinster with some higher status figures, *The Book of Hours of
Joanna of Castile*, British Library Add MS 18852
(*British Library Board / Topfoto*)

Souls being raised from Purgatory, British Library Add MS 37049
(*British Library Board / Topfoto*)

Fortune's Wheel, John Lydgate's *Troy*, British Library Royal 18 D II
(*British Library Board / Topfoto*)

INDEX

INDEX